"In nature you can sense and feel the rejuvenating intelligence, beauty and peace that inspired the creation of this remarkable book and its practical self-improvement process. *The Web of Life Imperative* offers more tools, knowledge and personal power for good than most therapies and spiritualities. It enables us to reverse our destructive relationships by empowering us to make thoughtful sensory connections with genuine nature. The connections responsibly satisfy the aching, ever-wanting hole in our psyche that has been produced by our excessive separation from nature and that leads us astray."

> **- Susan Chernak McElroy,**
> Award winning, N. Y. Times best selling author of *Animals as Teachers and Healers* and *Heart in the Wild.*

"We dramatically increased our program's effectiveness by adding the Natural Systems Thinking Process to it. It enables our participants to connect with their sensory origins in nature and use that peaceful power to improve their relationships with self, society and the environment."

> **- Dr. James Rowe,** Director,
> Outward Bound School in Costa Rica

"Here is an established, easily accessible alternative to the destructive pitfalls in the way we presently learn to think and relate. This foundation for a much needed improvement in education and counseling is a practical component for integrated learning. It enables contemporary humanity to co-create truly civilized relationships with our planet and its people."

> **- Dr. Douglass Cappogrossi,** President,
> Akamai University, Hawaii

Why This Book and Course?

"Scientific research is based on the idea that everything that takes place is determined by laws of nature, and therefore this holds for the action of people."

"Our task must be to free ourselves from (our) prison by widening our circles of compassion to embrace all living creatures and the whole of nature in its beauty."

- Albert Einstein

What Makes This Organic Book and Course Unprecedented?

Responses to this question by mid-career and other students who have completed the course in this book.

"It lets 'I want to make a difference' become 'I have a tool that enables me to make a difference'"

"*Helps us express love through acts that make our words trustable and our disorders subside.*"

"This social technology powerfully helps people reduce their conflicts and realize inner peace."

"*Presents a free, doable process that empowers us to implement Quinn's ideas in Ishmael.*"

"Substantiates natural systems theory with repeatable, first hand, experiences and observations."

"*If we want a peaceful and sane world, we must require every leader and parent to take this course.*"

"It sounds like it describes the workings of another planet until our experiences show us it is part of Earth and ourselves that we seldom get to see."

"*Scientifically engages us in a holistic natural systems process where attractions in nature unify our conflicted natural senses and ways of knowing.*"

"This practical science corrects the hurtful tendency of our best intentions to unintentionally produce our troubles."

"*Makes accessible presently missing information and energies in natural areas that we need to create socially and environmentally sound relationships.*"

"By heightening all my senses it saved me ten trips to the psychiatrist."

"*This invaluable educational tool helps me tranform irresponsible social and environmental elements of society into constructive planetary citizens.*"

"Presents the means for us to recover our soul by restoring natural systems in our consciousness."

"*Gives me an ally in nature that lends a hand in helping students improve their learning abilities.*"

"Its discovery is more useful than e=mc² because it frees the wilderness values within us. This helps us help our natural systems recover their integrity."

"*Authorizes us to benefit from our kinship with the purifying powers in nature that sustain health.*"

"Gives rise to the Internet becoming a courier for the wisdom of the global ecosystem."

"It could correctly be called *Earth's OK, I'm OK* or *Our Sensuous Planet.*"

Reviews of Michael J. Cohen's other books* and programs that the *Web of Life Imperative* introduces and updates.

"Dr. Cohen offers an environmentally sound, hands-on educational process that reduces apathy, motivates peace and promotes mental health. It fulfills our personal and economic needs, deeper ideals and spirit. His work deserves the attention of those who seek to reverse our troubles."

Dr. Robert Muller,
Chancellor of the University for Peace, United Nations; Assistant Secretary General Emeritus of the United Nations; recipient of the Albert Schweitzer Peace Prize and UNESCO prize for peace.

"Its impact lies in the fact that the author has lived its wisdom for these past twenty years. I have learned first hand that its theories prove themselves in the fruition that its education delivers. It offers the medicine that disillusioned humanity and the endangered environment needs."

Herb Alf, Ed.D.,
President, Environment Talent Development Ltd.

"Dr. Cohen's compelling application of ecopsychology connects us with the often ignored source of spirit and wellness found in nature. His deeply felt chapters catalyze conscious sensory contacts with the natural world and bind us to energies that heal our deeper being."

Dr. Larry Dossey, M.D.,
Researcher and author of *RecoveringThe Soul: A Scientific and Spiritual Search.*

"A pioneer in the environmental education movement. Participants learn to learn, learn that all subjects are interrelated with one another and themselves. Most of all they develop an interest in themselves."

The New York Times

"This is not a reading experience; it's a hologram. It is communicating through talking leaves, something of what whales communicate to each other...you are there."

Robin E. Lagemann, Native American activist

"Delightful, illuminating communication at its best--contains stories and guidance for experiencing Nature in the full thrill of her presence. "

Dr. Thomas Berry,
Author of *The Dream of Earth*

"Helps people make a profound connection between their psychological health, their sense of well being and the health of the environment by becoming aware of all the sensory experiences nature offers."

Maggie Spilner,
Walking Editor, Prevention Magazine

"A remarkable book: a do-it-yourself ecopsychology process that enables any school or individual to engage students in meaningful education filled with concern for creation."

Miriam Weinstein,
Author of *Making a Difference College Guide*

"This is the course that every civilized person will be required to take to reverse our disorders."

Charles Sierra, Counselor

"This book gently blends wholeness and critical thinking. It offers the powerful dimensions of intuition and sense of place to those who want to support responsible action toward nature."

Shann Weston
Project Wild coordinator, Oregon

"This fascinating literary work recycles your thinking. Cohen goes beyond simply exploring a relationship between psychology and ecology. He lets the natural world give us new ways to reason and consciously participate in our relationship with natural systems."

Chuck Lynd,
Education Forum Administrator, Compuserve

"Enables us to support and apply our good judgement, innate knowledge and visions for a better tomorrow. Here is an environmental educator who teams up with Earth to create a vehicle of hope."

Dr. Charles Yaple,
Director, Coalition for Education Outdoors

"This timely sound theory and well grounded experience demands its use by enlightened people. It should become mainstream in any society struggling to find connectedness and meaning in life. It allows the natural world to nurture a responsible growing edge of culture."

Bill Hammond,
Director of Education, Lee County, Florida

"The activities work; they move students. I see a significant improvement in their self-esteem and value. They discover an integrity outside themselves that they find to be a truth within themselves."

Mark Walsh,
Director of Wilderness Therapy, New Mexico

*Reconnecting With Nature   *Einstein's World*
Well Mind, Well Earth   *Prejudice Against Nature*
Across the Running Tide   *Connecting With Nature*
How Nature Works   *Our Classroom is Wild America*

Accompanied by study groups and trained to advanced degree levels, my unique twenty-eight year immersion in natural areas heightened my curiosity. In time, I and the others with me discovered how to think and teach using five imperative facts of life and forty-eight fundamental senses that we inherently register but that we normally socialize out of our awareness.

I observed how the omission of nature's fundamentals in contemporary thinking produces the destructive, hidden ruts that create our disorders, ruts that deepen each time we travel them. Without using natural system fundamentals our best efforts to increase inner and outer peace and personal and environmental health seldom succeed.

This book and course enable you to reverse our "destructive rut" phenomenon. It gives you a teachable process to help you and your community, in your locale, genuinely connect your thinking with its origins in the balancing, rejuvenating powers of nature. Personally and professionally you will learn how to bind with and support the health and peace of natural systems within and around you and in others. That's when things improve.

- *Michael J. Cohen*

Natural Systems Thinking Process
Educating, Counseling and Healing with Nature

The Web of Life Imperative

A Primer of Organic Psychology

The science of greening human services, education, and alternative medicine,

humanities, politics and spirituality.

Michael J. Cohen, Ed.D.

Co-Authors

Theresa Sweeney, Ph.D.

Sarah Anne Edwards, L.C., M.S.W.

J. Christina Brittain, M.A.

J. Marc McGinnes, J.D.

Susan Chernak McElroy, B. A.

Cyrus Rhode Jr., M.P.A.

Janet Thomas

Gary Leroy Hoover, Ph.D.

Jane Anne Jeffries, M.A.

Mark Brody, Ed.D.

Gerry Eitner, B.S.

Gaia Davies, M.S.W.

Maria Odum, M.S.

John Scull, Ph.D.

Marianne Salo

Peggy Garrigues-Cortelyou, M.Div.

Kacy Sigl, B. Ed.

Mardi Jones, Ph.D.

Janet LeValley, Ph.D.

Dave Paulsen, B.A.

F. Richard Schneider, Ph.D.

Allison Weeks, M.S.

Andrew E. Fister

B. James Rowe, Ph.D.

Charles M. McClintock, B.A.

Jan Goldfield, Ph.D.

Gretchen Grani, M.S.

David R. Givers, M.S.

Steve Smith, R.N., B.S.N.

Brigett Hurley-Camarena, B.A.

Carol Biggs, M.S.

Marie McLean, M.A.

Kaisa Naskali, Ph.D.

Cheri Wells, M.S., C.P.C.

Teresa Votlucka, R.N., M.S.

Kurtland Davies, Ph.D.

TRAFFORD

Project NatureConnect
Educating, healing and counseling with nature
books, scholarships, courses and degrees

Institute of Global Education
Box 1605, Friday Harbor, WA 98250
360-378-6313
Email: nature@interisland.net
www.ecopsych.com

NOTE: for review, subsidized, or quantity copies of this book, please contact the above address.

Printed on Chlorine free, recycled paper

Printed in Victoria, Canada

National Library of Canada Cataloguing in Publication Data

Cohen, Michael J., 1929-
      The web of life imperative : regenerative ecopsychology techniques that help people think
in balance with natural systems / Michael J. Cohen.
Includes bibliographical references.
ISBN 1-4120-0185-4
      I. Title.
BF353.5.N37C643 2003   155.9'1   C2003-901865-2

Acknowledgements

Special thanks to Marlow Shami, Bruce Conway and Christina Brittain and to the many co-authors, students and faculty who have helped edit and re-edit this program and the hundreds of Project NatureConnect students and interns who make and share conscious sensory contacts with nature during their coursework. To increase personal and environmental wellness, anonymously, they have donated for publication, here and elsewhere, the journal entries of their experiences. Their encounters ground this book in an authentic global reality that, to our and Earth's loss, we seldom learn to enjoy.

Contents

Advantages, Idiosycncrasies and Instructions

To the reader's benefit *The Web of Life Imperative* is also a course that may be taken or taught using this book as a textbook and guide. The course may be done online. For best results as a course carefully study and follow the Instructions in Appendix C.

> In the text of the book, instructions for online participants are usually boxed in grey or otherwise clearly indicated.

If your purpose is to just increase your knowledge, simply read the text of this book. In addition, to improve your thinking, wellness and relationships, read the text and do the activities fully. They are clearly identified. *For best results, keep a journal of what you discover in the activities and readings.*

Although the book has its own logical sequence, the chapters may be read out of context if you first read the Introduction and Chapter One.

To increase its effectiveness, the course optionally includes reading selections from *Reconnecting With Nature* by Michael J. Cohen, (Ecopress). Dr. Cohen's book *Einstein's World* further explores the use and potential of this book's web of life model in non-academic settings.

Lesson plans are being developed for each chapter and activity. If you create one and want to share it with others, please contact the author at nature@interisland.net or mjc100@dr.com

Because the course can take 12 days to 10 weeks to complete, this book repeats its important points in chapters and essays in order not to forget them. When using or presenting an isolated essay, this also eliminates the necessity for searching for related material it is based on. Although this makes parts of some pages repetitious, it enables the reader to separate out and use the book essays as complete study material in workshops, classes and presentations if they are preceded by the Introduction and Chapter One. The chapters contain activities, research, evaluations, experiences, essays, lessons, counseling techniques, healing skills and references. A handy overview of the book that may be distributed appears in Appendix E.

Most of the information and experience in this book have been documented in published references. In Appendix D, an article **Substantiation of the Natural System Thinking Process** contains statements that, by topic, support the information in this book as well as cite references to it. The article thereby serves as a course overview and lends scientific affirmation to the course subjects and conclusions.

This book's course is also known as the *Orientation Course* or *Psychological Elements of Global Citizenship*. It is taught online where activities and interactive participation can take place. *Doing the activities and sharing their results is an important part of the course. It provides irreplaceable empirical knowledge, evidence and energy for change.* It enables course participants to use each other's experiences and their reactions to them as a powerful textbook because experience is the best teacher. Doing this also serves to use these experiences to improve and widen relationships. Other books, courses, articles and degree programs that support this course are located at www.ecopsych.com.

This book and its course are the "real thing" in that for the past decade a wide range of people have applied the book's process and obtained the results we describe. However, just as you can not design a robot to substitute for a person and have it become a human being, with respect to the process offered here there is also no substitute for the real thing. As reasonable as a substitute may appear to be for parts of the process, it is also reasonable to remember that, so far, the way we have learned to think is faulty with respect to living harmoniously with people and the environment

A free course online, *Integrity 101* is located at http://www.ecopsych.com/giftpersonal.html . It is a useful introduction to this course and book. You may also give it as a gift to others.

" Oh, what a catastrophe, what a maiming of love when it was made personal, merely personal feeling.

This is what is the matter with us: we are bleeding at the roots because we are cut off from the Earth and sun and stars.

 Love has become a grinning mockery because, poor blossom, we plucked it from its stem on the Tree of Life and expected it to keep on blooming in our civilized vase on the table."

- D. H. Lawrence

"Nurture your felt love or respect for nature. Never deny it. That love is nature's voice, our origins in nature, the eons, the purifying intelligence, beauty and diversity of natural systems sustaining us in their perfection. It is the root source of our deeper hopes and ideals.

Our excessive disconnection from nature's attractive and intelligent perfection underlies the insanity of our suffering, greed and destructiveness. Unadulterated natural systems seldom suffer them.

To recover our sanity, we must reconnect our psyche with nature's genius and restore its strength and peace in our consciousness, thoughts and soul. In this book, a readily available Natural Systems Thinking Process empowers us to do this."

- Michael J. Cohen

Think for Yourself

Does Nature have recuperative and regenerative healing powers?

If not, how does nature create and sustain the perfection of its purity, balance and peace along with optimums of diversity, cooperation and life...without producing garbage, pollution or unreasonable abusiveness?

Isn't humanity part of nature?

The core of the organic science this book teaches recognizes that although we and our psyche live excessively indoor lives, separated from nature, we and our psyche are inherently part of nature. This means that the renewing, purifying and recycling powers found in natural systems can help us heal our injured psyche and thinking when we genuinely reconnect them with authentic nature. This reunification enables us to benefit from and further nature's powers. Although contemporary thinking often scoffs at this notion, others applaud the beneficial results this significant reconnection produces. We must keep in mind that the wellness of our thinking determines our health, relationships and destiny.

Doesn't the difference between the state of the unadulterated natural world and that of industrial society clearly show that while we suffer from warped thinking and relationships, unadulterated natural systems create and sustain nature's qualities and perfection that we inherit at birth?

Think for yourself. Reasonably explain to yourself the hundreds of substantiated findings, similar to those listed below, with respect to when we connect our psyche with natural systems.*

Given a choice between a scene with trees and one without, people of all ages and ethnic groups from all countries prefer the scene with trees.

People help rejuvenate and improve their lives by having a pet, going for a hike, keeping a garden or visiting a beautiful place.

Surgical patients have shorter hospitalizations, less need for pain medications, and fewer complaints about discomfort when they have hospital windows that overlook trees rather than brick walls.

Police report lower crime rates in areas of public housing developments that have a density of trees.

Prisoners with cells that provided views of rolling landscapes were found to need fewer sick calls than inmates whose cell windows overlooked prison courtyards.

Pets have positive effects on patients with dementia. Even patients with impaired mental abilities connect with cats or dogs.

Contemporary people who live in environments that are more natural, live longer.

Post-traumatic stress victims recover by connecting in nature to "something larger than themselves" in nature.

Nature-centered people and cultures seldom display or cause the problems that undermine industrial society.

*Irvine, K and Warber, S (2002). "Greening Healthcare: Practicing as if the Natural Environment Really Mattered" reviewed in *Alternative Therapies in Health and Medicine* September/October 2002 (Volume 8, Number 5).

Introduction

The Natural Systems Thinking Process

A powerful, sensory, nature reconnecting tool enables us to restore to health the numbed, nature-disconnected areas of our psyche that limit our reasoning and create our disorders.

SECTION ONE

A pioneer in nature-connected learning and psychology, Michael J. Cohen, Ed.D., recently passed by a homeless person lying on the sidewalk and successfully diminished a feeling of sadness that would usually overcome him. He became aware that the continuing degradation of people and the planet may have begun to harden him, as it has so many of us.

Cohen believes we subconsciously learn to numb ourselves to the state of the world because part of us has been hurt and given  up hope. We feel overwhelmed by our inability to produce the heaven on earth that our soul innately knows and constantly seeks. Globally and locally, we and the environment are bulldozed by power hungry, desensitized, big money stories and interests that exploit and control the natural world and people. Often helpless, sometimes in despair, we protect ourselves from the pain of this assault upon life's integrity, including the integrity of our personal lives. We are driven to find gratification where we can, too often in rewarding, immediate relationships that have destructive side effects and add to our troubles.

Cohen recognizes that we can neither implement our deeper ideals nor reverse our disorders if we do not have an effective, organic process that enables us to attain these crucial goals. He takes solace in the realization that through his tireless efforts the necessary process is readily available. He is heartened because people are increasingly benefiting from it.

Since 1959, Cohen has researched a sensory science, a unique way of relating that effectively addresses the core of our challenging personal and global problems. We who have become expert in his work have helped write this book because we know from experience that his process should not be ignored. Cohen sums it up in his description of a course he facilitates: "This course will teach you a simple, nature-connecting psychology tool that is easily accessible and practical. It will help you learn to use conscious, sensory connections with nature to reduce stress, heal disorders, improve your personal and professional relationships and enjoy more rewarding life-styles. It will give you the organic means to bring personal, social and environmental interactions into balance."

Our purpose in writing The *Web of Life Imperative* is to teach you important things about the natural systems within and around you that the powers of contemporary culture seldom want you to know. Industrial society usually urges us to suppress rather than nurture our inborn, natural way of thinking if for no other reason than it is cost free and independent. Empowering yourself with Cohen's Natural Systems Thinking Process helps you restore and enjoy the rewarding benefits of the way nature works to produce its balanced perfection.

Most people recognize that if we are to live in wellness and peace with ourselves, each other, and the environment, as have other cultures, it is imperative that we engage in a process that enables us to accomplish this task. Our great thinkers have provided us with hundreds of profound ideas about what is wrong and what should be done. What they have not provided, however, is a readily available process each of us can use to implement the best of these ideas. By following its instructions, this book teaches you that process.

NSTP results from an accidental discovery that Cohen made in 1952 while visiting a wild park area near Columbia University in New York City where he was a graduate student in Natural Science and Counseling. He observed in a group of students and faculty something that he had often felt in himself. While visiting this attractive natural area the group experienced a reduction of their stress and an increase in happy feelings and wellness. Cohen recognized that this was something he himself had always enjoyed when he was out in nature. Mentored by Dr. Paul F. Brandwein and Dr. Willard Jacobson, Cohen decided to investigate why this was so. Since that time he has concentrated on discovering ways to strengthen this valuable phenomenon because  he feels strongly attracted to relieve human and environmental suffering.

Cohen believed that natural systems in humans, as in the environment, have an inherent capability to build relationships that sustain life and health. He could see that the rest of the natural world does this with ease, but that contemporary humanity, although part of nature, had learned to ignore this gift. He has since taught thousands of people hundreds of short, fun, easy, principles and activities that help them discover and benefit from it.

Cohen has lived, learned and taught almost exclusively in natural areas for the past four decades. During this time, he has increasingly recognized that while people are part of nature, our excessively nature-separated lives remove us from nature's healing ways. This stresses and deteriorates our thinking, health and spirit. It reduces our nurturing by nature including its continual rejuvenation of our natural intelligence. This loss causes us to produce and suffer personal, social and environmental problems. In an Internet web site (http://www.ecopsych.com/integrity101.html) Cohen identifies this disorder as a distinct, destructive *Natural Attraction Desensitization Syndrome (NADS)*. More important, he has developed a preventative and antidote; a Natural Systems Thinking Process that helps us reverse NADS. The Process consists of scientifically developed activities, readings and interactive courses that are sensory and nature-reconnecting. They produce ordinarily absent empirical knowledge that empowers our thinking to participate in transforming NADS into more constructive and responsible relationships with ourselves, others and the environment.

Most people understand that our thinking's disconnection from nature can produce problems. It makes perfect sense to them, in theory, that reconnecting with nature must be a helpful solution. However, what most people have trouble understanding is why and how the Natural Systems Thinking Process (NSTP) works. Therefore, even when they see for themselves the beneficial results, they sometimes resist trusting the process and giving credibility to its use and effectiveness.

NSTP works because, back yard or back country, it enables people to create thoughtful moments in natural areas that let nature itself teach them what they need to know in order to restore into their consciousness the wisdom and integrity of their natural intelligence.

NSTP helps us heal our stressed and injured natural senses and sensibilities by interlacing them with the renewing energies inherent in natural systems. Because we are part of nature, when we make genuine sensory contact with it our natural intelligence becomes whole and can think with its powers. We enjoy and benefit from nature's balanced ways of knowing and relating. This makes us more resistant to NADS and we build more responsible relationships at every level. In this Process we realize the priceless value of natural systems within and around us so we further respect and protect them.

This Book's Key to Thinking and Relating

To understand how and why this NSTP book will work for you as it has for so many others, you must first consider the following key intelligence test question, one that ordinarily might help assess a person's mathematical aptitude and thinking ability:

"If you count a dog's tail as one of its legs, how many legs does a dog have?"

"Five," of course, is the correct answer for a math test. Intelligent people say "five" because it is valid in mathematical systems and contemporary thinking and is highly regarded and rewarded by our society. However, we don't solely live our lives or think in mathematical systems. Our natural sense of reason can consider what we know from our actual contact with a real, normal dog, too. That's when our multitude of other natural senses come into play: senses of sight, touch, motion, color, texture, language, sound, smell, consciousness, community, trust, contrast, and love. They each provide further information and help our sense of reason make more sense and a more informed decision. They enable our thinking to sensibly register that a tail is different than a leg, that a dog has four legs, not five, no matter what might be correct in mathematical logic.

It is a grave mistake for anyone not to take very seriously the difference between 4-leg and 5-leg ways of knowing and our learned prejudice for the latter. As this book shows, when they are not in balance the stressful schism between their two different ways of registering the world is significant. *Four-leg knowing* is a magnificent psychological and physiological phenomenon with deep natural system roots into the eons, the heart of Earth and our psyche. It brings our widely diverse multiplicity of natural sensory experiences into our awareness. *Five-leg knowing* produces important awareness through abstract imagination, labels and stories. However, when it does not also seek and contain organic 4-leg knowledge it results not only in our desensitization but in the separation of our thinking from the healing powers of Earth's natural systems within and around us. This profound loss produces the many destructive side effects of our artificial world that we can not readily solve.

Four-leg versus 5-leg discord creates an entrenched conflict in our psyche between how we think and how nature works. This is a point source of the stress and contamination our society produces in people and the environment. It generates our many disorders and troubles that are seldom found in nature.

It is important to recognize that by financially and socially rewarding us for getting "good grades" or for "making the grade" by using nature-isolated 5-leg thinking, our socialization habitually bonds, conditions, programs or addicts us to 5-leg thinking. In the process, 5-leg thinking often learns to demean 4-leg reasoning as childish, unscientific, or environmentalist (tree hugging, airy-fairy, Earth muffin). The result is that we become dependent on 5-leg knowing and relating. For example:

> "Aristotle thought there were eight legs on a fly and wrote it down. For centuries scholars were content to quote his authority. Apparently, not one of them was curious enough to impale a fly and count its six legs."
> **-Stuart Chase**

The Natural Systems Thinking Process reverses this psychological schism and its destructive personal and environmental effects by enabling us to reasonably gather information from both 4-leg and 5-leg sources. This lets us enjoy a whole, healing, 9-leg thinking process. The vital secret of NSTP is that by carefully following its instructions, we can enlist nature's restorative powers to overcome our bonded conditioning to destructive 5-leg thinking. In time, 9-leg thinking becomes as ordinary and healthful as brushing your teeth.

Disconnection From 4-leg Knowledge

Most of us recognize that we are biologically, psychologically and spiritually part of, and thereby lovingly attached to nature. We usually just say we "love" nature. Because we all need nature's "resources" to survive, we have a compelling attraction for these resources; an inborn affinity or love for sunshine, food, water, the land, air and healthy, supportive, diverse community.

Our greatest error is to ignore that we live extremely nature-disconnected lives. On average, we spend over 95% of our time indoors. This almost completely detaches us from and desensitizes us to nature. Over 99.99% of our thinking is 5-legged; it consists of stories that are separated from and out of touch and tune with nature's powers. We normally learn to know nature from 5-leg, abstract, "as if," or "objective" observations about it. We seldom enjoy or think with authentic, thoughtful, multiple-sense, 4-leg, natural systems contact. We substitute conjecture for empirical sensory evidence. This produces many conflicts and very

few satisfactions from wholeness. It becomes our destiny.

Our nature-estranged, 5-leg intelligence calls our extreme dismemberment of our psyche from its womb in nature "normal," "progress," and "excellence in education." We seldom register this way of thinking as a desensitizing, intellectual, emotional and spiritual amputation. As we suffer psychologically from this separation, Earth suffers from the impact of our emotional pain, insensitivity and ignorance.

We seldom realize that in order to escape or tranquilize the pain our separation causes, we often insensitively trespass or invade the integrity of natural systems within and around us. This produces many of our seemingly unsolvable problems. There is a solution. People who use the Natural Systems Thinking Process have an organic tool that helps them more effectively participate in  resolving our greatest challenges through 9-leg reasoning and acts. The tool works because it helps us reattach our dismembered psyche to its origins in nature in exactly the same way that a surgeon reattaches a dismembered arm to a person's body. The surgeon brings the arm and body together. This allows nature's attraction energies to biologically heal the separation as only they can.

Observations from reconnecting

For the past 42 years Dr. Cohen has lived, taught and researched in natural areas, often camping and sleeping outdoors year round. From this 4-leg contact with nature he learned that nature is not something fearful to be conquered in the name of civilization, safety and economic growth. Instead, he learned to treat nature's attractive peace with respect. He enjoyed nature as a powerful friend, teacher and guide as do the members of the plant, animal and mineral kingdoms. His admiration or reverence for nature helps him teach his students to seek and include 4-leg information in their reasoning. This increases their sensitivity, thoughtfulness and intelligence regarding our relationships with natural systems within and around us. Through NSTP, natural systems in your locale will help you enjoy these benefits.

Significantly, the major problems our society faces seldom exist in intact natural systems or genuinely nature-connected people. As a twig is bent, so grows the tree. Contemporary people seldom grow up in a nature-connected, 9 leg way. Our nature-disconnected society rewards 5-leg thinking and relating; it exploits and demeans nature and 4-leg experiences. This habitual practice and its detrimental effects have led to the demise of the natural people and natural areas that thrived in North America before our culture arrived.

Cohen's forty years in natural systems have taught him that we do not have just five senses, as Aristotle said, but over fifty inborn natural senses. Cohen identified and published these senses in 1990 and again in his 1997 book *Reconnecting With Nature*. Each of these senses is a natural love and intelligence. Each registers in our awareness as an attractive 4-leg connection with natural systems through which we can relate sensibly and sensitively to the environment and each other.   Each helps our thinking and relationships make more sense.

Since 1952, Cohen has researched, applied, and taught people how to incorporate parts of the Natural Systems Thinking Process into their personal and professional lives. NSTP enables us to rejuvenate our 53 natural senses and restore these senses in our mentality and interactions.

NSTP is presently part of several accredited, university training courses as well as degree programs. It has been reviewed and published in professional science and technology, psychology and education journals. It is available to anybody through books, workshops and the Internet. Cohen has written four other books that explore various aspects of it. In this book, we update what you need to know in order to use or teach it on an introductory level.

The history of NSTP

In 1959, Dr. Cohen founded a camp and school program based on reconnecting with nature. The National Audubon Society and many others called it the most revolutionary school in America. They said it was on the side of the angels. Participants traveled and thrived by camping out in 83 different natural habitats throughout the seasons. They learned to be aware of their thoughts and feelings. They learned to live out their commitment to have open, honest relationships with the natural environment, each other and with indigenous people(s), researchers, ecologists, the Amish, organic farmers, anthropologists, folk musicians, naturalists, shamans, administrators, historians and many others close to the land. The experience deeply reconnected their 53 senses to their natural origins. They reconnected their thinking and selves to the whole of nature.

The students loved to educate themselves this way and its effectiveness showed in its results:

Chemical dependencies, including alcohol and tobacco, disappeared.

Destructive social relationships were challenged and healed.

Personality and eating disorders subsided.

Violence, crime and prejudice were unknown in the group.

Academics improved because they were applicable, hands-on and fun.

Loneliness, hostility and depression subsided.

Group interactions allowed for stress release and management; each day was fulfilling and relatively peaceful.

Some students using meditation found they no longer needed to use it. They learned how to sustain a nature-connected community that more effectively helped them increase their resiliency to stress and disease. Others found the experience increased the benefits of meditation by attaching it to the peace in global natural systems.

Participants said they felt they knew each other better than they knew their families or best friends and knew themselves better than they ever had before.

Participants felt safe. They risked expressing and acting from their deeper thoughts and feelings. A profound, inborn sense of social and environmental responsibility guided their decisions.

When vacation periods arrived, neither staff nor student wanted to go home. Each person enjoyed working to build this supportive, balanced living and learning utopia. They were home.

Students sought and entered right livelihood professions.

All this occurred simply because community members made sense of their life by developing supportive, multiple-sensory relationships that restored their contact with the attractive callings of the natural world within and around them.

The 9-leg secret to each participant's success was to learn how to thoughtfully learn through 4-leg natural sensations and feelings that arose from their newly regrown sensory roots in ecosystems within and around them. These sensations acted as nature's guiding voice. The value and rewards of doing this freed the participants' 53 senses from their bonds to questionable 5-leg stories. It re-bonded them to their 4-leg sense of reason in congress with 52 other rejuvenated natural senses while these senses were connected to their origins and home in nature. This resulted in consensus based 9-leg thinking, literacy and relating that included information from, and the regenerative, healing powers of, natural systems. To many 5-leg thinkers, this sounds crazy, but year after year the beneficial results still speak for themselves.

From 30 years of travel and study in over 260 national parks, forests and subcultures, Cohen developed a replicable learning process and psychology that anyone can use at home, work or school today. It unleashes our suppressed 4-leg ability to grow and survive responsibly with natural systems in ourselves, others and the environment. By documenting that it worked and could be taught, he earned his doctoral degree and the school became a nationally recognized graduate and undergraduate degree program.

From 1985-92, Cohen translated his nature-connected psychology program into Project NatureConnect and the Natural Systems Thinking Process for public use, backyard or back country, via the Internet or in conjunction with local community members in real time.

Through NSTP courses, people recover their natural senses and integrity by sharing their attractions to hands-on, sensory, nature reconnections at home, work or school. This is done individually and is then contributed to small study groups either over the Internet or in person. Students also respond to 5-leg readings. An example of NSTP in action is reported by a student in the next section of this Introduction.

The beneficial results and outcomes of NSTP are located in this book's Prerequisites: Survey of Participants section (page 31) and the unedited journal entries of participants found in *Einstein's World* as well as links from the Survey and www.ecopsych.com.

Any sane person understands full well that we can't resolve our unsolvable problems using the same, nature-disconnected, 5-leg thinking that produces them. The critical contribution of NSTP is that it empowers individuals to create moments that let Earth teach in its sensory voice. It helps us responsibly unify 5-leg and 4-leg thinking. This 9-leg unification is a healthy, organic, superintelligent way of knowing and relating. It provides us with the missing essence of sustainable living and peace that we can enjoy personally, socially and globally.

NOTE: We have published the essence of this Introduction's description of NSTP and 9-leg thinking as a single page located in Appendix E. With permission, it may be copied and used from that page as an introduction to methods and materials you may want to distribute in sharing or teaching NSTP.

In the essay that follows, a Doctoral graduate student, Sarah Edwards, who learned this book's chapters in Cohen's online Orientation Course, describes NSTP from her initial, experiences with it. What she describes is normal for this course that has been given over 125 times since its inception in 1995.

The Natural Systems Thinking Process: Mother Nature's Path to Relief and Release

My adventures with the Project NatureConnect Online Orientation Course.

by Sarah Edwards
October, 2002

In the early 90's, the field of ecopsychology rolled onto the map with alarms blazing. A flurry of books by experts from Jungian analyst Marion Woodman, to cultural historian Thomas Berry, to social historian Theodore Roszak and social biologist E.O.Wilson proclaimed a vital relationship between nature and our physical, social and psychological well-being. But, the experts despaired, we've become so disconnected from this link  that both we and the environment are suffering – we in terms of proliferating stress-related disorders; the environment in terms of severe degradation of the ecosystem.

Since that time, despite such protestations, our disconnection from nature has only grown more profound. We work in a "cubicle culture" tethered 24/7 electronically by email and cell phones to our personal and career demands. As a culture, we suffer from more lifestyle-related stress disorders and manmade environmental problems than ever before.

To cope, we pop Paxil, Prozac or Excedrin PM. Americans spend 1.8 billion dollars a year on Paxil alone and anti-depressants are only slightly below blood pressure drugs as the most commonly used medication.

Most people either:

1) Remain unaware that their chronic fatigue, dis-stress, deteriorating or non-existent relationships and loss of community are related to a disconnection from nature and their own innate biological wisdom – or –

2) Are unable to do anything to change the pace, limitations and pressures of their lives to find less demanding and more harmonious ways to live.

Recently books like *Awakening to Nature: Renewing Your Life by Connecting with Nature* by Charles Cook have arrived in bookstores. These books suggest that taking nature breaks and bringing plants into our cubicles can help relieve our frazzled nerves. Unfortunately, while such suggestions may provide temporary relief from a stressful day, they are purely palliative, casting Nature in the role of a warm bath that will make our hassles more tolerable.

We seem helpless to change our fundamentally frazzled lifestyle. Or that's how it seemed to me before enrolling in one of Dr. Michael Cohen's online courses, the *Natural Systems Thinking Process.* Over a series of nine lessons, I learned that nature can be far more than a respite from our way of life. It can become our guide to a permanent cure.

I began the online nine-week course with a small group of total strangers from across the nation and beyond. Over our weeks together, we participated in a series of Nature Activities pioneered over the last fifty years by Dr. Cohen, a leading authority in applied ecopsychology and author of the book *Reconnecting with Nature.* We learned that:

1. Nature knows how to operate free of the disorders we suffer.

2. As part of nature, we, too, have this capability.

3. We can do this by using our innate abilities to think and operate as nature does, reconnecting with natural attractions that link us to all other aspects of life.

4. In this way, nature can become our teacher, showing us in non-verbal but irrefutable terms how to live joyful, fulfilling lives moment by moment.

At the beginning of the course, some of us urbanites doubted that we would be able to find places to do Nature Activities. But we learned otherwise. It is possible to do Nature Activities whether one lives in a Manhattan high rise, suburban condo or mountain chalet. For example, one participant in our group lives in an inner-city rental in a major metropolitan area in the Southeast. She wrote, "I am having trouble finding many 'nice' natural places to go to. I have no forests or windswept beaches or whatever near me."

Upon closer investigation, she noticed there was an almond tree and several citrus trees in her overgrown backyard. A grape vine grew rampant along the fence and beneath it there was hidden an ancient vegetable garden created by a previous tenant. Orange flowers poked out above the blades and clumps of grass. Before long she also found herself exploring the dog park where she walked her dog and discovered a lovely stand of salmon-pink eucalyptus trees she'd never noticed before as well as a nearby golf course. "This was all so far outside of what I'd been thinking of as 'nature' that I'd failed to see what was right in front of my nose," she explained.

So, once or twice each week, we shared our experiences in nature with one another and established a bond none of us would have thought possible between total strangers who have still never met face to face. During the course, we were all confronted with one or more travails of life: the loss of a job, moments of self-doubt, overwhelming time pressures, the death of loved ones, and career crises. But within a short period of time, we discovered how our growing connection with nature could ease us through unavoidable traumas and help us avoid others all together.

One busy career mother, for example, came into the course feeling stressed and pressed for time. "I have been juggling time ever since my kids were born," she explained. She'd even put off taking the course because she worried how she could add one more thing to her day. But once both her children were both in school, she seized the opportunity.

"So much of my daily interactions are around taking care of others," she wrote later, "especially their pain. Or as a parent dealing with mundane tasks or having to be a disciplinarian. It's hard to stay in touch with play and humor."

But this began to change mid-way through the course during a Nature Activity she did while visiting a friend who owns several acres of wooded property. There she walked to sit by a small pond and was especially attracted to the wind, watching it dance across the shimmering water. It was "playful, joyful," she wrote and suddenly she wanted to make something beautiful. Arranging a broken piece of birch tree limb, some bark with little lichens, a few acorns and a pinecone, she created a thank-you gift on a rock beside the pond for her hostess.

"The important message for me from this experience," she wrote, "is how much I need to revive the playful, joyful, creative parts of myself." Since then, she's begun making different choices about how to prioritize her time and where to put her energy. In doing this some things may fall by the wayside at times, she finds. The house isn't always as orderly as she'd like. Their meals are more basic. Her garden gets neglected at times and the checkbook isn't balanced every month. But she says, "I am starting to feel better. I have a lot more energy. I'm more interested in my work and I have a deeper connection with my husband and kids."

Another participant was able to put the shock of an unexpected job loss in perspective. The experience had left him extremely drained of energy but while doing a Nature Activity in a nearby park, he experienced both the physical and the mental healing effect of nature. As he drew near a strand of shade trees, "It quite literally reminded me of being held in my mother's arms as a very young child," he wrote. "It was as if the area was saying to me; come to me, let me hold you so that you can rest."

He lay down and fell asleep under those trees. When he awoke he "sensed how each thing around me was connected to the others for its survival. We're all part of nature, relying on one another. I knew I would be OK even though my job had ended. Change is constant and I'm not going through it alone. The natural world has been surviving much longer than I have, so why not learn from it?"

Another participant suffered the deaths of both a dear friend and her cat. On top of that she was accosted on the street. She wrote, "I have had a week where my self-esteem hit a low and I was faltering about the reason for being in the world, the grief and loss had overwhelmed me and I was at my most vulnerable."

That week she found that the nature-connecting activity "gave me a sense of self-love and pride in my ability to defend myself. It was like having a friend, a very dear friend, hug me warmly taking away a lot of sadness and pain and shock reminding me to trust myself and to keep taking risks in life, no matter how hard it can get because I have the strength and courage to make it through."

While each week's activities had specific healing effects on our lives, the cumulative effect was even more far-reaching. Some of us began to re-evaluate our careers, where we lived, our relationships with our loved ones, etc. One participant decided to move to another part of the state where she lived, concluding, "I have decided to move interstate to an area that is more aligned with my values and needs. I have a feeling I am not in a healthy place. So I will be preparing to move over the next few weeks." She moved before the course was completed.

Another participant explained, "This course helped me grow emotionally over the past couple of months. I gained great joy from the experiences that I have had and shared with my wife. I am less wanting and quite happy most of the time. I have a feeling of calmness which if it leaves I now know how to regain efficiently and effectively through simple reconnection activities. It gives me hope for the future."

This last comment sums up what I found to be the most important thing for me both personally and professionally. On a daily basis we tend to get bogged down in a myriad of worries, concerns, fears, habits, and issues that are unappealing, unpleasant and even painful to us. Nonetheless we cling to these stresses, unable to escape them. As helping professionals in psychotherapy and other healing processes, we assume that we must help people to figure out these problems. We don't consider that by following our natural attractions as nature does, we can make different choices to eliminate these stresses from our lives.

Since completing the course, I've faced several upsetting events in my life, but I find I'm handling them quite differently now.

Knowing how good I feel when I am connected to nature and knowing that I have the choice to feel that good at any time, I am no longer willing to give up that feeling, even if I am in the middle of a frightening or unpleasant experience. I've learned that at any moment, I can say, "No, that's not what I want." No matter how difficult the situation, I can choose to connect with nature, to move responsibly toward what attracts us in the moment, to choose wisely for myself, my loved ones, my community and my natural environment habitat.

The Natural Systems Thinking Process is a remarkable personal and professional tool that can be used to heal us of a vast variety of lifestyle stresses and the resulting depression, anxiety, and addictions that plague us. In the process we can learn to respect and value, and thereby preserve, the life-giving natural environment around us.

* * *

Additional essays by students regarding their experiences with the course in this book are found at: http://www.ecopsych.com/newbook4wli910a.html

References

Berry, Thomas (1988). *The Dream of Earth*. San Francisco, CA: Sierra Club Books.

Cohen, Michael (1997). *Reconnecting with Nature*. Corvallis, Oregon: Ecopress.

Cook, Charles (2002). *Awakening to Nature, Renewing Your Life by Connecting with Nature*. New York: Contemporary Books.

Roszak, Theodore, ed. (1995). *Ecopsychology: Restoring the Earth, Healing the Mind*. San Francisco: Sierra Club.

Wilson, E.O. (1984). *Biophilia: The Human Bond with Other Species*. Cambridge, MA: Harvard University Press.

Woodman, Marion (1988). "Abandoned Souls, Abandoned Planets." in Ryley, Nancy *The Forsaken Garden: Four Conversations on the Deep Meaning of Environmental Illness*. Wheaton, IL: Quest Book.

SECTION THREE

Identifying organic four-leg experiences and their value

Can you afford to ignore the following seldom recognized, but well-documented by research, phenomena?

Personal or professional relationships that are genuinely connected with nature are more enjoyable, successful and responsible than those isolated from nature.

Nature-isolated people suffer from excessive stress, conflict and destructiveness. Contact with nature helps them transform and recycle back into peaceful and responsibly balanced relationships.

If you have ever had a good experience in nature, you know far more about the Natural Systems Thinking Process (NSTP) than you might realize. We identify some 4-leg experiences, below, because our 5-leg thinking is usually conditioned to overlook their value.

NSTP helps you validate and explain these phenomena because otherwise, too often, we take nature's messages and benefits for granted. For example:
Have you ever:

-wanted to go to a natural outdoor area for your vacation?

-had a good experience in nature that made you feel happier to be alive?

-longed for a livelihood that further contributed to personal and global balance rather than exploited Earth and people?

-noticed that disorders tend to subside and stress fade in nature?

-loved a pet, plant or place that made life more worthwhile?

Have you ever:

-treasured a rock or totem that helped you through troubled times?

- felt greater love for a person or people while in a natural area? Noticed that it is easier to build and sustain relationships there?

- felt, at times, as drawn to Mother Earth as you would a caring human parent that you loved?

- noticed that in nature you can think more clearly?

Have you ever:

-had strong sensations about connections between yourself and nature or Earth that you know are real but you can't easily explain?

-felt angry or sad about how we injure or destroy the natural environment and/or its people and diversity?

-noticed that counseling, educating and healing are more effective when they include quality time in natural areas?

-discovered new phenomena or senses that connect you with life that are often absent in indoor environments?

Have you ever:

-read the scientific studies that document how reconnecting our thinking and feeling to our psychological and biological origins in nature has beneficial learning, healing, and environmental effects? (Appendix D, page 133)

The experience(s) with nature described above, or others you may have had, demonstrate that nature has its own 4-leg healing energies and perfection that attractively register in us because we are part of nature. You did not need special training or books to enjoy or learn from these experiences.

Ongoing research (Appendix D) shows that neither nature nor people(s) whose thinking is consciously connected to it, produce the destructive stress, violence and corruption too often found in contemporary society. People in contact with nature recover faster from illness and enjoy many additional benefits. It also shows that our addictive 5-leg thinking has been trained to downplay the value of our natural system experiences. It often calls them escapes, fuzzy thinking or recreation instead of re-creation.

The Natural Systems Thinking Process in this book empowers you with a teachable tool that safely increases, strengthens and improves these experiences and their benefits. It works well because experience is the best teacher.

Although we may give nature lip service, we routinely relate to it as our slave or prisoner. We normally manage, exploit or kill nature for profit even while knowing that we are part of it and it is our life support system. We have subdued within us the ability to actively recognize that as part of nature, we share its natural systems. We learn to take far too lightly that what we do to nature we also do to ourselves.

Our cultural prejudice against nature often prevents us from validating and celebrating our nature-connected experiences. We fail to recognize them as "in tune" moments; moments when nature fully touches itself in us, becomes whole, and purifies its wholeness in our awareness. Too often, we learn to overlook how nature-connected moments make sense, feel attractive and have healing qualities. We seldom acknowledge that because the rewards from these moments are more sensible and powerful than the rewards from our destructive, irrational, psychological addictions, the energies in these moments can help us to transform our destructive attachments into constructive relationships.

If you could bottle the effects of good moments in nature you could sell the product for a fortune.

The Natural Systems Thinking Process helps you recognize that this 5-leg bottling idea is foolish. With respect to nature, nobody has yet to find a substitute for the real thing and its eons of experience. To bottle it would be to disconnect it from the integrity of its wholeness and that is its secret to success. You would lose the very essence of what you thought you were bottling. That's what pills, media and technologies are trying to do now. They are often part of our problem; not the solution.

People who learn and practice the NSTP science of reconnecting their thinking with nature improve their personal, professional and environmental wellness. We invite you to engage in this process through this book and the course it contains.

The best way to learn this process is do the activities and then discuss them in community. For many of us, the most available community is online with us at Project NatureConnect. Enjoy the many new opportunities that present themselves as you do the activities. WARNING! With respect to self-improvement it is practically useless to read this book and not do the activities. Recognize that your socialized tendency is to know and understand NSTP with 5-leg thinking and resist doing the activities. Not doing them may get you a 5-leg "A" for a course that you actually flunk if your goal is to improve relationships beyond the superficial.

One important thing to note about NSTP is that it works well because it is a complete process. If your 5-leg thinking tells you to ignore or shortcut part of the process because you already "know" it, your 5-leg thinking is probably misleading you. You may know how to drive a car, but if you don't get in the car and drive it to where you want to go, you won't get there.

Although this book teaches you the Natural Systems Thinking Process, it cannot alone help you to reconnect your 4-leg natural thinking with your 5-leg socialized thinking and verbalization. An important part of this process is sharing with another person what happened when you connected with nature through an activity. You then learn from that person what they liked or found worthwhile in what you shared. Vice versa, that person sharing with you their results from doing the activity, and your response to them, is equally important. This sharing provides even greater benefits and learning if you are sharing with a small group of diverse people. In addition, if one of these people has already had some experience with NSTP, a deeper level of sharing can be achieved. When done correctly, such sharing enables us to 9-leg connect with natural systems in each other, even though we've never met. Significantly, we learn to know, trust and love each other through the natural attractions that are us, each other and nature.

Over the past 12 years, sharing via email and telephone has proven very effective. You can make  arrangements to engage in the sharing experience by email through our web site at www.ecopsych.com. Sharing is built into the online Orientation Course that this book represents, as well as all our other online courses. Online, NSTP becomes customized to help you reconnect your personal disconnections.

Sadly, many of us contain a natural part of our psyche that suffers from *Natural Attraction Desensitization Syndrome* (NADS). That part of us has become frightened, hurt and angry that contemporary society and its disconnected 5-leg thinking has painfully put it in a jail for crimes it never committed. There it suffers the discontents of guilt, shame, depression, greed, isolation, stress, dependencies, aggression, insensitivity, and the many other NADS disorders that plague us and society. That part of us has good reason to mistrust organized education, psychology and science. It is even afraid that the process that has created nature-connected learning and activities will harm it, even while it also knows that a long walk in the park is usually refreshing.

Each NSTP activity demonstrates to the NADS part of us that nature's healing ways and supportive community are much more powerful than 5-leg NADS disconnection and its discomfort.

It is well worth keeping in mind that some things this book touches upon may at first feel uncomfortable. This is because the book sometimes addresses inaccuracies in 5-leg thinking. Remember, it is the 5-leg part of you that is literate, doing the reading and so that part of you becomes confronted. Similar to validating a dog's tail as not being one of its legs, you may help yourself restore your equilibrium by doing the activities and obtaining valuable 4-leg information through them.

This Book as a Course

The Ecopsychology of Educating and Counseling With Nature

Updated from *Psychology Today,* May-June 1994

Course Scope and Purpose:

From the druids of the Celtic forests to the great tribes of American Indians, people have sought balance, peace and wisdom by living according to the laws of Mother Nature.

Unfortunately, this century will be remembered for unprecedented exploitation of nature—and widespread psychological disturbance of individuals.

No coincidence to Michael J. Cohen, Ed.D., pioneer of what he calls Integrated Ecology or Applied Ecopsychology. A synthesis of ecology and psychology, integrated ecology proposes that both the destruction of the Earth's environment and people's isolation, stress and dysfunction stem from a fundamental denial of our connection to nature and its sensory voice. And by psychologically reconnecting with authentic nature, we reverse our psychological disorders.

Western civilization emphasizes only the faculties of sight, reason, and language, forcing most of us to suppress our natural senses - all 53 of them, by Cohen's reckoning. Among them are : hunger, thirst, compassion, color, sex, place, community, nurturing and motion. They sensuously connect us to the world; we think with them to make sense. Spending over 95% of our lives cloistered and indoors leaves these natural sensory connections excessively wanting; human dysfunction and evils — cigarette smoking, greed, dependencies, violence — naturally follow to help fill the void.

Cohen is not a lone hunter of the bond between man and nature. According to Pulitzer-Prize winning sociobiologist Edward O. Wilson, Ph.D., of Harvard, people have an inherent biological need to be in contact with the out-of-doors. He calls it "biophilia", and believes that nature may hold the key to our aesthetic, intellectual, cognitive, and even spiritual satisfaction. Our childhood love of animals and natural myths and fairy tales may be early evidence of our basic affinity for nature and its

instructive healing properties. Our loss of this affinity creates needs for humans, relative to their degree of disconnection, to partake in counseling and building responsible relationships by reconnecting with nature.

Cohen has devised therapeutic home study training manuals, workshops, on-site and email correspondence courses, discussion groups and degree programs that offer activities, in backyards or backcountry, to re-create many beneficial relationships enjoyed by earlier hunting, gathering, and communal living peoples. In the American Psychological Association Journal "The Humanistic Psychologist" (Vol. 21, No. 3) and other professional publications, he reports that while taking part in these education programs community spirit and responsibility grow, participants' personality and eating disorders subside, learning and other cognitive abilities improve, and violence and prejudice dissolve. He and other participants learn to do, own and teach unforgettable nature connecting activities that produce these results throughout their lives. Gradually, a deep environmental literacy evolves that rejuvenates our natural senses, balance and joy.

From his home base at the Institute of Global Education, a special NGO consultant to the United Nations Economic and Social Council, Cohen offers books, workshops, training, degree programs and information about ecologically oriented education and therapeutic methods.

Course Description

TITLE: Psychological Elements of Global Citizenship: Counseling, Healing, and Educating with Nature.

SUBTITLE: The Web of Life Imperative and the Natural Systems Thinking Process.

DESCRIPTION: Discover how our excessive separation from nature stressfully dismembers our sentient inner nature and produces our psychologically bonded "unsolvable" problems. Learn to reverse this destructive process. Master thoughtful nature-reconnecting activities that dissolve stress by satisfying our deepest natural loves, wants and spirit. This course scientifically teaches lasting, hands-on, education, counseling and leadership skills that feelingly tap the "higher power" wisdom of nature's creation process. Using e-mail and telephone contacts between course members, members help each other reconnect with nature and nature helps us nurture warm interpersonal relationships, wellness and responsibility.

Course Mechanics

This book parallels a distance learning Orientation Course given on the Internet for students at several colleges and universities. It serves as a reader and administration tool for the course. For this reason, some of the online course instructions are included in Appendices C and F. These appendices assist readers in teaching or using this material later. This information is important to anyone to better understand the online program, its procedures, and the potential for you or those you want to reach. These online instructions are also occasionally identified by their appearance in screened boxes throughout the text of the book. You may disregard them, as you read the main text of the book if they do not prove to be of interest. Return to them when they become useful as an essential part of your personal exercises or teaching materials. Full course instructions appear in Appendix C.

Repetitive Course Materials

As mentioned earlier in the book instructions, several of the basic tenets in the course are repeated many times. Repetition serves to make course articles complete so that they do not lose their integrity. The advantage to you is that for instructional purposes, articles in this book may be taken from it and still make sense when used independently. Independent use of chapters would not be possible if the prime material upon which the articles were based was not included in each article. When material seems overly repetitive, simply note its location for future use, skip over it and go on to the next point.

Questions the Course Addresses

To help yourself observe how much you confidently learn on the course, apply the question and response below to each question on this page now, and again when you have completed the book or course. We invite you to add your own questions about the web of life to this list now and review them later, too. None of us has a monopoly on the knowledge of nature. Each of us contributing our experiences and understanding can help all of us reconnect with nature.

QUESTION: How confident am I that I can reasonably respond to this question?

On a piece of paper, record the course question numbers that follow along with the number below, that indicates your degree of confidence in your response to the question.

1	2	3	4	5	6	7	8	9	10
low confidence		medium					high confidence		

Course questions:

1 - How much of our ability to sense and feel do we inherit from nature?

1	2	3	4	5	6	7	8	9	10
low confidence		medium					high confidence		

2 - What are webstrings? Why are they often subconscious and how do we bring them into awareness?

3 - What are the major steps to letting nature help us reduce our destructive attachments?

4 - Do you deserve to have good feelings? Why?

5 - How many natural senses do you have? Do you think with them? How?

6 - What is the point source of contemporary society's environmentally destructive ways?

7 - What is the key factor that makes people different or separated from nature?

8 - What values are there in your safely feeling closer with nature?

9 - What is the greatest truth in your life that you can trust? (Clue: the answer is not God, love, honesty or nature.)

10 - What is the difference between a fact, a thought, and a feeling?

11 - How many natural senses can you name that you can know and learn from?

12 - Is there a relationship between our runaway social problems and our environmental problems?

13 - How does nature within you know how to relate responsibly to nature in others and nature in all environments?

14 - Life has a purpose. What is it?

15 - Can you be sane if you are a good citizen of an insane society?

16 - Is our innate ability to sense and feel of, by and from nature?

17 - Does our formal education or our leadership competently address the above questions?

18 - Why don't survival stories and dollar bills produce balance and purity like nature works?

19 - What is consciousness and who invented it?

20 - Do miracles happen in contradiction to nature?

21 - What is the relationship between nature and the human spirit?

22 - Do our major problems result from the differences between how we think and how nature works?

23 - Since nature produces no garbage, does nature practice unconditional love?

24 - In nature, does two plus two equal four?

25 - Where in nature do you find life abstracted?

26 - To be part of a system, you have to be in communication with it in some way. We are part of the global life system and vice versa; how does it communicate with us and we with it?

27 - What is the relationship between natural attractions and consciousness?

28 - How and where do you collect self-evidence?

29 - What is an ecozombie?

30 - Is nature a form of perfection that people can achieve and if so, how?

31 - What produces the wanting void in our psyche, the discomfort, greed and loneliness in humans that often fuels environmental disorders?

32 - What is the sensory relationship between nature, the Divine and the Human Spirit?

33 - We learn how to be who we are; what prime factor in modern education teaches us to produce our lasting problems?

34 - What important source of healing energy does our cultural bias omit, thereby sustaining our dependency upon healing programs and uninformed leaders?

35 - What is the force that produces environmentally and socially destructive economic relationships?

36 - Why do we continue to assault nature and people when this assault doesn't make sense and we neither like causing this pain nor its hurtful effects?

37 - What is the fundamental building block of nature that we can experience in natural systems in all areas?

38 - How can we restore to our thinking the missing 48 sensory intelligences that our socialization has buried in our subconscious?

39 - Why does contemporary society often identify a person's love of nature as "escapist recreation" rather than "peaceful re-creation?"

40 - What gives nature its power to recycle and purify itself?

41 - What readily available, inexpensive process enables us to strengthen our inherent ability to build relationships that reduce our problems?

42 - Are there negatives in nature and, if so, what are they?

Identify important values in NSTP experiences

Participants who make 4-leg connections with natural areas have reported the following 9-leg benefits for themselves while taking this course.

INSTRUCTIONS: On a scale of 1-10 note the importance that you attach to the findings reported below then in the indicator, circle or save it elsewhere.

Benefits identified:

1. An increase in being known as an interesting person and attractive to other people who are responsibly enjoying a natural area.

1	2	3	4	5	6	7	8	9	10
no importance		somewhat important					very important		

2. An increased sense of holding life, sensuous relationships and survival in common with nature and humanity.

1	2	3	4	5	6	7	8	9	10
no importance		somewhat important					very important		

3. A desire to share with others the joy and wonders found when in contact with attractions in natural areas.

1	2	3	4	5	6	7	8	9	10
no importance		somewhat important					very important		

4. A reduction in personal stress and/or a reduction in mental disturbance with regard to personal or professional problems.

1	2	3	4	5	6	7	8	9	10
no importance		somewhat important					very important		

5. An increased feelings of soul, wholeness and belonging to something worthwhile.

1	2	3	4	5	6	7	8	9	10
no importance		somewhat important					very important		

6. An increase in relating to attractiveness in people with differences. An increased immunity to being vulnerable to differences between others and ourselves.

1	2	3	4	5	6	7	8	9	10
no importance		somewhat important					very important		

7. Greater awareness and distaste for pollutants, garbage and activities that deteriorate natural areas.

1	2	3	4	5	6	7	8	9	10
no importance	somewhat important						very important		

8. An increased desire to live more in balance and maintain a sustainable relationship with the environment and people.

1	2	3	4	5	6	7	8	9	10
no importance	somewhat important						very important		

9. A spirit, holiness or belonging that extends beyond people.

1	2	3	4	5	6	7	8	9	10
no importance	somewhat important						very important		

10. A greater sense of confidence and self-esteem because participants and others have been empowered to do something that makes a significant contribution.

1	2	3	4	5	6	7	8	9	10
no importance	somewhat important						very important		

11. A greater connection with history and hope for the future.

1	2	3	4	5	6	7	8	9	10
no importance	somewhat important						very important		

12. An observed reduction in physical and mental pain in others and in the participants themselves .

1	2	3	4	5	6	7	8	9	10
no importance	somewhat important						very important		

13. An increased feeling of true self as a purer, more beautiful being and finding this to be true of other people and species, too.

1	2	3	4	5	6	7	8	9	10
no importance	somewhat important						very important		

14. A strong sense of nature as a mirror and manifestation of deeper feelings and the divine.

1	2	3	4	5	6	7	8	9	10
no importance	somewhat important						very important		

15. A pleasing increase in sensitivity, trust and respect for all forms of life, including human life.

1	2	3	4	5	6	7	8	9	10
no importance	somewhat important						very important		

16. An increased feeling for finding and embracing unifying and lasting things that we hold in common with others of different views and backgrounds.

1	2	3	4	5	6	7	8	9	10
no importance	somewhat important						very important		

17. An added trust in seeking information from immediate attraction moments with natural areas and/or people.

1	2	3	4	5	6	7	8	9	10
no importance	somewhat important						very important		

18. The means to thoughtfully obtain non-verbal information from nature that beneficially modifies destructive stories we carry.

1	2	3	4	5	6	7	8	9	10
no importance	somewhat important						very important		

19. An added, easily accessible source of higher power for recovery and for increasing spirit and wellness.

1	2	3	4	5	6	7	8	9	10
no importance	somewhat important						very important		

20. Even though nature is cruelly misunderstood, I have a feeling of being intimately involved with the easily accessible perfection of nature that feels welcoming, familiar and intelligent.

1	2	3	4	5	6	7	8	9	10
no importance	somewhat important						very important		

Challenges

1. We have asked people to think of a major personal, social or global problem that they were aware of. Most people agreed that if the 20 benefits, above, were applied to that problem, they would help others and themselves resolve the problem. Do you agree?

2. With the consent of an accomplished typist, two letters were interchanged on the keyboard of her typewriter. A year later, she still mistakenly typed the letters incorrectly whenever she was not thinking about the change. She concluded that although we often know what should be done, our thinking, unknowingly, is carried along bonded to old ways that often continue our troubles. To release our destructive bonds, we must reattach them to new, more responsible rewards. Do you agree?

EVALUATION: Natural systems within and around you and us sorely need help in coping with the effects of our excessive disconnections. Add up the points you scored above. If you scored over 130 total points it signifies that you will gain and give a great deal while doing this course online in the Orientation Course. You are also an excellent candidate for Certification in teaching the Natural Systems Thinking Process.

The Ecozombie Dance

Five-leg stomp on Four-leg ways and Circle Right.

Sherlock Holmes and his sidekick Dr. Watson, an accomplished expert in 5-leg thinking, science and speculation, went on a camping trip. They pitched their tent in an open area and turned in for a good night's rest. In the middle of the night Holmes awakened the good Doctor.

"Watson," Holmes queried, "What do you see and what do you deduce?"

Watson rubbed his eyes, looked at the open sky and replied, "I see the sky and I deduce that among all the planets and stars in the heavens there must be some planets like Earth. And if there are planets like Earth there is a high probability that there is life out there."

Holmes replied, "WATSON, YOU KNUCKLEHEAD! Somebody stole our tent!"

Some people find that the story in this chapter helps them recognize the often overlooked "missing tent phenomenon" with regard to the absence of nature in their lives. Some also discover that they have long been aware of the restorative benefits produced by the Natural Systems Thinking Process and that these benefits have become a "missing tent" as well. This article presents a point of view that brings these missing tents into your awareness. It reflects the changes that natural systems somehow experience as they flow through us. Within us, they become subject to the 5-leg way we are conditioned to think instead of the 4-leg guidance provided by their balanced origins and support in the natural environment. The following story attempts to overcome your unawareness of contemporary society's 5-leg emphasis and its destructive message "Pay little attention to 4-leg ways of knowing, learning and relating."

Mr. Arnold Sanders
127 Larkin Avenue
Richmond, Virginia 12746

Dear Mr. Sanders,

Thank you for your phone call regarding the Natural Systems Thinking Process and for the honesty of your statement, "Nature is dirty and dangerous; you've got to be crazy to want to learn how to think like nature works."

We hope you are well and happy today for, sadly, we bring you some distressing news. We have examined your record. As we previously told you, in our study on contemporary normalcy, for over 31 years you have been one of a group of people whose thoughts we have been monitoring by analyzing their actions. Our study shows that you have developed a numbed ecological sensitivity zone in your thinking that acts like a dead area. In that respect, you are normal; you and your numbed skull mentality are typical of a vast majority of the people in industrial society. This sensory deadened area helps to explain our society's many environmental problems. What might surprise you, however, is that it also explains many of our personal and social troubles, too. That's why the surest sign that intelligent life exists elsewhere in the universe is that it has never tried to contact us.

Please permit me to be blunt. Our research suggests that your missing environmental sensitivities have made you into a zombie with respect to relating to life in its inherent life-giving way. We call a person in this situation an "ecozombie" meaning "ecological death that walks."

Like any other zombie, you don't think or know you are an ecozombie because the part of your brain that would register this phenomena is the same part that has been deadened. This is why ecozombies suffer from delusions of adequacy. For the betterment of all, we suggest at this time that  you either rehabilitate your deadened thinking or you publicly declare yourself a misguided idiot. Do something right. Demand to be institutionalized in order to protect yourself from yourself, as well as protect neighbors and most other life on Earth from your destructive insensitivity.

We strongly recommend you choose rehabilitation, and offer you the means to accomplish it through the Natural Systems Thinking Process (NSTP). It is an antidote and preventative for ecozombification. It operates by enabling us to integrate our 5-leg and 4-leg thinking. Without it, we become prime candidates for natural deselection.

No doubt you think this is a prank or crank letter. Unfortunately, that is a typical ecozombie reaction. If you believe this is a joke, be assured you are as wrong as the belief that people must study pharmacy to become farmers. You are a typical ecozombie. I know because I am one, too. Let me explain to you what this means and how NSTP will help you do something about it (if this letter is not already in your waste basket).

Mr. Sanders, you, like me, became an ecozombie because you were born into a ecozombie community, a society that has numbed and blinded itself to the sensory callings of nature's attractions. In metaphor, our society is no different than the blind Governing Council of an island community that consisted entirely of non-sighted people. Citizens on that island were content and adequate in their unique ways, even though each was born totally blind. One day, Gulliver, a s h i p w r e c k e d castaway, half-dead, washed up on the island. Compassionately, many community members nourished and loved him to full recovery. Then he became the bane of their existence. He demanded things unknown to them in their blindness: windows, lights, books, television, painted colors and sunglasses. The Council investigated and discovered Gulliver's trouble. Gulliver had organs that could see. The Council took his sight away. They took it away by surgically numbing his optical nerves. He became a zombie with respect to sight and he physically and emotionally hurt whenever he was reminded of the loss of his eyesight.

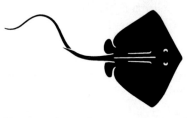

Similar to Gulliver, you and I have become hurt and desensitized with respect to how natural systems work within and around us. Our society has made us into ecozombies so that we will cooperate in its conquest of nature. Our society's intentions are honorable but wrong. It falsely believes it must conquer natural systems in us and nature in order to survive. Like many leaders or a broken computer, we probably don't fully recognize how insane it is for us to be encouraged to destroy our own life support systems. It is like getting directions from Amelia Earhart's *Guide to the Pacific Ocean.*

Ecozombification starts by learning to think with the lie that people are different than nature. Yes, we may often think differently than the way nature works and therefore behave differently, but biologically and psychologically, every other aspect of us is a natural system within us that is a seamless continuum of a natural system in the environment. You see, through its attractions, nature flows into us and vice versa, just as it flows into and through everything else in the natural world. Moment by moment we are supported physically and emotionally by natural systems. They provide attractive, fresh, pure food, water, air, sunshine and landscapes along with the uplifting joy and health that these things naturally give us. How much better this is

than cultural life where happiness can be experienced by seeing our boss's face on the back of a milk carton.

Mr. Sanders, we have already observed that you have had a few enjoyable experiences in nature at the beach, while skiing, and with your cat, Felicity. However, like most normally socialized individuals in our country, you and I are victims of contemporary society's long history of conquering and exploiting nature in the name of progress, safety and profit. Have you looked around recently? Although it is "normal," our undeclared war against nature is bringing about the pollution and death of nature and Earth (see Appendix B). We have fallen out of our family tree.

The numbed spot in your mentality is worse than Gulliver's blindness. Gulliver was at least aware of what happened to him. Your numbness prevents you from recognizing that since our natural senses and we are a part of nature, along with nature, most of our natural senses have been conquered and deadened in our consciousness. These senses that have survived our assault on nature are usually injured and often hurt. No offense intended but most of us are five pounds of sensory natural attraction hurt in a one pound bag. Even a small irritation of the bag lets the pressurized pain ooze into our consciousness so we become aware of it and hurt.

Because the war has numbed our natural ability to think reasonably with respect to ecosystem relationships within and around us, you and I have become ecozombies. The difference between the two of us is that I recognize this has happened and have learned how, to some extent, to restore my ability to think like nature works in balance. You, being 'normal,' remain an ecozombie because you have learned to think of nature as a natural resource that you can kill, exploit, and develop to your heart's content. Frankly, in this respect, you think like the south end of a horse headed north

Mr. Sanders, although every species and most nature-connected people acknowledge the facts that follow below, ecozombies reject and resent them. So prepare yourself; what I say next won't necessarily be comfortable for you and your pressurized hurt. Again, I don't mean to insult you, but as an ecozombie, you probably already have a numbed ability to think rationally about the fact that the essence of nature on Planet Earth is its self-organizing, natural system intelligence. This innate intelligence enables nature to produce and sustain its own perfection. It is perfect ™in that it produces optimums of life, mutual support and diversity without producing garbage. This means that nothing in nature is left out; everything belongs. This is a way to define perfection and describe unconditional love, too. People, being part of nature, inherit this ability, so neither ecosystems nor people whose mentality is genuinely nature-connected display or cause the destructive problems that plague industrial society. Connection with nature is not accomplished by ecozombies standing close to other ecozombies so that they can hear the ocean. It is accomplished by making sure your sensory connections register in your consciousness.

That nature has been conquered in our country is undeniable. Studies show there may only be one intact major ecosystem left in the USA and it is threatened. Thus, no matter what our leaders or ecozombie thinking say, since you and I are part of nature, the natural systems in us are also victims of society's undeclared war against nature. Think about it if you can. Strain yourself. How could it be otherwise? On this question, any one-celled organism can outscore us on an I.Q. test.

We each suffer shock from the conquest of natural systems within us and our trauma remains until we treat and heal it. However, we don't treat it. We don't even recognize it. We seldom even acknowledge that natural systems in our biology and psyche are part of, as well as victims of our war against nature. Ecozombies suffer from this distorted, deadened thinking and most of our leaders are the most wounded. In other words, they are profound ecozombies. They wrongly think we should not recognize, honor and treat ourselves as victims of this war. Why deny this truth? If we don't acknowledge and honor it, how can we begin to deal with it and its destructive effects? The first thing to do is stop our repeat environmental offenders by not re-electing them.

Our ecosensory deadening explains why, indirectly but knowingly, we senselessly, insensitively, continue to hurt people and other life forms. We see that happening all around us. We may not like it, but because it is "normal" behavior, we deny that it is a personal problem. However, we also know that with respect to living harmoniously with natural systems in ourselves, in others and the environment, part of us and those close to us have become death that walks. This, Mr. Sanders, alienates all of us from nature's global life community. In nature, everything mutually supports everything else or transforms until it does. In nature, death and conquest due to differing stories, belief systems, destructive stress, rewarded exploitation and mental illness are virtually unknown. As part of nature, we inherently know this. It does not enter our thinking, however, because ecosensory numbing is like having a photographic memory with the lens cover glued on.

As an ecozombie, you, like me, may have one of three discomforting reactions to the statement above.

You either disagree with it because you are too desensitized to recognize the sense in it, you agree with it and it embarrasses you, or you think this is a deja-moo: that you've heard this bull before. No matter the reason, the point is that you don't know how to stop this behavior so, against your better judgment and deeper ideals, your trespasses against life continue and all things needlessly suffer.

Our ecozombie socialization into contemporary society has taught us to excessively separate from nature and live over 95% of our lives indoors. We have, in addition, learned almost completely to detach our thinking from nature. Even when we visit a rewarding natural area our thoughts are usually about something else. They may be about a personal problem, the unfairness of our boss, ways to make more money, a new technology, a political topic, how to win a game, the desire for a mate, or some other activity that pulls our mind out of the present moment. Almost never is our mentality fully in tune with the attractive wonders that surround us in natural areas. Worse, when we are not in contact with nature's fullness, our mental disconnectedness increases immensely. Our indoor lives have given us a room temperature I.Q.

You are 52 years old, Mr. Sanders. As an educated adult, you probably don't even believe you can connect your thinking with nature or that it is worthwhile to learn how to do so. To our shared loss, even if you do believe it, you don't want to do it, know how to do it, and cannot teach it. It's actually hard to believe Mother Nature let you beat out 1,000,000 other sperm. How can I help you understand that connecting your thinking with nature can generate great health, personal enrichment, improved environmental relationships and greater peace?

I calculate that since you are normal, in your entire 52 years, your mentality, like the national average, has spent only nine hours and twenty minutes in tune with nature and its rewards. That is all. Think about it. You are not the sharpest knife in the drawer. If we spent only nine hours of our lives learning how to read and write, how proficient would we be now? We wouldn't be. Is it then any wonder that with respect to ecological literacy, the way we have learned to think has strayed from the unifying, peacefully balanced way that nature usually works for every other member of the plant, animal and mineral kingdoms? A significant part of your mentality has become a dehumanized cultural object. You have become a few bricks short of a load.

As our culture extremely separates our thinking from nature, it produces very destructive consequences. It is like removing an infant from its mother's womb; the infant dies unless it receives artificial support. And we know of no artificial replacement for nature. Let's face it; we still don't even know how to make milk or sugar. We cause many troubles because our deadened mentality remains on Planet Earth in our body. Being dead with respect to nature, it does not interact with natural systems, including those in people. Instead, idiotically, it trespasses these systems as would a destructive outlaw, a zombie, a bull in a china shop, like a cancer that deteriorates the planet and its people. It parallels how the Ku Klux Klan might celebrate Martin Luther King Jr. Day.

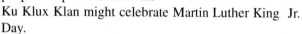

With regard to nature, society has carved our psyche to be like that of a person who has been raised in a closet. During 99.9% of our "normal" lives, our mentality has been closeted from nature and thereby taught and rewarded not to be in tune with the natural environment. Like a fish removed from water, our traumatized psyche gasps to survive while the trauma prevents us from recognizing that our great environmental and social problems result from tearing our mentality from nature's embrace. Psychologically, we have become like babies who without holding after being born, lose weight and eventually waste away. Our ability to think clearly about our relationship with the environment and the nature of each other has also wasted away. Our thinking has aborted from the profound nurturance of nature. Sometimes we discover and enjoy this attractive nurturance while visiting natural areas and we don't know any better than to call it an escape from reality. That's like writing "Sagittarius" where its says "Sign here" on a job application.

Mr. Sanders, our study shows that you psychologically suffer from your sensory and intellectual removal from nature. As if an arm has been torn from your body, you hurt. Since you don't recognize the cause of your hurt, you sustain yourself as an ecozombie because it is too painful to think about it. You become a few neurons short of a synapse.

You say that all this is unbelievable. Let me repeat: although overwhelming evidence shows that, with respect to nature, you think like an ecozombie, you believe you are normal because you think like the rest of us. And since the cause of your disconnection pain is protectively hidden from your consciousness, you neither believe nor want to believe it is true. However, being a ecozombie makes perfect sense when you consider that the effects of the deadened way you think produces personal, environmental and social stress and deterioration. Although this may be too painful for you to hear, it makes you feel such a reaction, too, Such a reaction, too, is normal. But how is it different than remaining calm when you learn your wife has a paramour because you don't care how she cuts the lawn?

Mr. Sanders, you want from the loss of nature in your life. Because you want, for you there is never enough. In replacement, you crave and psychologically addict to things that satisfy your greed, booze, tranquilizers, excessive technologies, competitiveness, arrogance, power and apathy. Where there's a will you want to be in it. These things often get out of hand and become unreasonable. They produce substance abuse and abusive interpersonal relationships, even when you know they are nonsense, destructive or greedy. Knowledgeably acting irrationally is typical ecozombie behavior. It encourages death rather than supports life.

Since we ecozombies can produce artificial substitutes for some parts of nature we have lost, we forget that there is no known substitute for all of nature, the real thing and its eons of intelligent, life supportive experience. Each substitute we create falls short of nature's perfection. This produces our destructive side effects, our pollution, garbage and relationship disorders. Wildlife flees our insensitivity as do our neighbors. We fear each other and thus feel lonely. We sense that we don't belong. These hurts cause us to behave so irresponsibly that, for the future of the common good, well-intentioned teachers want to give many fathers a gift certificate for a vasectomy.

Nature has the amazing power to sustain its perfection by purifying and recycling the things that would otherwise contaminate it; that is how nature produces no garbage. Because we are disconnected from nature, we don't turn to nature to help us revive and recycle our contaminated mentality. Our mentality suffers because it does not receive the restorative purification, healing and regeneration that ordinarily sustains the balance and health of natural systems within and around us. We instead celebrate our 5-leg intellectual prowess because it figured out that the white thing that came from a hen's butt was edible.

Let me again remind you that compassionately natural systems within us hide the pain of our separation from nature from our awareness to keep us from constantly feeling this anguish. However, anything that even suggests further separation of our self from any kind of support weakens the bag and brings our five pounds of hurt natural attractions into consciousness. Calling you an ecozombie instead of your name triggers pain. Being questioned in some way because of your fashions, lifestyle, technologies, job, education, taste, religion, music, race, speech, ideas, desires, politics, drugs or other attachments also triggers pain. When you don't feel accepted by our 5-leg society, you suffer. Even the difference between an academic grade of A and B can produce this uncomfortable effect. Watch out. Over time, it can dumb you into taking three hours to watch 60 Minutes.

Mr. Sanders, each possible rejection from our 5-leg ways can bring some hurt from disconnection back into your consciousness. For this reason, your ecozombie life often consists of walking the thin line that keeps you from being rejected. That sterile, disconnected way of relating, Mr. Ecozombie, is apathy; an emotional death. It restricts freedom and demands pacifiers. It destructively erodes our politics, economics and spirit. When it becomes unbearable, depression, suicide, arson or murder can result. Much of the remainder of our lives is spent seeking substitutes for our sensory disconnection from natural systems. We gain rewards for transforming from natural people into cultural objects. We are filled with that B.S. In fact, that's how I discovered NSTP was helping me. I went to my doctor because I had a black line suddenly appear around my neck and I became concerned. The doctor said the line showed I was a recovering ecozombie. It indicated that instead of being full of B.S., I was down a quart.

Mr. Sanders, do you recognize that through dogmas, business, political, spiritual and academic leaders deliberately aggravate your hurt? Do you see how they then sell you a multitude of products to pacify your discomfort? Buy, buy, buy means goodby to natural habitats and ecosystems. Rampant consumerism only temporarily satisfies our hurt, fears and wants. We turn to our leaders for help, but because our sentiently disadvantaged ecozombie thinking selected them as leaders for their outstanding ecozombie achievements, our situation usually worsens. We feel helpless, so we celebrate what is left of our lives by dancing on the deck of our sinking ship.

"Back to back, mon, belly to belly
I don't give a damn 'cause I'm stone dead already;
Oh, back to back, belly to belly
It's a zombie jamboree."
   - Conrad Eugene Mauge, Jr.

There is some good news, Mr. Sanders. There is hope. Five-leg thinking definitely shows that nothing in contemporary society is perfect. This means, neither you nor I are perfect ecozombies. Somewhere in our thinking and feeling we recognize there may be a grain of truth in the observations I have shared here. If this were not so, why would you have read this far? And if I was a perfect ecozombie, could I have written you this letter? For entertainment? Out of curiosity? Not possible. Perfect zombies are too dead to experience them, so dead that they get hit by parked cars.

To honor our ecozombie imperfection, let me offer you an important, short, two-part message. In it, the alive part of me directs itself to the alive part of you where our collective thinking is connected to nature. This nature-centered part of you will find my message completely accurate and very useful. Ready? Test yourself:

1. Since our nature-disconnected senses and thinking cause disconcerting personal, social and global ecozombie problems, learning to genuinely reconnect with nature can help us use its regenerative powers to heal our mentality and solve these problems. ( ) YES ( ) NO.

2. Our intact, non-zombie, natural selves can learn how to use the Natural Systems Thinking Process, an antidote to zombieism. NSTP enables our thinking to genuinely reconnect with authentic nature, benefit from nature's recycling and purifying attraction powers and promote personal, social and environmental wellness. ( ) YES ( ) NO.

Mr. Sanders, do you realize that you can play an AM radio in the afternoon? Do you realize that the non-ecozombie answer to these questions is YES? NSTP enables you and others to recover from ecozombie disorders. It will teach you how to psychologically reconnect your many senses with nature and nurture them back to health...backyard or back country... and make your thinking more sensible. Although it sounds strange to your ecozombie numbness, your remaining sensibilities can use NSTP as a self-empowering, grassroots, missing link to healthful thinking and enhance your life and all of nature. If this doesn't make sense to you, it shows the extent of your ecozombie disease. Your antenna is not picking up all the channels.

To realize hopes and ideals, we must have a process that enables us to implement them. That process is NSTP.

In conclusion, let me update you on Gulliver and his relationship with his blind community. I realize that the ecozombie part of you won't let you believe what I will say here but many others and I know it is true because we've experienced it. Gulliver discovered that often when he visited natural areas many of his innate senses became stronger and registered in his awareness. Visiting nature became a memorable occasion. In Nature he enjoyed life and related through at least 53 natural senses, not just the five used in ecozombie society. It was similar to the joy of walking in the park or along a beach. This was so empowering and supportive to Gulliver, he figured out how to scientifically strengthen the process and direct it towards his ecozombie desensitization. As his connections to nature grew stronger his eyesight un-numbed and began to recover. He told his blind friends about the resilience, energy and sensibility he had found through the process, and the delight of improving his life and health and some who heard him speak tried connecting with nature and thrilled to similar results. In turn, they helped others increase their thinking power, wellness and pleasure and became thoughtfully, passionately protective of nature because it made sense and felt right.

Mr. Sanders, my congratulations to you for reading this letter. I encourage you to use the material and activities in this book to help your thinking process get out from under the 5-leg ecozombie yoke that directs it to disregard the valuable 4-leg information in natural systems within and around you. You'll find it more useful than calling talk show hosts to discuss if a hearse carrying a corpse can drive in the carpool lane.

Best wishes,
C. King Helpnow, Director,
Ecozombies to Reverse Ecozombie Disorders.

And now, back to reality:

From CBS News 3/7/02: A professor of psychology, psychiatry and pharmacology at Vanderbilt University, says of NSTP's benefits: "People can get the same gratification from material things such as a teddy bear or a favorite blanket. The key is to determine what works for you and do it."

Whoa, hold on a minute Professor, isn't that what we are doing now? On this kind of advice, you make a living? "Because it works" for some people is why General Motors is building a new, 16 cylinder, 1000 horsepower Cadillac. It's image and power satisfy. Cigarettes satisfy, too. Would you recommend them?

Dr. Psychology-Psychiatry-Pharmacology Sir, when do you start teaching General Motors and us that we are part of nature? How we can become healthy by thinking and acting as if the health of Earth and its natural systems matters? Please, please help me with this. I'm having a deja-moo.

Course Prerequisites

Reach your greatest potential

A Survey of Participants

It is important that the prerequisite Survey in this chapter is studied before doing this book as a course. It prepares your ingrained 5-leg way of knowing to integrate with your 4-leg potential for wholeness. The Survey helps you identify your possibilities and interests that the course has helped others achieve. Without doing the survey preparation first, many people are unaware of the potential of the book or course for themselves and that escapes their awareness when they encounter it.

This book and course empower students with a process, a tool that helps them improve their relationships and meet their deeper hopes and ideals. If learned and used correctly the Natural Systems Thinking Process (NSTP) adds a component to counseling, education and healing that supports the United Nations manifesto for environmentally sound personal growth and social justice.

It is no longer heresy to say that the greater a person's desensitization or disconnection from nature's voice, the greater are the problems that person suffers and causes. Conversely, genuinely reconnecting with nature may be our salvation for it enables us to transform our disorders into unifying, constructive relationships, personally and globally. We hold nature, Earth and survival in common; they are unifying factors we learn to overlook in our conquest of them.

To repair our mentality's destructive disconnection from nature NSTP does the seemingly impossible. It enables anybody to safely make and share thoughtful, conscious, sensory contacts with natural attractions in nature, backyard or back country. This energizes nature's voice to register in our thinking as attractive felt senses, logic and desires.

An informal study Dr. Cohen made of people who visited wilderness areas disclosed that most of the time they were there, their mind was elsewhere. Although immersed in natural systems, they mostly thought and talked about relationships, technologies and problems at home or internationally. They were in nature, but not in tune with nature. Their consciousness was engaged in 5-leg stories rather than with the 4-leg ways of relating to their immediate environment. Ironically, the latter was often the perfection that they sought to discover and benefit from on their visit. This phenomenon is predictable in a population whose mentality is disconnected from nature 99.9% of the time.

NOTE: Since this book is also optionally used by participants in this course online, instructions for online participants are included and shaded or otherwise clearly indicated.

ONLINE COURSE PARTICIPANTS:

1. If you have not done so, write a 1-2 paragraph letter of introduction to your Interact group. Include a brief biographical sketch and the reasons you are taking this course. Save this statement and share it with your online participants list on the starting date. At the end of this statement please assure them that they can trust you to supportively participate and complete the course with them.

2. Read this chapter's Survey of Participants. Identify in Part 2-6 what you think are the two most important statements in each part and why they are important to you.

3. On the course starting day email 1 and 2 above to your Interact group address list. You will, in turn, receive this same information from them.

IMPORTANT: After completing the Survey, be sure to carefully read the Instructions in Appendix C.

Below is an example of what the course looks like when it is running smoothly. This is accomplished by mastering the Prerequisite material and instructions in this section.

Preparation: Carol, an online course member, has done her preparatory "homework." She read through the introductory course and web site material, submitted her application to the course and received a course participation confirmation. She ordered her optional *Reconnecting With Nature* book and this book, completed the required prerequisite activities and her self-introduction, and set up a group mailing list from the addresses sent to her by the course organizer. Then she carefully read the instructions you are reading now.

The specific dates for her course were made for the convenience of all and send and receive dates for email assignments were set. Group guidance roles were offered to participants, the co-facilitator was identified, and the email addresses were checked to assure that they worked properly.

Attitude: "Enthusiastic" is the way Carol feels about the course. She knows what is important in it to her because in the prerequisite material she identified areas of interest and results that others found important to them. She also tried some of the activities with friends and knows they work well for her. They help her thinking reasonably co-create with nature's intelligence, balance and beauty by safely connecting with it. She recognizes that with respect to nature's eons of balanced relationship building experience, there is no known substitute for the real thing. Substitutes often pollute or deteriorate naturally balanced relationships.

Schedule: Carol reads her course instructions online from a "Base Camp" web page. She learns from them what activity she and her email partners, who live in many different countries, will do on this scheduled day in their local park, backyard, or even with a terrarium. In general they have been doing two activities a week. The schedule they use is posted at their Internet Base Camp web page whose address they were given when the course began.

The role of attractions: As Carol begins this day's activity she seeks what's most attractive to her in a local natural area at this moment. Unexpectedly, she becomes aware that the delicate sparkle of a water droplet on a fern attracts her. She does additional activities that reinforce this nature-connected sensation and she becomes aware of other things that come to mind from the total experience. They include other times she has felt its joy and meaning as well as her past disconnection from it, what caused it and the effects of the loss. She discovers the droplet being attractive to her was not an accident. It was subconsciously attractive to parts of her that sought the fulfillment of the balanced tenacity, brightness and refreshment it provided. Contact with the droplet brought these parts of her into her awareness.

Written material: Carol then reads, or has already read online, (and optionally in her *Reconnecting With Nature* book,) material which helps her understand and model various aspects of the activity she has just done and how she might apply them to improve and further enjoy her daily relationships with people and the environment.

Guidelines and process: Carol closely follows the twelve guidelines that come with the activity instructions. At some convenient time on the due date for the completion of the activity and readings, Carol goes online and shares with her 7-person Interact group her thoughts, feelings and reactions from her nature connecting experience. She also downloads, reads, and later reacts, to the attractions she finds and things she has learned in all the emails she receives from the group by the due date. They become the course textbook. They convey her group members' experiences in nature with the same activity and readings she just did. Later she reads their reactions to the experience description she just sent to all of them.

Unity: Carol finds the course process is enjoyable and educational. She feel relieved that participants hold something important in common and are therefore supportive and not bogged down in "flaming" arguments about differing viewpoints, ideologies, religions, politics, etc. Carol feels alive and spirited, sustained by her email partners' genuine responses and the group's rejuvenating reconnections to nature.

Value and self-empowerment: Her day brighter and energized, Carol looks forward to applying the activity by using it to further connect with people and natural places that attract her. They gain new value and she becomes aware of an often unrecognized natural worth in herself and others along with additional values in natural areas. She has new confidence for she has done the activity and known its effects. She owns it, can teach it and gain its rewards at will.

Why the process works: The course work sounds and feels simple to Carol, but explaining to others how and why it works challenges her intellect and spirit in fun ways. The process and its effects are so steeped in nature's balanced ways that for most people they are, like nature's perfection, beyond words. To be known and understood the process must be experienced first hand. To our loss, in our nature disconnected society that is often "suspect."

The prerequisite survey that follows addresses our disconnection phenomenon. It helps you prepare yourself to engage in the process as you learn it rather than simply become aware of it as a 5-leg story. You may be able to recite the story but that does not necessarily help you improve your thinking and relationships or help you teach others how to accomplish this.

If you truly want to master this material, teach it to somebody else who wants to learn it.

Prerequsite: A Survey of Participants

A Research Questionnaire Validates the Natural Systems Thinking Process Webstring Approach to Personal and Global Wellness

> Reminder. Online participants be sure to follow the instructions for the Survey in the grey box on page 29.

Since 1990, The Department of Integrated Ecology at the Institute of Global Education, in association with the United Nations Department of Public Information, Portland State University and Greenwich University, has developed and taught a Natural Systems Thinking Process (NSTP) that was researched for 20 years. NSTP is an easily learned, scientific means to consciously gain wholeness through tangible sensory contact with natural areas and people's inner nature.

Dr. Jan Goldfield, a retired psychologist, helped survey adults in a variety of occupations, who, during a three year period, learned to use NSTP by completing a 30 day Internet course. The findings show NSTP to be an effective vehicle for catalyzing personal and global wellness. They affirm the findings of other studies and educational programs that added to this survey report as **PART 5** and **PART 6.**

SIGNIFICANCE

This study shows that through conscious sensory contacts with natural areas, the Natural Systems Thinking Process psycho-logically reconnects people with nature's ways and reverses challenging personal, environmental and global problems. Since these problems are neither displayed nor caused by nature connected people, the study suggests that our excessive separation from nature creates abnormal wants that drive us into irresponsible relationships.

The Natural Systems Thinking Process offsets our society's excessive disconnection from nature. It enables us to endow our thinking and relationships with the wellness, balance and beauty of nature's ways.

The Process is rooted in its basic element, "Thoughtful, shared, sensory connections with attractions in nature improve our thinking, relationships and spirit."

Part 1

SYNOPSIS OF RESPONSES (AVERAGED):

People who use the Natural Systems Thinking Process:

-attain greater wellness with respect to pain, anxiety, community, learning, self-esteem and spirit.
-notice many disorders subside including depression, sleeplessness and loneliness.
-become more environmentally and socially active; their apathy becomes positive energy.
-significantly improved their personal and professional life and their relationship with the environment.

Study the results carefully in parts 2-6. Become more aware of your hopes and ideals by identifying the results that you feel are important to you and your community. Would you enjoy experiencing and teaching them?

Participants added statements to the survey responses with respect to their increased balance and wellness. This document presents a review of the results of the survey, including the statements.

Additional statements and reactions are found at http://www.ecopsych.com/millecopstrand.html

Part 2

THE SURVEY RESULTS:

PARTICIPANTS

The survey participants represent 37 different occupations/professions, many nationalities and ages 22-55.

The participants responded on a 1-10 measurement of agreement to statements about the NSTP course and its effects. The number in parenthesis after the statements below is the average measurement response rounded to the nearest decimal.

NSTP was taught in conjunction with Project NatureConnect (PNC) and the survey used the PNC acronym when referring to the process. In this context PNC is being used to refer to the NSTP in the personal effects of the nature reconnecting activities and webstring experiences.

Reaction Indicator

Strongly disagree   **Don't know**   **Strongly agree**

| 1 | 2 | 3 | 4 | 5 | 6 | 7 | 8 | 9 | 10 |

1. (9.8) The PNC experience helped me improve my personal life.

2. (9.4) The PNC experience helped me improve my relationship with the environment.

3. (9.0) The PNC experience helped me improve my professional life.

4. (9.6) Significant positive change would occur if a large segment of the population became involved in the PNC process.

5. (9.2) The PNC experience motivated me to help others build responsible relationships.

6. (9.0) The PNC process enabled me to bring environmental concepts into my consciousness that I have always felt but could not verbalize.

7. (8.7) The PNC experience gave me hope for the future that I did not previously hold.

8. (9.5) PNC is a process that every person in our society must learn if we are to reverse our present destructive ways.

9. (9.4) PNC is an effective vehicle to bring about personal and global peace.

10. (9.3) I would recommend the PNC course to students in any discipline.

11. (9.3) PNC enters and influences my thinking and relationships daily.

Part 3

UNSTRUCTURED INFORMATION:

Participants were asked to submit their own statement about the process that conveys to them an important essence of the NSTP as taught by PNC.

PNC is a part of a new process of knowledge.
The PNC exercises had a profoundly positive effect on my experience of the world around me.

I was an activist for the environment but could not cope with feelings of despair or hopelessness that positive changes would occur. PNC methods and materials helped me find good feelings, cope and move forward in my activist work.

PNC is easy and fun.

PNC helps me make relationships with others who are learning the same things I am.

PNC provides logical step-by-step methods of working through day-to-day problems with the good of all as the outcome. It teaches analyzing, decision making processes which make life easier and more fun when I use them.

PNC offers a unique process of connecting us with nature, with others,  with ourselves, and with our Higher Power.

Our planet cannot be saved with intellectual resources alone; we must have a personal connection to the natural world, as PNC provides, to save it.

PNC offers a set of principles to live by that leads us to peace through personal growth and responsibility.

PNC classes connect people at a deep level, resulting in sincere life-long friendships.

PNC has motivated me to make behavioral changes in my life that benefit the planet.

PNC creates experiences where individuals learn to honor their own developmental processes in relation to nature and to honor those same processes of others.

PNC helps to relieve physical and mental pain and positively affects people suffering from chronic physical or emotional illness.

PNC creates worldwide connections between nature-loving people, connections that would not exist otherwise.

Getting to know yourself in a fresh way is one of the perks of PNC.

The coursework of PNC creates opportunities for wellness and fosters inner growth.

New respect for the living global community is a by-product of the PNC program.

Teachers who take the PNC course are more apt to relate with their students from the standpoint of potentiality.

Self discipline is taught gently in the PNC program.

To be able to love the natural community is the first step to be active and to find solutions for environmental problems.

My self-esteem has been greatly enhanced by PNC.

PNC has taught me how to retrain my thinking process.

PNC has helped me restore my sense of belonging and place in the world.

PNC methods helped me discover that nature continually is available to support me emotionally, spiritually, mentally and physically in a non-verbal but powerful way.

I use PNC activities often as a support in my Alcoholics Anonymous recovery program; specifically, for me, as a form of prayer or "conscious contact" with my Higher Power.

I find the stress factor in my life has significantly decreased after PNC experiences.

Taking the PNC course helps you improve your skills in relating to people.

PNC can help students with self-esteem and other emotional problems open up, connect and develop healthy relationships with those around them.

PNC has enhanced my sense of social and environmental community.

PNC has value to the business community.

Part 4

SPECIFIC LIFE EXAMPLES

Participants were asked to write a statement that provided specific examples from their life, or their observations, of any of the points in Section 2 or of any other areas where PNC had proven valuable. A representative sampling of the wide-ranging, freely made statements appears below.

"The value of PNC to me is that it has led me to a direct personal relationship with life. For the first time I have the sense of being connected to the flow of living. Many people talk about being in the here and now but PNC has enabled me to DO it."

Chuck M.

"Since completing the PNC activities, I find that I tend to emphasize my similarities with others rather than differences. I tend to be less cynical about society and our future. I find myself picking up any trash I might find while hiking and have become more outspoken on issues related to protection of the environment. I contribute more of my time and money to causes which promote social welfare and environmental sensitivity. I found the PNC process to be truly life-changing. My daily behaviors and attitudes now reflect a larger faith and understanding that I am not separate from the world around me but an integral part of it. I have a unshakable faith in the process of life and all its manifestations. The PNC activities have helped me realize that I am a whole made up of many parts which are themselves whole. They have helped me realize that I, too, am a part of a whole greater than myself."

Bob H.

"With both the PNC list and two of the PNC courses, my life has been greatly enriched. Where I was very depressed in regards to the future of our planet and all life on it, I am now convinced that with encouraging people to participate in the exercises of Reconnecting With Nature....there is a very good chance we can heal the wounds of abuse and neglect we have thrust upon the Great Mother. Both my personal and professional lives have benefited from PNC...My interactions with employees, family and friends have improved greatly. My stress levels have dropped tremendously, migraines have been non-existent for about 2 months and I am sleeping through the night instead of waking 4 and 5 times.

The most important gift I was given with the list and the courses, has been the ability to interact with nature on a personal level....my inner child is being allowed to grow and emerge as a valid and needed part of myself."

Patricia A.

"PNC has provided a number of important experiences for me, most of which I not only remember but also bear fruit for me on a continual basis. It provides  a tool for almost immediate grounding and centering of my self, which is important to me and enables me to be part of my social and professional community; a participant in the human web of life.

PNC has value to the business world in that it can provide centering or grounding of a business team in pursuit of its goals. It has value to the larger community in that PNC teaches/develops realization of the web and inter-connectedness of our social structures, and as such can stimulate sustainability by organizations learning and subsequently feeling in supporting their community over the individual; cooperation over survival of the fittest.

What I am trying to say is that to exist as an individual, family, community or nation I need to connect with integrity with the larger picture. PNC activities enable me to do that.

Putting aside the academic rhetoric, I have taught PNC activities in a business class with good results - students responding positively to the outcome and coming back for more, similar experiences."

Rick R.

"The PNC course has given me a very important tool to work with environmental problems; an effective practical link between feelings and rational explanations of interactions with nature and people. It gave me the necessary inspiration, the will to share as an individual and a teacher my profound love and respect for life. As a scientist I use it for a more ecological aspect in my research. It has improved my health in ways I could not have foreseen. It is easier, simpler and more effective than meditation for me. Most important I have gained a very valuable gift from Michael Cohen's ecopsychology course, one that I had lost a long time ago about the tragic global planetary situation: HOPE."

Ruth

"I was in a supervisory role with a young woman, in a "back-to-work" job training program. She was in continual conflict with her peers and had just had a verbal match with a community member. This had come to the attention of the top administrator, who had full intentions of " firing" this young woman. I requested 30 minutes with the woman in order to prepare her. I anticipated the result of the meeting with the administrator would leave this young woman with feeling she had "nothing to lose" and that would reinforce her unworthiness. I was given only ten minutes. I wondered what I could tell her that would help her through what was to be a challenging meeting. My objective was to get her to stay calm and leave with dignity. I had ten minutes and not enough time. Instead of using words I decided to try an exercise from Michael Cohen's course. In that very short time the young woman was able to receive some guidance through her connection to a rock that provided a new awareness of he own nature and her choices. I introduced the activity and we did it together. Then she went in to face the "fire" and came out smiling and still holding her job. I asked her how she managed to keep her temper and her job. She pulled the rock from her pocket showing me that one side was rough, the other was smooth. She told me, "I kept the rough side hidden."

June L.

"I was moving a great distance from my 15-year-old son. I was very concerned that I was mistaken in my decision to leave him with his father (we were separated some years before I did an activity to determine where my son was "at", with this circumstance. I discovered so much in the 1/2 hour we shared. It was about me as a mother. I became aware as we progressed through the activity, of how ready he was for this separation and how tightly I clung to my role of mother. My son was ready for the next phase, a phase his father was ready and able to provide. I had to let go. I am glad I did."

Judy M.

"Organizing workshops has allowed my 13-year-old son to be part of a community of people who actively care about and value the natural world. Through PNC workshops, he had to help raise money for a wildlife crisis center which I feel was empowering for him. Similarly, through organizing these RWN workshops I became closer to my own family and made new friends who live nearby me but I had never met before. Many of us stay in contact now on a semi-weekly basis, continuing that feeling of community and further modeling community building and nature-connecting for my son. Additionally, I felt a feeling of happiness that I could be giving back to Nature and supporting the Earth by making PNC methods available to others. This gives me good feelings because the Earth is so generous with me all the time (for example by providing air, water, sunlight, food as well as unconditional acceptance, etc.). These methods allow people to receive and to give back to Nature and thus reestablish the web of connections we were designed to function optimally within."

Sea G.

"I have been using PNC in my personal life as well as with students at risk in an alternative high school for over 5 years. I have obtained over $30,000 in grants and have obtained very positive and sound results using PNC with these students.

I have just completed an exhaustive review of the literature in the ecology, environmental science and ecopsychology fields. I am dismayed by the fact that so few writers have any concept of specific solutions to our society's disconnection from nature and the resultant destruction of our biosphere. Michael Cohen is one of the few who has a model that works. It appears simple, but it is not. It requires some major shifts in perception. I have spent over a year studying with Michael in an in-person small group structure and I have taken and continue to take Michael's Internet PNC courses. Both have been invaluable. Although the Internet course is in an individual and written format, my group members have also become my teachers. Michael answers all calls and is always available if we stray or need help."

The NatureConnect model is revolutionary and what the planet needs. Michael also walks his talk. He continually opens his 53 senses as he sleeps outside year-round surrounded by the natural sounds and senses of the night."

Kurt D.

"PNC has helped me take responsibility for my life and the choices I make in a way the makes sense. I experience profound well-being and security I never thought would be available to me. It quite literally has changed my life."

Vicki S.

"I have shared many of the points and experiences with others. I believe that as this world grows towards a total technological world there must be a counter balance. A natural world that is not forgotten. With the many moves towards interactive TV, computers and software, Mother Nature is the greatest interactive action we will ever take.

Something I learned is that, Balance and Harmony are not only a place to be, but also an action to take."

Rick D.

"I have been a Type 1 insulin dependent diabetic for 38 years. Every 3 months I have an A1C test which tells me what my overall diabetic control has been like for the previous 3 to 4 months. During the period between March and June 1994, I was very much involved in doing the activities created by Mike Cohen to help us reconnect with nature, and I was also working hard to co-ordinate an Ecopsychology workshop in the San Francisco area. Although organizing the workshop was stressful, each day I would go to a park, or just into my little backyard, and for a short time I would just connect with the trees, birds, clouds, flowers, and my own internal peace, and I would end up giggling, or singing, or relaxing, and definitely feeling refreshed and wonderfully alive. Because I was not doing my normal diabetic routine of exercising as much as I should, I was worried about the A1C test results in July. To my delight, the test results showed a significant drop in my overall blood sugar levels over the previous 3 months!! I attribute this to the major increase in my sense of peace, relaxation, well-being, and even support that I get from connecting with the natural world.

Presently, I combine exercise, healthy eating, and most importantly, daily reconnecting with nature to keep my diabetes in very good control, and thereby greatly reducing my risks for serious complications in the future.

The other major thing that my connection with nature has done over the past 2 years, is completely alleviate my use of drugs for the control of anxiety disorder. I am forwarding here a copy of part of a letter I wrote in regards to this:

In 1983 I was diagnosed with panic disorder, a severe form of endogenous anxiety. For 2 years I suffered extremely bizarre and disconcerting physical and emotional symptoms, including depersonalization, agoraphobia, nausea, dizziness, headaches, and a disabling fear of impending death. My treatment consisted of addictive medication, psychotherapy, and a hard-line approach called voice fighting. While I no longer suffer from constant attacks, I am occasionally bothered by some of these same unpleasant feelings. In the nature-connecting activities offered through Applied Ecopsychology, I have made an astounding discovery. For me, connecting with nature within and around me definitely dissolves the more mild forms of panic/anxiety attack symptoms and fears. By enabling me to fully sense my natural affinities toward stability and peace, the connecting experience endows me with feelings of wholeness, wisdom, and a sense of my rightful flow towards profound well-being.

Statistics indicate that 10 million Americans suffer from some form of endogenous anxiety, with recent studies revealing that more children in the teenage years are now affected by this disease. 100,000 of these people are severely disabled, unable to leave their homes, unable to walk to their mailboxes, unable to fully live. In my experience, panic/anxiety attacks disconnect me from support, safety, love, and peace; using the Applied Ecopsychology nature connecting activities positively reconnects me with these senses and feelings, as well as the senses of nurturing calmness, emotional stability and well-being, trust, empowerment, and self-esteem. The very senses and feelings that are stripped from panic attack sufferers are re-awakened and re-enforced by using these nature connecting activities.

In addition to the above, my connections with nature have also given me two very precious gifts: The gift of trustable supportive friendships, and the gift of laughter!!! My sense of fun and playfulness has increased tenfold, and I have discovered what many have said before, that laughter is a most powerful tool for healing just about anything. Reconnecting with nature has awakened in me the feelings of fun, peace, love, joy, support, and vibrant life that I believe we all deserve."

Linda C.

"My involvement with PNC has brought hope that something (the exercises in PNC) CAN be done by ordinary people, in ordinary circumstances that can and will help turn around our behavior toward the ecological sustainability issue that we are facing. It is a way to sensitize without criticizing people's relationships with themselves, each other, and all life forms with which we share the resources on this planet. I believe that as we let down more of our barriers to feeling how we feel in regard to the current ecological situation, we will make the changes we need to make. PNC activities enable a person to allow those barriers to gently dissolve as they connect with the forms of nature around them.

The most important help I have received is in my practice of quieting my mind enough when I am outdoors to be receptive to what in nature is calling to me at that moment. As I follow the attraction and attune myself to the energy, the energy within my body becomes more balanced, my emotions become more tranquil, and a feeling of thankfulness flows from my heart. This practice has become an essential ingredient in my meditation practices that put me in touch with the consciousness of healing and wholeness."

Mark B.

"PNC activities have influenced every aspect of my life in a very positive way. I feel more confident, more relaxed, more healthy and happy. I feel I have found a greater capacity to love others and myself. In the past I was often very pessimistic and depressed and fond of complaining. Now, I feel more empowered and optimistic. I find joy and many simple attractive pleasures each day. I have let go of a dismal, materialistic downward spiral, and have spread my wings to fly up on a wonderfully positive natural thermal. I feel high on life. I gain new insights and challenges as I climb. I am now able to let nature's infinite wisdom flow through me to share with others who are attracted to it."

Heidi W.

"Reading about others' experiences reinforces my view that the environment has a strong influence on defining who we are as individuals and as a people. Positive environmental experiences produce positive-minded people. PNC appears to bring individuals into positive relationships. Research printed in environmental education journals I have read indicate that programs like PNC are the best way for individuals to adopt life styles that reduce our impact on the environment."

David G.

"PNC is unique in that it offers guidelines to live by that have not been interpreted (or mis-interpreted) by humankind. What I see in nature is also within me, and I KNOW and TRUST that totally.

I am a ministerial student, and PNC has become such a deeply ingrained part of me that it will surely be a large part of my ministry. PNC teaches that all of nature is based upon attraction (love); it teaches there is no judgment in nature; it teaches connections with the total of our senses rather than in some limited intellectual way; it teaches that nature exists in the moment; and it teaches that there are no negatives in nature. These, and many more, are parallel to spiritual principles, and I trust them.

I recommend PNC for anyone, and I will be sharing it with others throughout my life."

Jim S.

"PNC causes me to pause and reflect on the world around me. To slow down, listen and feel when before I would only look. It solidified certain ideas I had learned intellectually about interconnectedness of all life. I feel I have become more sensitive to certain practical things around the house, like recycling, water usage, habitat destruction on my own property and use of electricity. I had done much personal self-work before doing PNC so I felt good about myself already but not as connected to nature. I can see how this would help others to do the same work, especially in groups. I also have more desire to be outside and enjoy the outdoors than ever, particularly at night which seems to be prohibited by many things in our culture."

Maggie S.

"My initial interest was kindled by both a professional interest in nature-based therapeutic methods but more importantly by my personal interest in spiritual matters particularly those related to nature and the spirit of Nature.

Personally my interest was driven by a crisis in my personal recovery from the addictive use of various chemical substances. As a direct result of my application of PNC methods to my daily life, I find my personal recovery has become significantly more stable. Also my recovery is more sustainable now because it is less dependent on any particular model of recovery. In essence my ongoing recovery was made possible through the reliable and trustable methods of PNC that on a moment-to-moment basis allowed me to be in conscious contact with the nameless intelligence and wisdom of nature.

Professionally I have used variants of these methods in my work as a mental health nurse with people of all ages to focus more on the here and now of the moment and less on often destructive stories that reside in their minds. It helps these people to become aware that these stories are not actually present in nature unless they decide to actualize those stories by acting them out. I also use PNC methods in the marketing of my professional services. I often talk of my marketing efforts as 'growth through natural attractions.'"

Steve S.

"Taking the course validated my precious experiences of connection with nature which has helped to make them a more frequent and influential part of my life. I also learned a lot about people, both good news and bad news, and how to relate to them and which ones to avoid. This latter was learned through the correspondence. One can learn something useful even from negative people.

My strong positive connection with nature helped me turn sarcasm into a learning experience, i.e., turn it into a G-G experience: How to spot non-GG people on line early and avoid/defuse them."

Emmon B.

"The PNC experience helped me improve:

-my personal life by being conscious of my personal sensory functioning

-my relationship with the environment by being aware of it as a community, not as a resource

-my professional life by specifically looking for natural areas to practice my job.

The PNC experience motivated me to help others build responsible relationships because it's a pleasant, constructive and peaceful experience. It enabled me to bring environmental concepts into my consciousness that I have always felt but could not verbalize by learning first to love Nature. I had a true and personal experience that helped me to be aware of my true deep and fundamental nature. It's a way of living and thinking that brings wellness and peace. Now I know what I want and I don't feel aggravated by people anymore. Nature is now my personal guide. When I want to make a decision I go into nature and it helps me to find the best. New respect for the living global community is a by-product of the PNC program."

Frank B.

"I've gotten myself so messed up by being disconnected from something I never even knew I was supposed to be connected to. I literally almost died twice from buying into the world's stories. I truly feel that PNC is my road back to health, sanity and living a life of joy. I was filling the nature-separated void in my life with all the wrong fixes, but PNC has given me the key to real life again."

Theresa K.

"The awakened consciousness interacts with surroundings in a responsible way—from the heart—and always with Hope. In moving (through PNC) to a deeper understanding of the pure potential we can create for others in a world clearly in need of an understanding of responsible action, we can become catalysts, through education, for the support and nurturance of Nature, the living global community and Earth Mother herself. With even just a thimbleful of courage we can reconnect with our innate capacity to heal ourselves and honor life and 'all of our relations' including the great forests, the rivers and seas: the mountains and eagles and whales and deer and little lichens and four-leaf clover...and rejoice in rainbows and dance in moonlight and sing together by campfires as we seep out under the stars and as a human species finally come into our wisdom phase."

Jane-Anne N.

Part 5
RESULTS OF OTHER PROGRAMS

Dr. Cohen's Applied Ecopsychology story is not to conquer nature, but to flow, dance and balance with nature and each other, as do all other species. It says that nature consists of attractions; that pain, fear and stress are natural attractions, part of nature's perfection. These natural discomforts are nature's way of telling us we don't have sensory support in this moment. They attract us to follow our other immediate natural attachments. Our discomforts in nature intensify our natural attractions to nurturing, community and trust. They support our fun and survival.

Findings

The students in this study could not handle regular school programs. They were 180% below the poverty level, drug or alcohol addicted and suffered poor self-esteem and behavioral disorders. Some were homeless or in correctional settings. The results of Project Reconnect were overwhelmingly positive. The students' growth was later reflected in the improved psychological test scores and analysis which show lower depression and drug use and higher self-esteem. The students now personally own activities and rationale for reconnecting with each other and with nature in the environment.

The students bonded as a community. They also bonded to a trashed natural area near their forthcoming new school. To protect the area's integrity and for future NSTP activities, these "incapable" youngsters successfully cleaned up, weeded and replanted it, wrote environmental protection grants *and effectively presented their work* to Education Boards and Administrators who were intent on paving the area as a parking lot.

The student's sensed that the natural area, like their nature, wanted to recover from the abuse received from society. They said that, like them, it had been: "hurt, molested, invaded and trespassed." "It wanted to become healthy or die." "It felt trashed and overwhelmed." "It had no power; it needed a fix or help to recover."

They wrote:

"This wilderness community is being choked by alien plants and stressed by pollution, abandonment and major loss. We, too, are being choked by drugs and alien stories that pollute our natural self. We feel abandoned by our society, treated like garbage, and cut off from nature which fills us with grief. By protecting and nurturing this ecosystem we find the strength to open our minds, hearts, and souls for the survival of our Mother Earth and ourselves."

The state of Earth and its people indicates that mentally and environmentally, we are distressed. This suggests that Project Reconnect used in conjunction with daily stress situations, instead of artificially programmed stress activities, could serve as an ecologically sound citizenship education preventative for chemical, food, social and environmental abuse.

Analysis of Pre and Post Data

As the raw data easily shows, the group improvement was significant. The average scores changed dramatically.

The group score on Beck's Depression inventory reduced from 12.2 to 1.5.

Scores on the Stress Test went from 19.8 to 12.

Coopersmith Self-Esteem Inventory changed from 9.5 to 5.

Average scores of the Barksdale Self-Esteem Inventory rose from 22 to 36.2. (The rising score shows improvement in this test.)

Finally, the Sleep Inventory scores improved from 9.7 to 7.3.

In addition to the improved test scores, every student's attendance and academic progress improved while they were in Project Reconnect. No indications of chemical remission were observed 60 days after the program ended.

Part 6

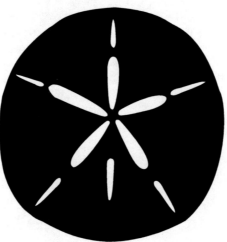

RESULTS OF EDUCATION BASED ON RECONNECTING WITH NATURE (Repeated from Introduction and Appendix E)

In 1959, Dr. Cohen founded a camp and school program based on reconnecting with nature. The National Audubon Society and many others called it the most revolutionary school in America. They said it was on the side of the angels. Participants traveled and thrived by camping out in 83 different natural habitats throughout the seasons. They learned to thoughtfully and feelingly live out their commitment to have open, honest relationships with the natural environment, each other and with indigenous people(s), researchers, ecologists, the Amish, organic farmers, anthropologists, folk musicians, naturalists, shamans, administrators, historians and many others close to the land. The experience deeply reconnected their 53 sense inner nature to its origins and self in the whole of nature.

Because of the participants' romance with educating themselves this way in the school community:

Chemical dependencies, including alcohol and tobacco, disappeared, as did social disorders.

Personality and eating disorders subsided.

Violence, crime and prejudices were unknown in the group.

Academics improved because they were applicable, hands-on and fun.

Loneliness, hostility and depression subsided.

Group interactions allowed for stress release and management; each day was fulfilling and peaceful.

Some students using meditation found they no longer needed to use it. They learned how to sustain a nature-connected community that more effectively helped them increase resiliency to stress and disease.

Participants knew each other better than they knew their families or best friends.

Participants felt safe. They risked expressing and acting from their deeper thoughts and feelings. A profound sense of social and environmental responsibility guided their decisions.

When vacation periods arrived, neither staff nor student wanted to go home. Each person enjoyably worked to build this supportive, balanced living and learning utopia. They were home.

Students entered right livelihood professions.

The 9-leg secret to each participant's success was to learn how to thoughtfully learn through 4-leg natural sensations and feelings that arose from their newly regrown sensory roots in ecosystems within and around them. These sensations acted as nature's guiding voice. The value and rewards of doing this freed the participants' 53 senses from their bonds to questionable 5-leg stories. It re-bonded them to their 4-leg sense of reason in congress with 52 other rejuvenated natural senses while these senses were connected to their origins and home in nature. This resulted in consensus based 9-leg thinking, literacy and relating that included information from, and the regenerative, healing powers of, natural systems. To many 5-leg thinkers, this sounds crazy, but year after year the beneficial results still speak for themselves.

From 30 years of travel and study in over 260 national parks, forests and subcultures, Cohen developed a replicable learning process and psychology that anyone can use at home, work or school today. It unleashes our suppressed 4-leg ability to grow and survive responsibly with natural systems in others, the environment and ourselves. By documenting that it worked and could be taught, he earned his doctoral degree and the school became a nationally recognized graduate and undergraduate degree program.

From 1985-92, Cohen translated the school's operants into a publicly available Natural Systems Thinking Process (NSTP). Today, backyard or backcountry, people gain from its readings and activities at home, work or school via the Internet. This survey conveys its results.

ONLINE COURSE REMINDER: Carefully read the Instructions in
Appendix C before starting the course in Chapter One that follows.

READERS: Appendix C provides important guidelines if you want to do
or teach the course actively.

Chapter One

Building Relationships as if Nature Mattered

(*Be sure to read the Introduction to this book before proceeding with this chapter.*)

"I go to nature to be soothed and healed, and to have my senses put in order."
- John Burroughs

Experiences are facts

This course engages you in the Natural Systems Thinking Process and its nature-connected, psychological science. It has a distinct rationale and methodology that respects and reinforces your ability to think and feel.

Living by the laws of nature is not a completely new way of thinking. As the quotes that are used throughout the course will demonstrate, it has been around as long as people have been thinking.

Since this can be a new way of thinking for some people, or maybe just a slightly different twist, it makes good sense for you to try this suggestion. Open up a new, fortressed, empty room somewhere in your mentality; maybe in the place you daydream on your screen of consciousness. Into that uncontaminated space carefully place the reasonable experiences, thoughts and feelings the course helps you discover. They are often 9-leg ways of knowing. There, they can remain intact and strong for your use at will. When you need them, simply open the door to the room and avail yourself of the attractive, reasonable integrity it will contain because you protected it. Otherwise, like the environment, that integrity becomes polluted by the nature-disconnected way of life and thinking that fuels so many of our problems.

In time, you will begin to notice that words are written on the door to the room. They say: "The Natural Systems Thinking Process: in nature within and about us, attractions are real, intelligent, healing, and conscious of themselves."

Thinking with the contents of this room is a key to success in personal and professional relationships.

Nature connecting activities

Nature activities must be done with authentic nature. Like reading a book about driving a car, if you actually want to get someplace, you must get in the car and drive. The main idea here is to let nature's intelligence show your mind that it is reasonable to enjoy and benefit from nature-connected thinking. It is attractive and sensible in and of itself. When connected to nature's intelligent and guiding ways, the activities enable your 5-leg verbal, reasoning mind to reconnect with your 4-leg feeling, sensory mind, your sensuous and spiritual mind. You remember how to fully think in the organic way that nature works.

The more natural the area you visit, the better. Just about anywhere can be very effective, whether it is a wilderness area or nature preserve, a vacant lot, a national or city park, a backyard, a potted plant, another person's inner nature, or a goldfish. Just as long as it's not a nature video or even this nature book.

The following is our first example of reconnecting with nature, in this case with your own inner nature, the natural systems in you. Almost all of the activities are best done in the most natural or wild area that you can access.

You are a part of nature's intelligent and sustaining ways. In the grand scheme of things, your inner nature is *as* important – but not *more* important – as any other part of the natural universe. We are equal in the world in that we hold in common the seamless continuum of natural systems that build and sustain relationships around and within us.

So, we'll start this organic journey of remembering with this very important part of you, the natural systems within you.

The Activity: Thoughtful Contemplation

Think about a prior good experience you had in nature. Think about where you were, how you felt, what you sensed, then ask yourself if you would want to repeat that experience. (It is especially helpful to write your thoughts and feelings in a journal.)

Ask yourself these questions, and write down your thoughts and answers in your journal:

What was feelingly enjoyable or rewarding about the experience?

What 4-leg sensory attractions were involved in the experience? Colors, sounds, feelings, aromas, sensations, moods, contrasts, textures, sizes, distance.

Were you 5-leg taught to have this good experience in a class? From a book? A person? Or was it your natural sensory attraction connections to the natural area that provided the rewards?

Do you recognize from this experience that there are intact, inborn parts of you that inherently have the ability to register and retain attractive sensory contacts with nature? Do you acknowledge your nature experiences as facts...natural facts of life...facts of your life?

Optionally complete this summary evaluation:
SUMMARY STATEMENT A:

Because I am naturally a sensory being, in this activity sensory contact with attractions in the natural area provided most of the rewards I obtained from my good experience in nature.

Either in your journal or on a piece of paper, record the SUMMARY STATEMEMT letter code (A) along with the number on the continuum scale below that indicates the extent of your agreement with the Summary Statement:

1   2   3   4   5   6   7   8   9   10
disagree   partially agree   fully agree

Supportive Reading

How can we help our thinking reasonably help us come to our senses?

A responsible society acknowledges its destructive effects and acts to eliminate them. The destructive effects of industrial civilization are undeniable with respect to its impact on the web of life. The web is nature itself, a biological, connective, balancing, natural system process that the natural world and the inner nature (inner child?) of people hold in common.

Our basic relationship with nature has been to conquer nature and be rewarded in the name of progress and survival. We have done this so successfully that we are in denial that the rewards have psychologically conditioned or addicted us to some abusive, unsustainable ways of thinking and relating. For this reason, our personal, social and environmental problems have become runaway. We no longer know how to stop assaulting nature although we know we should. With respect to our relationship with the web of life, we must go back to the basics. We must learn how to be part of the web in a constructive way.

What is the web of life?

Experts often depict the web by gathering a group of people in a circle. Each person is asked to represent some part of nature, such as a bird, soil, water, etc. A large ball of string then helps members of the group see the interconnecting relationships between things in nature. For example, the bird eats insects so the string is passed from the "bird person" to the "insect person." That is their connection. The insect lives in a flower, so the string is further unrolled across the circle to the "flower person." Soon a web of string is formed interconnecting all members of the group, including the one or two who represent people.

Dramatically, people pull back slightly and sense how the string organically and peacefully unites, supports and interconnects them and all of life. Then one strand of the web is cut signifying the loss of a species, habitat or relationship. Sadly, the weakening effect on all is noted. Another and another string is cut. Soon the web's integrity, support and power disintegrates along with its spirit. Because this activity reflects the reality of our lives, this has brought some participants in the activity to feelings of hurt, despair and sadness.

Earth and its people increasingly suffer from "cut string" disconnection, yet we continue to cut the strings.

Something to think about:
To my loss, do I unknowingly cut or injure strands of the web of life within or around me? Do I know how to stop myself from doing this?

Every part of the global life community, from sub-atomic particles to weather systems, is part of the web of life. The intelligent process by which they interact produces nature's harmonious, supportive ways and prevents our runaway disorders from occurring in nature. The process nature uses consists of interacting while in contact with the whole of the web through its web attraction strings. As part of the web, we, along with everything else, are born with this ability. Our troubles begin when we don't recognize or use it, deny its existence or hurt it. It usually remains alive in us but it becomes subconscious to protect us from constantly feeling its frustration or hurt.

Something to think about:
Am I aware of the strands of the web of life that I was born with and still contain? Do I use

them and their ways to build responsible relationships with people and places? Have I been taught or forced to make them subconscious?

Dr. Cohen often asks the web of life activity participants if they ever went into a natural area and actually saw strings holding things together there. They say, "No, that would be crazy." He responds, "If there are no strings in nature, what then are the actual strands that hold the natural community together in balance?"

It is always very, very quiet.

Pay close attention to this silence. It flags the missing organic link in our thinking, perception and relationships that produces many troubles. The web's strings are a vital part of survival, just as real and important as the plants, animals and minerals that they interconnect, including ourselves. The strings are as true as $2 + 2 = 4$, facts as genuine as us. As part of nature, we are born with the natural ability to know them (4-leg thinking and awareness) but we learn to seldom recognize or exercise this ability. Without seeing, sensing or respecting the strings in nature and our inner nature, we break, injure and ignore them. Their disappearance in our consciousness produces an organic void, an uncomfortable psychological emptiness in our thoughts and lives that we constantly try to fill. We want, emotionally and materially, and when we want, there is never enough. We become greedy, stressed and reckless as we try to gain webstring fulfillment. This places the Earth, others, and ourselves at risk.

Now, NSTP's nature-reconnecting activities enable us to bring webstrings – natural sensory attraction relationships – back into our lives. Their presence in our thinking helps reinstate balanced personal and environmental relationships.

Something to think about:
Am I aware of the strands of the web that lie within and around me? Is it important to me to stop thinking in nature-disconnected ways that place Earth and its people at risk?

Source Of The Strings

The strings are biologically of, by and from nature. Since you are part of nature, the strings are in you and you can learn to nurture them and relate harmoniously to them through an organic, nature-centered, self-improvement process that helps us let the strings consciously teach us their knowledge. Many people disbelieve this because we are taught to conquer, not respect, nature including the webstrings. We have also learned that the strings, which manifest as dozens of senses in natural systems within us (our inner nature,

child, inner self), are taboo, flaky, subjective, spiritual, unscientific, bad, wrong, etc. Thus, many webstring senses can have hurt attached to them, hurt that blocks the webstrings from freely entering our consciousness, where they can be felt, into our values and thinking. Often, out of hurt and frustration, the strings disappear rather than support us when we need them.

Something to think about:
Is my 5-leg thinking prejudiced against the strings and nature's ways to the point that it influences my relationships?

To connect with nature our thinking must include a 4-leg sensory way of knowing. Our senses connect us with the living Earth around us in every moment. If we don't understand our interdependence and relationship to nature, it is because we have disconnected our senses from their source. We have dismissed them as irrelevant. We have forgotten their significance.

Throughout history, many people have cherished their webstring senses and recognized their importance, as follows:

"We cannot live for ourselves alone. Our lives are connected by a thousand invisible threads, and along these sympathetic fibers our actions run as causes and return to us as results."
- Herman Melville

Scientifically, it is clear that natural systems organize themselves with webstrings. Moment by moment, organic systems are 4-leg attracted to create additional strings and connections that increasingly weave, balance and repair the web of life. This is not done haphazardly; rather it forms an attraction intelligence that produces nature's optimum of life, diversity, cooperation, balance and beauty. It is worth remembering that the process is inclusive and caring enough to globally produce and sustain the web of life without creating garbage. At the macro level, nothing is left out, unattached or unwanted – a way to define unconditional love.

Something to think about:
Can I allow myself to believe that natural relationships contain, or are, a form of unconditional love?

Attraction Energies

From subatomics to solar systems, common sense and experts, including Albert Einstein and Jonas Salk, recognize that all intact relationships, physical or otherwise, must be held together by something. Without this glue, they would fall apart. That "something" is an essence of nature, the natural attraction energies Cohen calls webstrings. By definition alone, this makes sense. What we call repulsion can just as easily be recognized as attraction to something more immediate and important. For example, when in a dangerous situation do we run away in fear (repulsion) or run for our life? Both are survival attractions. Was the "big bang" a profound explosion or a profound attraction to growth?

"From atoms and molecules to human beings with developed consciousness, all entities feel attraction for one another. . . attraction is the law of nature."

- P. R. Sarkar

Elements of Regeneration

Attraction energies in nature are the heart of its recycling and purification process. These unifying forces are the power in natural systems that reconnect detached natural attractions and thereby eradicate contamination and pollution. This helps nature sustain its wellness, balance and beauty. For example, nature purifies contamination through attraction energies that beckon air to flow through people and natural areas. In so doing, air nourishes people and nature with each other's "waste" products. In the process, air also recycles its own purity as well as strengthens the diverse integrity of the plant, animal and mineral kingdoms.

It is most significant that on atomic as well as global levels nature's recycling of air is fueled by attraction energies, a fundamental, organic, binding force that some might consider spiritual.

Something to think about:
Can I believe that nature is a perfection of its own that does not produce any garbage because it consists mostly, if not only, of attraction relationships?

Whenever we safely make contact with attractions in nature, they trigger our brain to release Dopamine, a neurotransmitter that produces the good feelings that we seek. These good feelings are a vital gratification reward. They help our thinking become aware that a beneficial survival connection to natural attraction energies has been made, a connection that contributes to replenishing, regenerating and sustaining all of life. Thus, each attraction sensation, feeling or emotion in nature is a rational, sensory, rewarding way of knowing and relating that we biologically inherit from and hold in common with nature. Neuroscientists identify attractions as Freud's "drives" that they call "seeking urges." Each encourages and shapes good citizenship and recycling in the global life community. Sensing and appreciating the role these attraction energy webstrings play is 5-leg thinking at its finest. Reasoning that includes them is 9-leg thinking.

"This world - the shadow of the soul, or 'other' me - lies wide around. Its attractions are the keys which unlock my thought and make me acquainted with myself."

- R. W. Emerson

Something to think about:
How much do I believe that nature's encouragement of natural attractions in natural areas is an origin of my ability to feel good?

Properly designed nature-connecting activities help us create moments that let genuine contact with natural attraction energies organically realign and recycle the misguided attachments in us that draw us into destructive relationships and dependencies.

At night, I open the window and ask the moon to come and press its face against mine, breathe into me.
Close the language door and open the love window.
The moon won't use the door, only the window.

- Rumi

A major solution to many problems is to genuinely enable our thinking to return to the organic "Garden of Eden," and use its natural attraction wisdom to help us recycle our destructive thinking and co-create a brighter future for the Garden and ourselves.

Life is a finely woven net in which all worlds are joined - ancestors, spirits, humans, animals and the natural universe - bonded by the timeless eternal spirit of that which has always been and is.

- T. C. McLuhan

Need for connection

We are mentally, more than physically, isolated from the natural world. The disconnected way we think is polluted and produces behavior that pollutes natural and social systems. We seldom recognize the need for our thinking to be genuinely connected with nature, be renewed, and contribute to life's welfare as part of nature's restorative processes. This misjudgment produces a hurtful omission in our reasoning that pollutes and disables our ability to think through organic 4-leg attractions, like nature works.

Something to think about:
If nature is guided to its balanced ways by natural attraction energies, am I willing to let them influence me?

Because we are so disconnected from nature, our leaders seldom recognize that our sensory appetite for air (our desire/attraction to breathe) is a sensation and wisdom we can respect and learn from. Neither do they recognize that we need nature to help purify faulty thought processes, heal and simultaneously contribute to life's welfare as part of the natural recycling process. Conflict and suffering result from this omission.

Something to think about:
Do some of my problems stem from a hurtful omission in my reasoning that has led me to enter destructive relationships?

The attractiveness of God

Attraction energy reasoning recognizes that many issues and differences between various beliefs regarding God are today, as through the ages, a major source of human conflict, death and suffering as well as joy. Each person or group is so strongly attracted to his or her God that they are at times willing to argue, fight, shed their life or take the lives of others to honor their God relationship. This and the passionate forms of worship people practice strongly suggest that one of God's qualities is attractiveness. God is naturally very attractive.

Natural attractions being an observed essence of the materials and energies in the natural systems of our universe, nature, Earth and ourselves suggests that God created this universe from His/Her attractiveness. He/She may have made other universes from His/Her vast knowledge, power or size. If, however, we are to be true to ourselves and trust our senses, rationality and

experiences, it becomes reasonable to consider that our universe may be constructed of God's attraction energies and that to know God while bypassing nature creates disorders.

"I believe in God, only I spell it Nature."
- Frank Lloyd Wright

Something to think about:
Is there room in my thinking to know, or accept that some people know, natural attractions as an expression or essence of the Divine that we hold in common with the natural world? What difference do I see between natural attractions and pure love?

Natural systems and nature-centered people don't display the runaway war, abusiveness, pollution and mental and environmental disorders that plague our lives. These problems arise because our estrangement from nature prejudiciously and addictively deprives our thinking from conscious contact with webstrings, their intelligence, nurturance and energies. (If you don't believe this is a psychological addiction, just try to get a group of people to make contact with webstrings.)

We spend, on average, less than 12 hours per lifetime in conscious sensory contact with nature. How well could you read, write or think if you only spent 12 hours of your total life learning to do it? Without ongoing sensory contact with our sensory origins, for example, our thinking still foolishly lets us obtain rewards from smoking cigarettes while fully knowledgeable that they contain poisons. In addition, our "stringless" solutions for runaway personal and global problems are as ineffective as the warning labels on cigarette packages.

"There must be the generating force of love behind every effort that is to be successful."
- Henry David Thoreau

An essence of separation

It is common knowledge that, with the exception of humanity, no member of the web of life relates, interacts or thinks through words. The web is a non-verbal "illiterate" experience consisting of in-the-moment direct attraction relationships (webstrings), not words, stories, videos or images. No plant, animal or mineral string of nature's ancient web consists of literary communication or attachments to it.

Language is a great asset to human survival when we use it to help make and sustain sensory contact with the web and its intelligent ways. Language, however, becomes a source of our problems when it, through nature-disconnecting stories, excessively removes our thinking from our sensory origins in the web and its wisdom. For example, sensory discontents initiated by our separation from nature psychologically addict us to the story that we must conquer nature to fulfill our natural senses: hunger, thirst, taste, love, etc. Since we are nature, we addict to conquering each other and ourselves thereby producing mental anguish and war. To find lasting peace, we must heed a new story: "Learn how to reconnect your ruptured sensory webstrings with their brilliant, fulfilling, organic origins in the lifeweb."

Something to think about:
Am I a victim of thinking in 5-leg language and stories that isolate me from the unifying web process that peacefully holds the global life community and people in balance? Do I have symptoms of this, such as undue loneliness, sadness, stress, excessive wants, depression, lack of attention, or underlying anger?

In contemporary society, 99.99% of our feeling and thinking being separated from nature painfully dismembers our psyche from its origins. It silently suffers a profound loss of contact with its nurturing sensory and sensibility roots in nature's webstring ways and intelligence. We contain this bag of hurt. Any word or incident that reminds us of our psychological dismemberment, of our abandonment, breaks the silence. It releases the emotional pain of dismemberment into consciousness and we feel it. As reflected by the state of the world, indoors or outdoors, our mentality is often guarded, stressed, ill, wanting and destructive in response to our painful deficiency of nature's attractive peace, wisdom and beauty. We become "ecozombies;" our thinking is deadened to the ways and values of natural systems within and around us.

Something to think about:
How much of the frustration I experience is due to my environment actually not supporting me and how much is subconsciously triggered by memories of my dismemberment from nature?

Restoration through reconnection
NSTP enables us to reverse many of our troubles because it effectively addresses their source. The process starts by having us learn how to consciously make enjoyable, non-verbal, sensory contacts directly with the life web and its members, not with substitutes for them. With respect to the perfection of nature's eons of experience, there is no substitute for the real thing. These sensory contacts enable us to consciously and sentiently reattach the strings within us to their origins, the strings

in the web. We can feel and enjoy the orgnic connection; it is an attractive experience in nature.

The process then helps us safely translate our sensory attraction feelings into verbal language and share them. This lets our sensory connections with the web feelingly validate themselves in words to the thinking and reasoning part of our psyche. It is important to recognize that without this verbalization and sharing, NSTP is like an engine without gasoline; it can but doesn't produce action.

"Nothing is more indisputable than our senses."
- Jean Le Rond d'Alembert

By using NSTP as a tool, we help nature guide our thinking to work like nature works. We sensuously enjoy nature's harmonious wisdom and support as it enters our relationships. In this psychologically organic, nature-reconnecting process, the natural world, be it potted plant or wilderness, becomes our classroom, mentor and library. It helps us peacefully co-create a sustainable future with the global life community.

Something to think about:
Does it make sense for me to want to learn through contact with natural systems? Have I prejudicially learned that doing this is "flaky" or "fuzzy thinking" and may make me look foolish like a "hippy" or "Earth Muffin" so I won't do it?

NSTP helps us recognize that the strings are  actually natural attractions. Every atom and its nucleus consists of, expresses and relates through natural attractions. All of nature, including us, contains these attractions.

As suggested earlier, webstring attractions feelingly register in our consciousness as sensations we call senses. For example: as natural loves for sight, touch, and sound; as our attractions to water (including thirst); color and community; as attachments for nurturing, belonging and trust; as affinities for reason and contact with nature; for wholeness. Senses of place, gravity, pain, motion, temperature, and trust, are each attractions that, when energized, register and help guide our conscious thoughts.

Wouldn't my relationships be more rewarding if I could learn to increase my sensitivity to natural attraction energies in people and places around me?

People and things think and love through at least 53 different sensory attraction strings, not just five as we are usually taught. Each string is an intelligent way of knowing that inherently attracts to and blends with other strings to build and be guided by the common good.

"The senses, being the explorers of the world, open the way to knowledge."
- Maria Montessori

Nature helps create, sustain and balance life through these powerful 53 sensitivities in concert. To our loss, our excessive separation from nature addicts us to think and relate with less than six of them. The loss of this sensory wisdom unbalances our thinking.

"The moment my inner attraction string for color touched the color string of this woodland, I experienced a special joy."
- Raymond Sierra

A metaphor concerning seven blind wise men touching and 5-leg arguing about an elephant conveys the dilemmas of our blindness to nature and our natural senses. In the story, each blind man argues his case based upon what part of the elephant he is touching. While one calls the elephant a pipe (the tusk), another says the elephant is a snake (trunk) or like a rope (tail).

Such differences often lead to demoralization, hate and war because we psychologically bond to, and fight for, stories we know to be "the truth." We seldom reconcile our differences by making further common contact with the integrity of the whole elephant or whole web of life. Satisfying many of their additional natural attraction senses would have led each wise man to further explore the elephant and discover the diverse integrity of the animal, each other and themselves.

"It is difficult to get people to understand something when their salary (or other reward) depends upon them not understanding it."
- Upton Sinclair

Has my extensive disconnection from nature unknowingly blinded me to the existence and value of my sensory attraction strings?

Our thinking blindly loses contact with the truths that it needs to recover from the absence of these truths. That is why, in our nature-estranged society, it is best to learn NSTP by **doing it.** The Process helps you let your 53 natural senses plug directly into their attraction origins in nature and energize. This recharge brings the web's supportive string signals further into your consciousness, thinking and being. This helps you let contact with nature increase your sensibility, balance and wellness. In addition, you give natural attraction energies a chance to organically recycle and purify on their own as only they can do. You feel better and your outlooks and relationships improve. Anybody who has had a good experience in nature has enjoyed this phenomenon. Through NSTP, these moments and their benefits become available at will.

"The beginning of wisdom is to call things by their right name."
- Confucius

Verbal reconnection

Through NSTP, each of our natural senses is identified by their right name, "Webstring: A seamless sensory attraction energy string of the global web of life community within and around us." Webstrings feelingly help us bring nature into our awareness and thinking at will. No offense intended, but to call webstrings anything else, as we are often trained to do, (senses, feelings, God, instincts, needs, drives, spirit, desires, blessings, beliefs, subjective, bias, angels, attractions, energies) tends to keep our thinking disconnected from the wholeness of the web of life and its organic ability to establish balance. In our nature-separated society, we are bonded to think and know through 5-leg words that produce separation. That disconnection is the psychological heart of many insurmountable personal and global problems.

"There's nothing either good or bad...but thinking makes it so!"
- William Shakespeare

Am I missing contributions that my natural self can make to my relationships? Was I trained to deny my natural self?

The success of NSTP and the webstring model is its accuracy. It helps us recognize a secret aspect of how nature works, a secret we too often learn to ignore or conquer. The secret is that webstrings are attractions; nature primarily works by attractions. This means that each webstring we experience as a non-attraction (for example, fear, pain, spiritual distress, excessive thirst, hunger, temperature, motion, etc.) is actually also an attraction, a natural love. *It attracts us to find more rewarding natural attractions–when danger lurks, to seek safety.* For example, we become aware of attractions to coolness when a fire becomes too hot, or to less painful areas when thorns are sharp. These warning messages are attractive. We would not survive without them. It is when we don't, or can't heed or honor them that trouble arises.

Something to think about:
Do I negate or demean the contributions that some webstrings make because they interfere with my immediate plans, wishes or enjoyment? Have I been trained to see them as negative, or overcome them and thereby upset a natural balance?

"The laws of the universe are not indifferent, but are forever on the side of the most sensitive."
- Henry David Thoreau

Sensible education

Making space in our lives to do activities that reconnect us with nature has proven to produce responsible relationships. Once we learn how to do a reconnecting activity, we own it and can teach it to others.

The web of life only exists today because yesterday, through attraction contacts, every component of the web consensually "educated" its environment about how it supported its immediate environment. This basic consciousness process occurs moment by moment in nature; it is an essence of all life relationships and survival. As part of nature, it is true in humans, too.

Cultures that exist today only exist because they are successful in educating their members about how the culture works and its value; they, in turn, carry on the culture. Today, globally, the Internet empowers people to engage in this webstring education process by enjoying and teaching webstring-connected consciousness through distance learning activities, courses and communication. In local communities, person-to-person webstring activity education occurs as well.

"One touch of Nature makes the whole world kin."
- William Shakespeare

Considering the vital natural and cultural survival value of webstring education, it is no surprise that, genetically, our mind and bodies, our inner nature, learns only 15% of what we read but 90% of what we teach. If you want to personally and globally come into balance, teach what you have read here: Thoughtful, continuing, consensually shared, sensory reconnecting activity attractions in natural areas bring into our consciousness the webstring connections with Earth that help us build balanced organic relationships. The sensory webstring of reason demands that we engage in the activities.

Earth and its people are at risk. ***Isn't it time that we come to our senses*** by letting the 4-leg attraction strings bring us to them through enjoyable nature reconnecting activities? The strings can do this because they are natural sensory loves, an essence of life itself. D. H. Lawrence beautifully validated this when he said:

"Oh, what a catastrophe, what a maiming of love when it was made personal, merely personal feeling. This is what is the matter with us: we are bleeding at the roots because we are cut off from the Earth and sun and stars. Love has become a grinning mockery because, poor blossom, we plucked it from its stem on the Tree of Life and expected it to keep on blooming in our civilized vase on the table."
- D. H. Lawrence

By thoughtfully learning how to become conscious of webstrings and teach this awareness, we reattach our ability to love to its roots in nature. This restores love to its fullness and heals our bleeding.

Something to think about:
Do I want to professionally and personally further my life and all of life by learning to let contact with Earth itself nurture my inner nature's isolation, hurt and fear of additional rejection? Can I really get to know who I am and help people and Mother Earth if the thinking part of me seldom registers, validates or reconnects my inner nature and the web of life?

Confucius say: In the web of life model, if you call each of your senses and feelings a "webstring attraction" you will help your life and all of life improve because the word webstring signals "a guiding web of life attraction" rather than "an isolated sensation." In the web of life model, webstrings are as real as 2 + 2 =4.

On the courses we've been calling the attractions webstrings, webloves or NIAL strings meaning Nameless, Intelligent, Attraction, Loves. People who can't make sense of some situations are often found to be in deNIAL.

Something to think about:
Does my 5-leg tendency to call my sensuous experiences "senses" and "feelings" deprive me from consciously knowing and enjoying the 9-leg wisdom of respecting them as attraction energy strands of the web of life?

As the examples below demonstrate, readily available sensory activities that produce conscious connections with Earth make a difference. The sensory webstring of reason demands that we use them.

Connecting with nature, 9-leg examples:

Stress
"This morning I was battling the remnants of some depression I had been feeling about my family and life "stuff". I was doing the sensory attraction activity, looking around enjoying the day, the breeze, the sun, the beautiful trees and the sounds of singing birds. In a flash of good feeling, I realized that these feelings are what is so good about living on Earth at this time. It was enough, if for no other reason, to be here, to experience the beauty of this planet. This was a major breakthrough for me, because I battle the reason for being here quite a bit in my recovery work. This happened before noon, and it is now 6 pm, and I still feel great!!!!!!!!!!!!!!!!!! I wanted to share this because I am so happy!!!!!!!!!!!!!!!!!!"

Peace and Support
"I was never taught to ask permission to relate to people or the environment. I just take that for granted, as we all do. However, this activity required my senses to learn how to ask an attractive tree covered area for its consent for me to walk through it. The area continued to feel attractive, but something changed. It was the first time in my life that I totally felt safe. It felt like Earth's energies were in charge of my life, not me. It gave me a wonderful feeling of having more power to be myself. I felt in balance with nature and the people here because I could distinctly feel their energies consenting to support me. I never experienced nature and people that way before. It was like a powerful law protected not only my life, but all of life. I felt very secure and nurtured as I walked under those trees. I learned that when I seek permission from the environment and people I gain energy and unity, I belong."

Chemical Dependencies
"I want to share with the group that I feel different from when I started this course. I have always struggled with chemical addictions, and these last few weeks, I find I hardly have cravings at all anymore. At times, I do, but then I can go into nature, right outside my backdoor, and feel a connection that is real. I have been through therapy as well as currently working a twelve-step program, and I feel these nature activities have really helped me, more than I have words for. This is definitely an attraction, I cannot label it, have no words for it, yet I know in my heart something has changed."

Global Intelligence
"My, how my mind does chatter with words that can mislead me. When I make contact with nature and think with nature's intelligence, it guides me with a wisdom that helps me keep in balance. The contact is non-verbal because nature does not communicate with words. As I worked through the Introductory Course,  I began to use the [*Reconnecting With Nature*] book's methodology to quiet my mind. As I went through the activities, I began to sense a subtle, but perceptible shift in my ability to attain a non-verbal awareness. Then one day, as I was doing one of the activities that asks us to "jam" the verbal mind with a word ("unity" in my case) I suddenly connected. WHAM! There it was, non-verbal awareness. No naming, no concepts, just being. What a relief! It didn't last long, but it did change my life. Since then, I have extended my abilities to just be. Now my "mind chatter" is only a murmur when I ask it to be. This has opened up experiences so far beyond anything I even dreamed of a few years ago."

Healing and Wellness
"The activity helped me become aware of my attraction to the crescent moon as it hung over two hills near my home. Soon, its mellow glow, framed by peaks and trees, embraced me in a wordless, ancient primordial scene. Timeless power, peace and unity swept me up. I just wanted to stay in that state of awe. I felt in balance with all of reality. I was simply "BEING," No tension, no pressing goal, just truly belonging to the global community. This natural energy captured my stress laden pulse and seduced it to the rhythms of Earth. The sleeping disorder I have battled all my adult life dissolved in this

power. For the first time in decades, I gently fell asleep after dark and arose shortly after dawn. I celebrated the breakthrough and I thanked nature. I thanked the activity, too, for it lets me reconnect whenever I choose."

Something to think about:
Would my health and happiness improve if most of the time my mentality and relationships felt like I feel when I'm having a good experience in nature?

If you want to reach this goal, start by remembering other good experiences you have had in nature. Then apply the information and your thinking in this chapter to each of those experiences.

If you are only reading this book and not doing the activities, you might be interested in the course instructions to online participants that follow. They show you a vital, 9-leg part of NSTP that increases its potency.

Book Option

If you have the book *Reconnecting With Nature,* read Chapter 3 for a stronger understanding about the Reconnecting With Nature process. You need not do the activity in that chapter.

ONLINE COURSE PARTICIPANTS:

Thoughtful Verbalization:

Important guidelines: Complete each Part of the course by journaling it and posting it to your study group. The guideline list below in this book is also in Appendix C and on the last page of this book for handy reference.

Online: Start your post to the group with the Subject (GROUP NAME OR NUMBER)_____: PART 1, YOUR NAME, so that other course members and readers can identify it, read it, and share their thoughts and feelings about your experiences and vice versa. Submit your attraction experiences, thoughts and feelings from the material on this page to the group along with the following Twelve Interact Catalysts:

The Interact Catalysts

Journal and post your response to these guidlines with your online study group or other interested people who are familiar with this chapter.

1) A general description of how you did the activity and what happened, along with quotes you like from the readings and how they added meaning to the experience.

2) The three most important things you learned from the chapter and webstring connections.

3) How you   would feel about having the webstring attractions you experienced in the activity taken away from you.

4) Whether or not the activity enhanced your sense of self-worth and your trustfulness of nature.

5) The part of you, if any, the activity identified or re-educated inside or outside of you.

6) Your reactions to what you found attractive in the postings you read from the other group members. Be sure to save the Interact postings of yourself and others that are attractive to you so that you can refer to them and quote them in the final paper for this course.

7) What value, if any, there was to doing the Summary Option (if you did it.)

8) Write one or two keywords that convey what important thing you learned from this assignment.

9) Write one or more complete, single, short, power sentence "quotes" that convey a significant contribution that this assignment makes to improving our relationships.

10) Integrating Dream Time: Get a night's sleep before doing the next activity. While your 5-leg mind sleeps, your 4-leg mind rides the inroads to consciousness made by the activity and reading. Note, upon awakening, whether any changes have occurred with respect to your outlook or the way you feel.

11) Conclude by identifying what things you have put into the trustable, uncontaminated, thought and feeling room/space you built into your psyche as suggested in this chapter.

12) Remember: You will increase your learning from this activity by 75% if you teach this activity to another person. You may co-facilitate this course online, upon completing it. The use of these twelve Interact Catalysts will enhance your learning experience and that of the others in the course as well.

Organic Psychology

After World War II ammonium nitrate munitions began to be used as a food production fertilizer while organophosphate nerve gas was used in developing powerful insecticides. To avoid the environmental and social detriments of this as well as chemical additives to food, by the late 1960s the production of natural and organic foods arose. Today, organic crop farming and gardening are a welcome, well established and steadily growing $4.2 billion industry in the U.S. alone.

Similar to the need for organic food and other products as an alternative for detrimental farming and food additives, the Natural System Thinking Process is an organic alternative to the detrimental psychological and educational relationship building practices caused by the excessive disconnection of contemporary thinking from natural systems within and around us. The strongest roots of NSTP stem from Dr. Cohen's determination in 1965 that Earth's global ecosystem acts like, or is, a living organism. By definition this makes NSTP an *organic psychology* because it is of, relates to, and is derived from the integrity of living organisms without the employment of contaminating substances, stories or other adulterating factors. *Organic* means fundamentally relating to or arising in a bodily organ or organism and affecting its structure to help form an integral element of a whole. NSTP meets this definition.

"Even a child can recognize that as long as we continue to be psychologically bonded to contaminated materials and tainted thinking while building relationships with people and the environment, many personal and global troubles we suffer today will continue. Learning how to think and relate using the organic psychology tools of NSTP has given me access to unadulterated sources of information and energy. It has helped me transform my destructive bonds into constructive relationships and create a healthier personal and professional path for myself."
- NSTP Participant's Anonymous Course Evaluation

Sadly, the psychologically addictive rewards from money, substances and power socialize you and us into being well-adjusted citizens of industrial society along with its all too many nature-abusive substances, relationships and technologies. Because we are part of nature, our psyche, health and happiness suffer from this "normal" abuse and this helps produce our many troubles.

Our major disorders and discontents persist because we treat them with contaminated solutions that cause additional problems and we seldom treat them as psychological addictions.

Organic relationship-building and substances support, rather than abuse, nature and our inner nature. Thus, if your thinking, psychology and technologies are not organic, you, as part of nature, to some extent unintentionally support your personal and our collective troubles.

NSTP gives you an Organic Psychology learning tool to help you constructively transform the destructive bonds that underlie your harmful thinking and relationships. It enables you to think and relate organically and reap the rewards of personal and environmental wellness. This gives you a vibrant edge in obtaining support for your deeper hopes and goals.

By adding important holistic and environmental dimensions to psychology, medicine, education and most relationships, NSTP helps them and you become more effective and responsible. It is an integrity-building, whole-life component that you may beneficially incorporate in any human service or means of learning, relating and healing.

"We have done hundreds of these organic psychology activities with people of very varied backgrounds, ages, mental health, education, vocation and physical fitness. We have never met one person who has not had a positive experience. The greater majority of those we have taught have expressed enormous gratitude for this work."
- Gaia and Kurtland Davies

Take a good look around you locally and at the world at large. Note that even though we know and feel that our inappropriate relationships are dangerously hurting us and the environment, psychology as it is presently practiced has not prevented the mentality of contemporary society from continuing to injure natural systems in people and places. This is because contemporary psychology mostly deals with social interactions, not with the organics of natural system relationships that inherently produce balance and renewal. Most psychologies are not organic. Rather, they are adulterated because they suckle on our society's nature-disconnected thinking, rewards, therapists, exploitive relationships and pollution. As they help solve one problem they often intensify another. They are similar to using non-organic gardening, non-organic food and other questionable products. They seldom operate as if nature matters.

As long as our thinking, learning, psychology and consciousness are disconnected from communication with the balancing and healing powers of natural systems, the systems and therefore we suffer the troubles caused by our disconnection. NSTP offers us a easily accessible, personal and global instrument to reverse this disorder. Uniquely, this organic addition to psychology and learning enables any individual, discipline or organization to make "The answer is blowing in the wind" a practical reality because NSTP helps us find the answer there. The chapters that follow teach you how to put NSTP into action.

Chapter Two

Trusting How Your Nature Works

Underlying Principles of Relationships: How our 5-leg socialization manipulates webstrings.

ONLINE COURSE PARTICIPANTS:
Posting Schedule (shaded areas for online only)
Posting days 2A and 2B (7 days total in the default schedule)
PART 2A Sections 1-4: Do these in the first three days (Wednesday-Saturday in the default schedule)
PART 2B: Do these in the last 4 days (Saturday-Tuesday in the default schedule)
Course members have the option to on their own time, take a day for each of these sections, or find a partner or two who want to do a section a day and post to each other. Please invite the facilitators to participate or react to the postings. Do not let this disrupt the course schedule, however; during this period continue on to Part 2, 3, 4 etc. as per the index schedule.

Instructions:

Do the following sequence of activities while you have immediate contact with the most natural area that is convenient: a park, potted plant, aquarium or backyard so you can experience them in conjunction with nature. Space out the activities. If possible, do one or two per day.

Please identify one or two attractive things you find most significant in each of the following ten sections.

Section One:
The Sensory World. Who are You?

"I sense and feel, therefore I am." Would you place your name here_____as a person who believes the statement in quotes?

Please note this factual truth:
2 + 2 = 4   (X) True (   ) False.

Mathematics is considered to be the purist of sciences and fact. However, the fact that we each sense and feel webstrings is as true, if not truer, than mathematics. We are not born knowing mathematics; we must learn it just as we learn names and labels for the world. However, we are born with the inherited ability from nature to sense, feel, think and learn through webstrings. We share this on some level with all of nature.

Do you trust your inborn senses and feelings as much as you trust mathematics or definitions? For example: pinch yourself gently. Do you trust that you felt something?

Now, pinch yourself too hard. Do you trust that a webstring sense (pain, reason or both) intelligently calls to you to stop pinching yourself that hard? Sensations and feelings offer self-evidence that you may reason with. (Optionally, further explore this in Appendix A.)

Who are you? We largely build our lives and our knowledge of who we are around the intellectual 5-leg truths of mathematics, science and technological artifacts. Through this process, we come to know ourselves as "cultural objects" (teachers, mechanics, actors, our names, etc). We are often taught to do so without also learning from experiences in nature, the webstring attraction truths of what we naturally sense and feel. We often know ourselves better by our names and prejudices than by how and what we think and feel. For example, with respect to living in balance with Earth, each other and ourselves, most people sense that we have gone too far. They feel we are too abusive and destructively out of control. Although we strongly sense this, we are presently unable to stop, yet we seldom call ourselves "senseless," "uncivilized," "out of balance," "disconnected from Earth," "stupid," "insane," etc.

Section Two:
The Purity of Balance

Very little, if anything, is out of balance in healthy ecosystems.

Do you have the ability to trust the sensory webstring truth ecosystems convey to you? For example, if you go to a natural area and love a sunset there, do you believe that your love for that sunset is as true or more true than 2 + 2 = 4? If you do recognize this, you have great potential to help yourself and others learn to think in globally balanced ways, and to live in greater peace and responsibly with yourself, society and nature.

> **CREATE A MOMENT THAT LETS EARTH TEACH**
> **Follow the Box Instructions in Section One**

Section Three:
5-leg Domination

Look at the colored circle design on the back cover. If you apply a story that the colors are more important than the black and white portion, or the colors are in the foreground, doesn't the picture take on a three-dimensional quality that it did not have before?

The influence of a story on natural sensitivities can be seen in the starry night sky. Look at the stars as if the small and light stars are farther away and the larger brighter stars are closer. Does the sky become three-dimensional for you? Your perceptions changed based on a lie. Some bright stars are farther than dim stars.

> **CREATE A MOMENT THAT LETS EARTH TEACH**
> **Follow the Box Instructions in Section One**

Section Four:
Bonding to the Word or Image

This is a color design of black and white colors and shapes if you turn it upside down or keep it moving.

If you apply a label to it and call it faces, you will see faces and the vase disappears.

If you label it a vase, you will see a vase and the faces will dissappear. In theory, it is not possible to see both simultaneously.

Consider this critical observation about the effects of the 5-leg stories we hear. If I tell you the story to think that the color white is important or closer to you, you see a vase and the faces disappear. This also happens with the color black and the faces, the vase disappears. In other words, the authorities whose stories place meaning on the world can determine how and what you perceive. They can engage you in making parts of the world disappear. For example, during the Vietnam War, when Vietnamese people were labeled "gooks" it became easier to kill them. The word dehumanized and demeaned them.

A crucial question: Does identifying Earth as a "dead natural resource" or a "wisely balanced living organism" make a difference in
-what you think?
-what you feel?
-how you act/relate?

> **CREATE A MOMENT THAT LETS EARTH TEACH**
> **Follow the Box Instructions in Section One**

> **PART 2B**
> Post your response to the four sections above to your Interact group at this point (Saturday on the default schedule).

Section Five:
Effects of Repetition

An elephant was chained by its leg to a post to prevent it from straying. It hurt when it pulled on the chain so, in time, the elephant did not stray past the chain length thus avoiding the pain. A rope that the elephant could break was then used to replace the chain. The rope also triggered some pain so the elephant remained in place. Then rope was removed and replaced over time by a string, and finally nothing, but the elephant never went far enough from the post to discover it was free. Its psyche now contained the chain. It had been socialized not to stray.

The authority that punishes us unless we obey instructions can determine how we know the world.

Do we learn to know and relate to nature from our direct sensory experiences with it or from our culture's nature conquering stories, labels and rewards about it?

> **CREATE A MOMENT THAT LETS EARTH TEACH**
> **Follow the Box Instructions in Section One**

Section 6:
Bonding to the Familiar

A group of subjects was shown 15 meaningless Chinese-type figures of calligraphy similar to these, (but these have meaning):

Some figures were shown only once; others were shown as many as 25 times. The subjects were then shown all 15 figures and asked which ones they liked. They consistently liked the figures to which they had the most exposure. The figures that had the least exposure were least appreciated. *

Your Thoughts: What significance does this study have with respect to the fact that, on average, we spend 99.9% of our lives in our indoor, artificially-built surroundings and stories, separated from nature on a conscious sensory level?

> **CREATE A MOMENT THAT LETS EARTH TEACH**
> **Follow the Box Instructions in Section One**

Section Seven:
Effects of Rewards

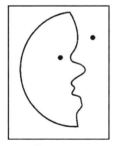   

figure a   figure b

In an experiment, people played a card game in which they randomly selected cards.

They were given a dollar reward whenever they received a card with the *figure a* image above.

They forfeited a dollar whenever they received a card with the *figure b* image above.

After an extended period, the players were shown *figure a .b*

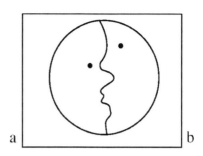

Most of them easily recognized *figure a,* the money winning figure, but *figure b* was often very difficult for them to perceive. *

What implications does this demonstration have with respect to our relationship with nature and our economy? Can you see a relationship between it and Upton Sinclair's observation, "It is difficult to get people to understand something when their salary depends upon them not understanding it."

> **CREATE A MOMENT THAT LETS EARTH TEACH**
> **Follow the Box Instructions in Section One**

Section Eight:
The Nature of Subconscious Relationships

Sharon, an adult woman, had an adverse reaction to a blue block of wood she had selected, sight unseen, from a bag of wooden objects. She blindly selected the block because she was attracted to its shape and smoothness when she groped and explored it by the webstring of touch. At first, she did not know why she didn't like it when she saw it. In time, she realized it was a subconscious reaction. The block was the same shade of blue as the walls of her room where, as a child, she had been molested.

The existence of subconscious memories and their effect on our daily relationships has long been established. Although these memories seldom enter our rational thinking, to protect us, the hurt webstring feelings attached to them often come into play as a natural warning device when an experience or story presents similar attributes to the original hurt.

Without awareness of the suppressed webstring subconscious source of our discontents, we have no choice but to relate in hurt ways to each other, the environment and ourselves. Oblivious to the reconciling knowledge held in our subconscious webstrings, even in safe settings, like watching a scary movie, we often feel vulnerable, frightened or angry. This produces the stress, depression, and addictiveness to destructive gratifications all too common in our lives. $1 + 1 = 5$ is an untrue, wrong statement if you can't see the number $3 +$ that appears in the space that precedes the statement. The number 3 is like webstrings and nature in a nature-disconnected culture. They are seldom recognized or appreciated because they are largely absent in our indoor environment and in our consciousness and thinking because they have become subconscious. When we connect with natural areas and know them by their names, such as "tree," "cloud," "genus," "animal," etc., webstrings and nature remain a number 3 because nature is "non-literate," and is proud of it. (That, by the way, is the biological source of our sense of pride). Nature has no name by which it knows itself or its elements. In nature, the word or number 3 is like the blank space that precedes the numerical statement.

You are part of nature and nature is part of you. Can you think of examples where you know yourself as $1 + 1 = 5$ and therefore think you are wrong, bad, asocial, inept, etc?

> **CREATE A MOMENT THAT LETS EARTH TEACH**
> **Follow the Box Instructions in Section One**

Section Nine:
We Are What We Label

Blank 3 x 5 cards were distributed to a group of people in a classroom. At the bottom of 50% of the cards appeared the word BARBELL. At the bottom of the remaining cards appeared the word GLASSES.

glasses

barbell

The first image in the figure above, was shown to the study participants for 10 seconds and then removed from sight.

The participants were then asked to draw the image on the card they had.

People who had the word GLASSES written on their card often curved the line connecting the circles to accommodate the shape of the nose. Some drew ear hooks on the glasses.

People who had the word BARBELL written on their card often thickened the size of the bar. Some wrote the weight of the bells or the # sign by the circles. *

Implications:

The 5-leg labels, values and processes we place on the world influence webstrings subconsciously and shape the way we know the world to be and how we describe it. For example, when adults are asked to pick any number from one to twelve, except five, most will pick seven, or seven will have been their first thought. Subconsciously, the request to remove five from twelve hooks our webstring of reason into its conditioning to subtract the numbers and the result appears automatically. Similarly, houses come with lawns, no matter that lawn care products are one of the greatest water pollutants, and wildlife habitats are disappearing continuously.

* Note: For these and other similar studies see Vernon, M.P. *The Psychology of Perception,* Gretna Louisiana: Pelican, 1971.

> **CREATE A MOMENT THAT LETS EARTH TEACH**
> **Follow the Box Instructions in Section One**

Section Ten:
The Rewards of Sensory Connections

Each phenomenon that occurs in Sections 1-9 arises from an aspect of life that we learn to overlook in our 5-leg disconnection from nature. Moment by moment, life and survival are attractive and rewarding. In each moment, one or more of our many webstring senses experiences a degree of gratification as it is fulfilled by contact with the environment, be it our built-society, indoor-story world or the natural world.

Once a sense is rewarded, it naturally tends to seek that reward again for further gratification and survival. The reward feels good because connecting with it produces endorphin and dopamine neurotransmitters that naturally produce good feelings to encourage us to follow natural attraction energies. The sense begins to bond to that reward. The attraction and reward are psychologically/emotionally fulfilling and important. Thus, our webstring perceptions of our relationships and ourselves tend to warp based on how we are rewarded. Good grades, approval, status, money and connectedness with people reward us for being literate. There is value and gratification in knowing something by its 5-leg name, label or story.

Revisit Sections 1-9 and locate the rewards of sensory connections and their effects in each section.

What value or reward can/did you find in making space in your life for enjoying sensory connections directly from and in natural areas?

Are you aware of the often overlooked secret of nature, that enjoying sensory connections in natural areas is rewarding in itself and is environmentally friendly, too?

> **CREATE A MOMENT THAT LETS EARTH TEACH**
> **Follow the Box Instructions in Section One.**

Do you think that the natural attractions you found in the CREATE A MOMENT THAT LETS EARTH TEACH parts of each section were purely accidental or do you think that they may have been attractive to you because part of you was subconsciously seeking balance after reading the puzzle presented in the section? This is similar to when you are thirsty, water becomes more attractive.

It perhaps sounds strange but remember that webstrings in nature and you non-verbally organize themselves to produce the balanced perfection found in nature. The puzzles may have set the webstrings in you off balance so they selected fulfilling balance in nature. This is similar to the projective psychological functions involved in Rorschach and Thematic Apperception Tests. They legitimately address social relationships. The puzzles here legitimately address the 5-leg socialization of nature's 4-leg attraction relationships.

As demonstrated in examples 1-10 in this chapter, when we focus and attach the energies of our webstrings to any one story, our other webstrings and stories tend to have less energy and may drop out of our awareness and thinking, eroding their balance and unity. In addition, we can be conditioned/brainwashed for our webstrings to attach or bond to certain stories. This includes stories that applaud the 5-leg verbal webstrings and demean following our other 4-leg webstring attractions to nature, calling them childish, flaky, tree hugging, fuzzy thinking or wrong.

In considering Sections 1-10, do you think the following descriptions have any application to how we learn to know nature within and around us in our nature estranged society?

Brain-wash-ing: A body of knowledge that centers on changing people without their knowledge.

No exchange occurs; communication is one-sided.
Organization remains fairly rigid.
Change occurs primarily to improve thought reform effectiveness.
Uses an instructional mode to persuade.
Takes authoritarian and hierarchical stance.
No full awareness on the part of the learner.
Is deceptive.
Uses improper and unethical techniques.

Brain-wash-ing: Keep the person unaware of what is going on and the changes taking place.

Control the person's time and, if possible, physical environment.
Create a sense of powerlessness.
Covert fear and dependency.
Suppress much of the person's old behavior and attitudes.
Instill new behavior and attitudes.
Mystical manipulation.
Doctrine over person.
Put forth a closed system of logic.
Allow no real input or criticism.

Conclusion:

Every part of the global life community, from sub-atomic particles to continents to weather systems, is part of the web of life. Their webstring attraction interconnectedness produces nature's balanced integrity and prevents runaway disorders. In the web of life demonstration model, dramatically, people pull back, sense and enjoy how their web of life string peacefully unites, supports and interconnects them and all of life.

The web of life is an attraction string that forms itself and each web member. Through webstrings, it interconnects all members of the web, including people.

One webstring is that of verbal language, a recently evolved attractive survival tool that, through stories, uniquely brings the web and its parts into human consciousness. Our verbal stories, however, are foreign to the plant, animal and mineral community, for they are non-verbal, non-literate.

The loss of 4-leg input into our 5-leg stories removes webstring connectors that would ordinarily reach others who have attached to different stories. We become argumentative and separated from wholeness and attach to people who hold similar attachments. As demonstrated in politics, religion and nationalism this can prove disastrous and lead to divorce or war.

The webstrings in our internal natural systems keep our lives healthy so we may best support life. Doesn't our mental and physical health deteriorate when we are robbed of our webstrings 4-leg energies by destructive, 5-leg, vested interests? Doesn't this help explain the nature-connected health phenomena identified on Page viii that precedes the Introduction (Page 9) to this book?

To enjoy how webstrings have always peacefully united, supported and interconnected all life, including people, it is wise to learn a process that enables us to genuinely reconnect with webstrings in natural areas and keep them alive in our thinking as much as possible. As natural attractions, they have the innate ability to unify. Most conflict resolution procedures bring them into play but seldom applaud them as an attribute of nature. If we acted that way with each other, we'd call ourselves plunderers.

The Challenge of the Unknown

It is easy to recognize that spending 99.9% of our sensory lives consciously disconnected from the web of life leaves blank areas, a wanting blind spot of deadened webstrings in our thinking and knowing. This is blatantly seen when we ask even environmental specialists, "What are the strings?" and nobody says anything. This blind spot becomes like one step beyond, a venture into the unknown. When our psyche hits a blind spot it fills it in with what it does know, usually the same nature disconnected 5-leg way of thinking and perceiving that has brought us to today's dilemmas. An interesting demonstration of this phenomenon may be seen at http://serendip.brynmawr.edu/~pgrobste/blindspot1.html.

"Most people don't become involved in the Natural Systems Thinking Process. They are too fearful to break free of what they know. I just heard of a very disturbing experiment that was done on cats that grew up in a cage and were then shocked. The cage was all they knew. The "scientists" opened the door to the cage, giving the cats an out, but the cats just stayed in it being shocked to their death. This shows how being in the familiar, as painful as it can be, can override our ability to find freedom. This cruel experiment is a very strong statement."
- Course participant

Significant Psychological Questions:
Does identifying the thoughts, sensations and feelings that register in your consciousness as being "webstrings" make a difference in
-your connectedness to the web of life?

-what you think?
-what you feel?
-how you act/relate?

Is there a value in recognizing that psychologically you may be conscious of the world either through contemporary humanity's verbal label/story webstring or through 52 other webstring attractions in addition? The chapters that follow help you strengthen and improve your 9-leg ability to create webstring moments that let Earth teach.

ONLINE COURSE PARTICIPANTS
1. Share the one or two significant attractions that you found in each of the ten sections above with your Interact group.
2. In a single paragraph that incorporates the material presented in this chapter, write a short statement about how your destiny may be influenced by how we have learned to separate from and think about nature and its values. Share this statement with your Interact group by email.

In a single short paragraph describe, if you can, how the information in this chapter affects your answer to the question "Who are you?" Share this statement by email with your Interact group.

Summary Option:

Optionally, complete this summary evaluation:
SUMMARY STATEMENT B:
Because I am mostly rewarded by people and society, I tend to habitually know and think about the world through the perceptual filter of our nature conquering society.
Either in your journal, or on a piece of paper, record the SUMMARY letter code (B) along with the number on the continuum scale below that indicates the extent of your agreement with the Summary Statement:

1	2	3	4	5	6	7	8	9	10
disagree				partially agree			fully agree		

Record and retain your score.

Supportive Reading

Nature Disconnected Education

On April 18, 1972, Karen, a high school junior who was quitting school, said to her principal, "Dr. Miler, you can't teach me what I want to know because what I want to know is how not to be like you." Karen's words come to mind more and more as I watch well intentioned folks I love, hurt themselves, each other and Earth. Their best thinking about how to solve our runaway problems has proven not to be as thoughtful as it needs to be.

Karen, after many attempts to "adjust," had decided to drop out of school. She was an excellent student and Dr. Miler pleaded with her to remain. He pledged that he would teach her anything she wanted to know. That's when she told him he did not have the ability to do that. She explained that the effects of his thinking and relationships depressed her. They showed that neither he nor the faculty knew what she wanted to know, no less how to teach it. That knowledge was unavailable to the public in 1972. It is, however, available today through the Natural System Thinking Process.

Although they played their role well in school, Karen's faculty was a cross section of society, then and today. For example, despite the warning labels, 30% of them smoked cigarettes. Because they protected others from the smoke by providing themselves with a smoking area, they were within their legal rights. Smoking was not, and is not, illegal. Karen felt that if cigarettes became illegal, smoking and its adverse effects would not stop. In her social studies paper she wrote, "It would be like deer hunting. In many states more deer are poached illegally than are legally killed during hunting season." In that paper Karen also said, "We can't make sense of how our society educates and governs us because it is not sensible."

Karen discovered what most people tell me they know. With respect to helping us sustain happy, responsible lives, the education we receive, in and out of school, is often no more effective than the warning label on cigarettes. Karen was different than many students because, in counseling, she learned something extra. She discovered the integrity and value of her subconscious thinking. She started to sense the strings. She found that she wanted and deserved more than school provided. She began to realize that the world and its people were at risk. Her paper said, "We are in jeopardy. We don't just need information, we need an effective process. I want to learn how to build respon-sible relationships. That is not happening in this school." She wrote, "To teach it or learn it, you must live it. I have tried, in vain, to make this happen here."

At a meeting, the faculty pleaded with Karen to stay in school, for she was an excellent student. "I'm afraid to stay," Karen said. "The abusiveness in the world scares me." She choked, "We are on the brink of nuclear war. And the natural environment is deteriorating so quickly there may not be a world for me to live in." Her tears flowed freely. "There is nothing abnormal with me feeling depressed at times. The hurt I feel is real. It comes from knowing and watching people being killed and bird species decline. I am tired of putting medicine on that hurt in counseling and thinking there is something wrong with me personally. That hurt will only disappear as abusiveness disappears and as sensitivity, peace and birds reappear. That is not happening here. This school is contaminated; it's a subculture, a breeding ground for our problems."

Mrs. Cook tried to speak. "Let me finish please," Karen said, and continued, "The school has just bulldozed the natural area on the building's west side to build still another lawn. That area was not only a nesting and feeding habitat for birds. It was a womb for all forms of life, a place that I loved, where I could find peace at lunchtime and after school. Compared to being in class, or even in counseling, that place made sense. It was beautiful; it felt right. I could go there depressed and safely feel all the beauty and life that flourished there. In just a few minutes, I would feel much better. I refuse to be touched by the thinking here that has been bulldozed into such stupidity as to bulldoze that natural area."

Dr. Miler interrupted, "Karen, there was no choice. That was part of a legal contract from years ago. We had to fulfill that contract or be sued. And some students smoke marijuana in that area."

"I don't smoke marijuana," said Karen, "I feel sad for those that do. I feel even sadder that the law says that I must spend half of my waking life indoors in school. This environment is bulldozing paradise to make still another lawn. Dr. Miler, you once told me that we learn more from the world around us than we do from books and lectures. I simply refuse to trash paradise or learn to do it. I refuse to let you rub off on me any further. What's wrong with that? It makes sense to me." She seemed stronger for her statement and its intensity.

"Earth and its people are at risk," Karen continued. "Every year in this country, five thousand square miles of nature are bulldozed into oblivion. How can you possibly teach us to deal with such a massacre when you are engaged in it? What are you thinking? What sense is there for me to sit in Social Studies class to discover that our nuclear generating plants are dangerous yet their total electrical output equals the energy this country uses just to run hair dryers? That makes no sense. What do we learn here that helps us stop using hair dryers? To be accepted here, I feel pressured to use one, not to desist. Where is the sense in that? In Biology, we learn that a decade ago Rachel Carson showed the danger in using pesticides and chemicals. Since then, we have introduced thousands of new chemicals every year into the environment. What are you thinking when you use these chemicals on our lawns here? I don't want to learn to think like that. What kind of a world is school teaching my mind to build?" she asked passionately.

Dr. Miler calmly advised Karen that the school did the best it could. If she left, she would be truant and there would be consequences. She would not be able to attend college. Karen replied, "I don't care. I choose to learn elsewhere. It's too stupid in school. Here, society sentences me to live in an irresponsible mold, a change-resistant, indoor learning environment that assaults the natural foundations of life. This environment is so boring, controlled and stifling that most students are drugged out or into something that is outlandish, self-destructive or socially harmful. I'm spending close to 18,000 hours of my most impressionable, developmental years in this nature isolated school closet. That's like growing up in another culture, and a destructive one, at that."

Mrs. Cook, the English teacher, objected, "I, and other faculty members, have taught you repeatedly that these things don't make sense." "Not really," Karen retorted. "You merely say these things don't make sense. What you really teach me by forcing me to be in this setting is that I must adapt to being part of runaway stupidity. You don't teach me how to successfully deal with it. Wake up, Mrs. Cook! You don't know how to stop it so how are you going to teach it? Am I supposed to just accept your belief that the Communists and minorities cause our problems? At church, we have a conflict as to whether it is right to subdue the Earth as the Bible says. Isn't there a separation between church and state? You are not compelled here to subdue the Earth, so why do you do it and teach it?"

"This has nothing to do with religion," said Mrs. Cook. "Maybe not to you," Karen replied, "I have friends for whom that woodland was a cathedral. Think about it, weren't the lives of our greatest spiritual leaders shaped by profound experiences in nature?" Smiling, Mr. Langley, the Social Studies teacher said, "Karen, cheer up. You are going to be the first woman President of the United States." Wiping her tears, Karen stammered, "Oh

sure, the first president with a prison record. State laws say I will go to prison if I am truant. That sucks! I don't care; I'll take my chances. Go ahead, turn me in. The law has me jailed here right now anyhow. The big advantage to being in this jail is that I can walk out and find a better way to learn. That's what I'm going to do."

Karen's words bring to mind a study done by a sociologist in Maine. It showed that the students' level of morale in a high school was the same as that of prisoners in a state penitentiary. My research shows that this does not happen if you teach people techniques that enable their thinking to tap into the strings of the web of life. As shown below, today, Karen would not want to leave school if the Natural Systems Thinking Process was part of the curriculum.

The following semester, Karen enrolled in the outdoor school Michael J. Cohen founded and directed. So did Mr. Langley, as a university graduate student and intern. Today the webstring program lets contact with nature and nature-centered people teach students of any age how to be more personally environmentally and socially responsible by learning Cohen's Natural Systems Thinking Process. Along with it they learn the academics they need to build responsible relationships.  Karen went on to become a successful environmental lawyer, professor and advocate for sustainability.

Cohen says, "Sadly, today, as in 1970, protests, letters and petitions for improving peace, social justice, the environment or mental health are relatively ineffective because they omit using and offering the webstring component for unity that this book contributes." He believes this omission in other sectors of society prevents the reduction of health and social disorders and their ever increasing budgets.

For some thoughts and humor concerning Karen visit http:www.webstrings.org/karen2.html.

Thoughtful Verbalization

These instructions are located on the last page of this book. Once you complete them, return to this page.

Optional:

Read Chapter 6 in *Reconnecting With Nature* for additional information about the relationship of words to webstrings. (You need not do the activity there for this course).

Chapter Three

Sensing and Feeling Webstrings

To be part of any system, a person, place or thing must be in communication with that system. Earth is a global ecosystem and we are part of it. Through natural attraction webstrings, Earth communicates with us, and all other beings in supportive ways. Webstrings are nature's voice. They contain a unifying logic that our nature-conquering society often teaches us to ignore.

The activity below helps us register Earth through psycho-logic, the 4-leg logic of our sensations, feelings and emotional abilities that we biologically inherit from nature.

This activity is from the book *Reconnecting With Nature* by Michael J. Cohen and is used by permission.

STEP 1. Consider the following: Human beings depend on reasoning and language to survive. We are the only species on Earth with the ability to communicate and think with words. Unlike us, the global life community sustains its beauty and balance via non-verbal attraction communications and acts, not words.

We cannot teach Earth to speak English or any other verbal language. We can, however, learn to participate in Earth's non-verbal, webstring ways since we, as part of all of nature, are born knowing them and able to register them. This is part of our natural substance and inheritance. When you sense that you are ready to learn how to safely communicate with Earth, proceed to STEP 2.

STEP 2. Go to the most unspoiled attractive natural area or thing available to you, be it a potted plant, weed, pet, backyard, park or sanctuary. Go to a real natural area, plant, animal or mineral, not to a picture, video, visualization, memory or spirit of nature.

Let your webstring of reason work for you in connection with nature. It is reasonable to want to feel safe and seek good feelings. If you sense anxiety producing or discomforting webstring signals from

some things, seek another attraction instead. It will prove to be safer and more rewarding.

STEP 3. Thoughtfully try to know the natural place or thing that attracts you in a non-verbal way, similar to the way Earth and nature knows it. You may accomplish this way of knowing by focusing your thinking and feeling to the word "attraction." It is a variety of natural attraction webstrings that hold the Earth community ecosystem together in balance. Say "attraction" repeatedly again while touching, smelling, hearing, and viewing the attractive colors, sounds, shapes, motions, smells and sensations that are present in the natural area. Do this with eyes both open and closed. You may also enhance your connections to nature by using the word "webstring," "sensation," "feeling" or "connection" to bring to mind how natural attractions register in people. Note which of these attraction labels work best for you and record them in your journal. Keep in mind they are all different names for webstring attractions, otherwise they tend to lose their identity as parts of you, Earth and nature.

Choose one special natural attraction that is present, such as, a vibrant leaf, breeze, view, a delightful smell, flower, or shape, captivating bird, sound, motion or texture.

STEP 4. Notice the ways in which this attraction feels good. Thank it for giving you comfortable feelings. Enjoy the good feelings for a moment. (If the natural place or thing does not feel good to you, find another attraction that does. Don't forget that the sky is part of nature.)

STEP 5. Now translate the truth of your experience in this enjoyable natural moment into words. Write the sensory attraction experience you just had in the space provided in the following sentence.

"My experience in nature shows me that I am a person who gets good feelings (by, from, when, etc.):_____."

For example, an individual attracted to a bee in a flower said,

"My experience in nature shows me that I am a person who gets good feelings from silently watching and hearing a bee in a flower. I love watching different things in nature nurture each other. They have a special beauty. They tell me that nature and I can safely, enjoyably dance."

As in the above example, you may write up to three additional sentences about how and why this experience feels good and what it means to you. Recognize that this writing is usually "9-leg" in that it combines 4-leg and 5-leg ways of knowing and being.

STEP 6. Read your statement to yourself and/or share it with others in your Interact group and elsewhere.

STEP 7. Think about the experience you just had and what value or meaning it had for you. What did it suggest to you? How did it let Earth speak? Repeat the activity whenever you so desire. You will continually find new attractions, good feelings and meanings in nature.

STEP 8. Go to the web page http://www.ecopsych.com/guestbook.html, and read statements from others who have done this activity. Select the three that are most attractive to you. Do you recognize part of yourself and Earth being brought into awareness by the statements that attract you? Can you identify and honor that natural part of yourself and others?

Insight

The Activity statement "My experience in nature shows me I am a person who gets good feelings from_____" is significant because it is 9-leg in that it contains the following trustable relationship building elements:

My: sense of self, being and connectedness
Experiences: multi-webstring attraction, hands-on, trustable information in the moment.
In nature: the natural webstring world itself, not an indoor image or disconnected story, is the source of this information.
Show me: a reasonable, trustable story as well as sensory experience, balance and validation.
I am: self-identity, beingness, webstring registration, participatory, immediate
I am a person who gets: human identity, interactiveness, openness, connnectedness, natural functioning and the ability to register webstrings.
Good feelings: indicate conscious contact with webstring attraction origins in nature that signal connectedness and resonance with the web of life.

From: a willingness to be open to webstring attraction signals in nature.

Activity Summary:

At any given moment, the totality of Earth, including us, consists of every part of Earth in some non-verbal attraction link with its immediate environment.

In congress, these webstring attraction links interconnect and govern the global ecosystem. We biologically inherit at least 53 distinct natural sensations (senses) that feelingly bring these attraction links into our consciousness For example, thirst connects us with water, color connects us with sunsets, etc. Our senses are ancient, non-verbal "inventions" of, by, and from nature. They serve as natural survival mechanisms that enable us to feelingly, consciously, experience and more thoughtfully relate to the global ecosystem.

In moments when we focus ourselves on our natural attractions to nature, we make sensory contact with the Earth community network and our origins there. We may feelingly describe and communicate this contact in words. This process enables us to translate our sensory relationship with Earth into a life-supportive verbal story that includes our Earth-connected natural attraction feelings and loves.

Optionally, complete this summary evaluation.
SUMMARY STATEMENT C:
Natural senses and feelings are attraction strings of the web of life that can psychologically help a person make conscious sensory connections with the web.

Either in your journal, or on a piece of paper, record the SUMMARY letter code (C) along with the number on the continuum scale below that indicates the extent of your agreement with the Summary Statement:

1   2   3   4   5   6   7   8   9   10
disagree   partially agree   fully agree
Record and retain your score.

Supportive Readings (1 of 2)

Read, find and share what is attractive to you in the following short letter. It shares a professional affirmation of the nature-reconnecting process.

PsychoScience Journal
Dr. Mark Germine, Editor-in Chief
P.O. Box 71786
Loma Linda, CA 92354

May 15, 1995

To: Dr. Michael J. Cohen
Project NatureConnect
Box 1605
Friday Harbor, WA 98250

Dear Mike,

I attended the May 1-5, 1995 Meaning of Life and Death conference that was conceived and coordinated by former United Nation's Assistant Secretary General, Dr. Robert Muller. I came, like many other people, "looking for something," not the "answer" to the question of the meaning of life and death, because I don't think that question can be answered in words. I think people can speak and listen to words endlessly without it having as much influence on them as a single experience. That's how I felt about the conference. The meetings were good, but the important experience I took with me was the connection with "green" that I experienced in your Applied Ecopsychology session. It was the most valuable thing at the conference to me, and to many others as well.

I'm a psychiatrist and have done or know just about every kind of therapy there is. You have developed a kind of basic and applied science for reaching down into the ordinarily unconscious area of pure feeling, an essence of nature. The many natural senses you have experienced and describe are, as I see it, senses that form a network of basic feeling within and between people and nature. This is not psychobabble but is based on the serious ideas of process philosophers from Plato to Whitehead. I'm affiliated with the Center for Process Studies and Center for a Postmodern World in Claremont. Your work fits well in both the process and postmodern views of how reality is constituted.

Some people may be having trouble with the green on green and green/orange analogy in your article Counseling and Nature in the *Interpsych News* article (see Chapter 4). It is a metaphor for either validating or denying basic feeling (our senses). It is intuitive, so hard to intellectualize. But I think your Applied Ecopsychology therapy has enormous potential for both ordinary people and the mentally ill. I've done hypnosis and other techniques and have not seen such a deeply unconscious state brought to the surface before. The perception of "green-green" has stayed with me, it was a kind of insight, which makes it all the better.

The problem of humanity's interconnection goes further than appreciation of nature. Ecopsychology, to me, is based on the knowledge that we are part of the cumulative experience of the living world and the universe, and to everything that is. We are in dire need for contact with each other and with other living things. There is a very strong scientific and philosophical basis for this, but talking about it is not going to re-establish this connection. Our ability to cognitively abstract our contact with the world constantly takes our sensory experience and hides it under a veil of thought. The resulting loss of connection is, I think, the greatest ill that plagues humankind. It is the cause of many problems in the individual and in society.

It is important that your nature-reconnecting methods not be lost to the wider needs that they can serve.

In friendship,

Dr. Mark Germine
Editor-in-Chief
PsychoScience Journal

Supportive Reading (2 of 2)

Conflict, Natural Attractions and God.

NSTP attraction reasoning recognizes that issues and differences between various beliefs regarding God are now, as through the ages, a major source of human conflict, death and suffering as well as joy. Each person or group is so strongly attracted to their god that many are willing to argue, fight, shed their life or take the lives of others to honor this relationship. From the many passionate forms of worship that people practice, the ones based on a belief in God, describe Him/Her as attractive. God is naturally very attractive, or the most attractive.

In considering God, (since natural attractions are an observed essence of the materials and energies in the natural systems of our universe, nature, Earth and ourselves,) NSTP goes out on a limb. It suggests that this is not an accident, that it is reasonable to assume God created this universe from His/Her attractiveness. He/She may have made other universes from His/Her vast knowledge or power but if we are to trust our senses, rationality and experiences, our universe must be constructed of His/Her attraction energies.

In the natural world we don't observe some parts of nature fighting with other parts of nature over God. We learn from contact with nature the value in this, and the means to gain it, so we do likewise. Thus, in NSTP, we find it reasonable, by consent, to relate to and through the natural attractions that we experience in people and places without referring to them as God. People who experience natural attractions as God are applauded for their wise observation. They are equally applauded for their natural attraction to promoting nature's peace by not making others accept this observation...to honor the observation that nature does not place words or labels on itself.

While some people find it helpful to consider nature to be their Higher Power, isn't it the 5-leg labels we learn that often cause troubles?

> *"The name that can be named is not the eternal name. The Nameless is the origin of Heaven and Earth."*
> **-Lao Tzu** circa 600 B.C.

Some NSTP participants recognize the connections that Christian leaders had to nature. Jesus is reported to have shaped his ministry from 40 days in the wilderness and Moses had a similar experience that led him to the Ten Commandments.

Many NSTP participants celebrate that wholeness and holiness are the same word, as are sanctified and sanctuary. Some revere St. John of Yosemite and St. Henry of Walden. Many are attracted to three quotes with respect to nature and God: One is from St. Francis of Assisi to the effect that the natural attractions we seek are what is doing the seeking. Another is Kahlil Gibran to the effect that Nature is God gazing at himself in a mirror. Here's the third that was quoted earlier:

> *"I believe in God but I spell it Nature."*
> **-Frank Lloyd Wright**

In *Reconnecting With Nature* Appendix C, "The Ecology of Spirit" makes a fascinating contribution regarding God and Genesis.

Thoughtful Verbalization

These instructions are located on the last page of this book and the end of Chapter One. Once you complete them, return to this page.

Optional:

Read Chapter 9 in *Reconnecting With Nature* to further understand the ecopsychology of community relationships. (You need not do the activity there for this course).

Chapter Four

Natural Consensus

If you are attracted to a more naturally balanced and sane way of life, it is reasonable to become closer to the beauty, intelligence, equilibrium, and peace found in nature. This is what the majority of us try to do when we escape to natural areas on our vacations or when we retire. Since nature's ways are already a part of us, it is simple to learn to thrive and grow through supportive relationships in the same manner that nature does.

We are biologically and psychologically constructed to sense natural attractions. Our attractive experiences in nature consist of many senses, such as color, touch, temperature, sound, fun, and belonging. Nature-centered people know that following their natural sensory attractions in the environment and in others is the key to survival in balance. We each inherit this ability but often take it for granted. Have you ever considered giving thanks to nature for it?

Wander outside and find some aspect of a natural area or thing that calls to a sensory part of you that appreciates it. Take note of this fact. It is a biological attraction relationship between you and an aspect of nature. It may be a combination of many attraction senses. You are "built" to naturally sense it, it registers in your awareness, it is a love that is alive and well in you. This sensory attraction invites and welcomes you. It feelingly encourages you to enjoy this moment. On a feeling-sensation level, it gives you permission and invites you to be here. Do you feel thankful for it and your sensory self?

Further validate this attractive connection relationship or webstring to your sense of language by putting it into words.

Write and say, "I know my inherent sensitivities to natural attractions are alive and well because I could enjoyably sense and feel _____." Include whatever you sensed such as colors, forms, shapes, textures, pressures, temperatures, fun, motion, emotions, etc. Note that you also can have these same sensations and feelings about people. Although they exist without verbal language, they are a form of connectedness shared throughout all of nature. You can and should learn to trust them for the facts that they are.

The Activity:

Just imagine how life on Earth might be more at peace and in balance if people in every nation learned to deal with the underlying ecological and psychological causes of their personal, environmental and social imbalances.

Too often, our efforts to sustain unity and wellness on Earth do not meet the goals of others. Our mentality's estrangement from nature's balanced energies produces our apathy, resistance to change and addictive prejudices. This is far more than a social disorder. It is an ecologically-rooted psychological problem...a problem that begs psychological solutions.

For this reason, use and teach the following activity called "In Balance with Earth." It is a unifying nature-connected psychology experience for use year around. It enables anyone to create and share moments in nature that let Earth's regenerative qualities sensuously touch us and teach us its peace, equilibrium and cohesiveness.

This activity empowers us to reverse our irresponsible tendencies because it helps us release our destructive bonds and reconnects us to constructive relationships and participation with nature.

Activity Instructions:

(This activity, "In Balance With Earth," is drawn from the Applied Ecopsychology book, *Reconnecting With Nature: Finding wellness through restoring your bond with the Earth*, by Dr. Michael J. Cohen. The activity has been donated for public use.)

Introduction:

Although we are part of nature and it is part of us, the global life community does not exhibit our personal, social and environmental problems. Self-evidence shows that the Earth community knows how to cooperatively relate in ways that sustain an optimum of life, diversity and beauty without producing the runaway garbage, pollution, war, stress and abusiveness generated by some human communities. Biologically, psychologically and spiritually we inherit this natural system legacy. It is in  us. We often call it our deeper ideals, inner nature or spirit.

The deteriorated state of Earth's natural environments and peoples infers that we educate ourselves to separate from or injure the Earth community. This activity helps us discover immediate positive outcomes from treating the Earth community fairly, with respect, as a mother, an equal or as a friend rather than as something to further abuse or exploit.

Purpose:

To discover the means to treat Earth, people and our souls justly and with respect.

Object:

To learn how to obtain a natural area's consent for us to visit it and enjoy the benefits it has for us.

A Guiding Metaphor:

Bob: What would happen if you walked past a complete stranger, into his house, opened his refrigerator door, took out his sandwich and ate it?

Eileen: You would trespass on his bonded integrity and his territory. He would be frightened, upset and angry. A fight might break out and the police called.

Bob: How could this disruption be avoided?

Eileen: You could first make a friendly connection with the stranger, thank him for listening, communicate your desire for food, and respectfully ask for and obtain his consent for you to enter his home and satisfy your hunger. A valuable friendship might develop.

Procedure:

The following activity parallels the procedures used above in the metaphor about the sandwich. Follow the instructions below written in bold type and consider the explanations written in normal type.

1. Nature enables things to build balanced relationships through natural attraction energies. **Notice how you feel right now, then go to something in nature that you like, something you find attractive such as a park, backyard, aquarium, even a pet or potted plant.** Attractions you find in nature are tangible sensory connections. They invite, welcome and feelingly connect your consciousness to them. Just like thirst naturally attracts you to water, or contact with water sometimes makes you thirsty, you are biologically built to naturally connect with the Earth community through cohesive sensations. They are natural "webstring" loves that feel good. The more attractive a natural area or thing

is, the more worthwhile the results of this activity. A goldfish or a flower may be better than a wilderness area if it is more attractive to you.

2. Thank the natural attraction that brings you to this area for being there for you. Thank it for safely activating the good, rewarding feeling from nature that you are experiencing.

3. Recognize that as part of the Earth community, justifiably, this natural area or thing desires and has a right to exist, build beneficial relationships and grow, just as you do. Decide that you are going to respect its 4-leg integrity by obtaining its consent or permission to visit with it. Give it the opportunity to 4-leg signal if it is attracted to your wishes.

4. Silently, aloud or in writing, ask this natural area or thing to give its consent for you to be with it and to do this activity in its presence. It will not give you permission to visit if you are going to injure, destroy or defame it, or if it does not feel for you. In nature, negative relationships are not attractive. **Promise the area or thing that you will treat it honorably.**

5. Sense the area or thing for 10 seconds or more in silence and respect. Be aware of negative signals from stress, discouragement or danger, such as thorns, bees, poison ivy, ticks, cliff faces or unpleasant memories, thoughts or feelings. If they appear, thank them for their "attractive" message to help you find other attraction ways to obtain good feeling and rewards safely.

A. When the 10 seconds are up, note whether the area or thing still feels attractive, or has become more attractive. If it has, it has consented to your visit through a multitude of your natural senses. Proceed to 6.

B. If this natural area or thing no longer feels attractive, or is replaced by another attraction, thank it for its guidance and simply seek another area or thing that feels attractive to you. Repeat the gaining consent process (start with 2 above). Do this until you find a ten second period when a safe attraction feeling remains for a place, color, shape or other natural thing. When this occurs, you have multisensory permission to visit it. In this moment, many additional natural senses are connecting and consenting.

6. As soon as you gain a natural area or thing's consent to visit, genuinely thank it for giving its consent for over 10 seconds.

7. Compare how you feel about being in this mutually supportive moment with nature now to the way you felt when you first started doing this activity. Has any change occurred in you from gaining this natural area's consent through your attractions and thanking it for consenting? Does the area or thing feel

better or friendlier to you? Do you find it more attractive or rewarding now than before you received its consent and thanked it? Do you feel better about yourself and more in touch and supported by the life community? **Write down what occurred. If you obtained good feelings**
or rewards from doing this activity, describe what they were and whether you trust them. Share this information with people close to you or others who are doing the activity.**

If you find that thankfully gaining permission to visit a natural area or thing is rewarding, remember that whenever you want to feel rewarded again, you can choose to repeat this activity. Remember, too, that nature exists in the natural systems of people...we are part of nature. Thankfully, respectfully asking permission and gaining consent to relate to the natural attractions you find in people also provides rewards and helps build good relationships. It honors another person's life experience, who that person is or has become up to this moment.

It is also rewarding to thankfully request that people seek and obtain your consent to relate to you and your nature. Doing this activity may help them learn to relate to you in consensual ways.

Learn to trust the process and sensations in this consensus experience because they are safe, supportive, Earth linked, sustainable, in balance (multisensory) and they feel good. In them, lies hope.

Discussion Question:

Earth naturally produces a balanced optimum of life, diversity and beauty without producing the runaway garbage, stress or abusiveness found in some human communities. Do you think it is possible that it accomplishes this "miracle" by having each thing in nature somehow gain consent to survive in its form by establishing mutually supportive attraction relationships with its surroundings? Doesn't this cooperative, consensual ability make the things that survive the "fittest" to survive?

The Experiences of Others:

Below are reactions that previous activity participants have shared with each other. Many additional responses are located in the online archive at http://www.ecopsych.com/archive.html.

"It was hot. Soon after I asked for permission to visit with the grove of young trees, a gentle, refreshing breeze came through them. It cooled me, and the trees waved their leaves at me. It felt good, like the grove smiled its consent. Thanking the grove strengthened that feeling as does sharing the experience with you now."

"I was attracted to the sound of a raven on the rocks ahead. I stopped and sought its consent for me to enjoy its presence. It began to come closer and closer, increasing my delight and excitement. That was so fun and unforgettable. I feel thankful to that experience and this group."

"My whole attraction to the moss on the rock increased. I felt more intensely than when I first arrived; it felt like a hug from the planet."

"Many times, I have forced myself to back away from the deadlines and details of our super demanding lives and return to nature. In every case I have found the same welcoming feeling of self. In fact, I had to stop today (a particularly stressful day) and gain permission to connect from a beautiful maple tree outside of my office window whose leaves are just popping out of their buds. People often ask me how I stay so calm while they are all running around like crazy. When I try to share the ideas of this activity, so many people look at me as if I am the crazy one."

Summary Option:
Optionally complete this summary evaluation:

SUMMARY STATEMENT D: It is reasonable and helpful to seek permission, gain consent and give thanks in appreciation for the enjoyable feeling and senses we receive from visiting and building responsible relationships with places and people.

In your journal or on a piece of paper, record the SUMMARY letter (D) along with the number on the continuum scale below that indicates the extent of your agreement with the Summary Statement:

1	2	3	4	5	6	7	8	9	10
disagree				partially agree			fully agree		

Record and retain your score.

Supportive Reading

A reviewed and published scientific study supported by empirical evidence further validates the sensory incongruity between 4-leg and 5-leg ways of knowing and relating.

EDUCATION AND COUNSELING WITH NATURE:
A GREENING OF PSYCHOTHERAPY
by Michael J. Cohen. Ed.D.

UPDATED FROM: VOLUME 2, ISSUE 4
THE INTERPSYCH NEWSLETTER MARCH 1995
(Reprinted in *Reconnecting With Nature)*

Abstract

The study below identifies the natural world as an exceptional resource for learning how to therapeutically build responsible relationships. It also offers sensory activities that let nature teach its wise and balanced ways. Once participants identify and differentiate their "natural-sensory" and cognitive "language-reasoning" ways of knowing, a coloring task challenges them to express in words their natural sensory knowledge. The task induces stress, which disappears when language is introduced that validates their sensory way of knowing. This paper observes the dynamics of this transaction and examines its stress management and mental health implications. It offers unique nature connecting activities and home study training programs that reduce stress and reports their mental health and environmental effects.

Introduction

Many outdoor educators and therapists confirm my observation of a reduction of social and psychological problems when our clients are in natural areas. This reduction parallels the relative absence of psychological problems and insanity found in nature-centered tribal communities. It suggests that the purpose of modern psychology and psychotherapy is to heal the sensory wounds inflicted by Western Civilization's excessive disconnection from the natural ways and wisdom of the global life community. My findings confirm this, for by teaching my clients to use and own nature-connected activities and reasoning, their problems wane while their wellness, spirit and ability to learn increase, (Cohen, 1994).

Can sanity truly be measured by Western Civilization? Do we promote true sanity if we teach our clients to support and depend upon a society that knowledgeably spawns irresponsible relationships? This paper describes a practical answer to this question, a working model for responsibly creating personal, social and environmental balance. Since 1959, I have constantly

lived, learned and taught throughout the seasons in natural areas, the places Thoreau called "a civilization other than our own." That non-language civilization taught me how to let its "magic" therapeutically counsel people. I discovered and use counseling activities that let Earth itself teach its integrity, a wisdom, joy and beauty devoid of pollution, war and insanity. This was not difficult to learn once I recognized that as natural beings we are born with this ability. All I had to do was let Earth nurture this ability, and that is how I help others learn it now.

The natural world produces no garbage. On a macro level, it values everything from proton to planet. Nothing in nature is discarded or unwanted, a way of relating that defines unconditional love in action. Scientifically validating and connecting with nature's "unconditional love" and its effects allows us to enjoy and benefit from it.

We, as part of life, inherit the natural world's integrity as our inner nature, a profound globally shared creation blueprint which too often condescendingly we call "The little child within us," (Cohen, 1993b). True education includes learning to read this blueprint, to draw it out from within and resonate with it, validate it and support its integrity. Instead, to our cost, society often teaches us to conquer it within and about us.

Reading this blueprint connects us to our common origins so that we might start anew to co-create a truly civilized society rather than become even more personally and socially "bewildered" (nature-separated). In this article, I offer critical thinking tools and activities for reading the non-language blueprint. Appropriately, the tools come from modern knowledge, from experience with today's science, problems and relationships, (Knapp, 1988), not from other times, environments and cultures. The tools I use let familiar contact with natural systems teach us how to enjoyably walk in balance. Counselors, educators and interpreters increasingly use these tools to reverse apathy, stress and dysfunction.

Nature seldom sustains itself by using "techno"-logic meaning: "A thinking logic that creates artificial stories and techniques." Instead, the natural world uses "bio" logic. In people, bio-logic consists of being multisensory, of heeding each moment's natural attractions that call to our inner nature through our more than 53, not just 5, genetically inherited, but culturally devalued, natural senses and feelings such as thirst, smell or nurturing, (Cohen, 1997). These feelings are ancient, globally evolved memory signals, multisensory ways of knowing and being for harmonious survival. For example, not only is water a vital flowing foundation of life, so, equally, is our natural survival sense and feeling of thirst. Thirst is a biological memory that reconnects land beings to water and survival. Thirst fluctuates to self-regulate our water flow so we neither bloat, burst nor dehydrate. The feeling of thirst makes bio-logic sense as do each of our other 52 natural senses. And although we seldom describe it as such, most counseling is multisensory learning, a sensing or re-sensing (remembering) one or more natural sensations along with their degree of integration, fulfillment or frustration.

Too often, our techno-logic words and stories exclude our natural sensory wisdom. Each word, story or moment that doesn't bring to awareness our natural sensory interconnectedness further separates us from the support of nature's multisensory integrity, (Cohen 1994). However, an account by Rodney Romney exemplifies how multisensory experiences with the nature's web of

life sensibly modify human behavior: In Scotland, farmers were overturning their hay bales to exterminate rats that lived beneath them. A trio of rats tried to flee but, unlike the other fleeing rats, these three stayed closely together which limited their ability to escape. Upon investigation, the farmers found that the middle rat of the three was blind; its companions were guiding it to safety. I have witnessed similar behavior in local flocks of geese. Deeply moved, the farmers did not kill these rats.

The farmers responded to many natural senses and feelings triggered by the incident including consciousness, sight, nurturing, place, curiosity, hunger, motion, trust, empathy, sound, compassion, community and reason. We sometimes call this response human morality, values, ethics, or being humane. However, these words separate us from a truth of nature. They hide that natural senses are nature expressing itself, for natural senses are solely of, by and from the natural world. Note that the rats "morally" responded to the same group of senses and that rats have done so for millions of years before humanity evolved. We observe similar animal and plant behavior throughout the natural world. However, our culturally ingrained, prejudicial anti-nature stories prevent us from saying the farmers acted naturally, like rats, pigs or fungi.

Many researchers validate that psychologically and physiologically, a human being's inner nature consists of a variety of distinct, different natural sensations that we call faculties or instincts, (Cohen,

1994; Murchie, 1978; Pearce, 1980; Rivlin-Gravelle, 1984; Rovee-Collier, 1992; Samples, 1976; Stevens, 1993; Spelke, 1992; Wynne-Edwards, 1991). They include senses like color, thirst, language, smell, taste, consciousness, excretion, belonging, space, distance, form, temperature and touch. Each is unique. Each offers a specific message and wisdom. Each is a natural intelligence and consciousness at some level.

Note that reasoning, language and consciousness are also natural senses that serve a survival function in nature. In some form and intensity, each sense or sensitivity pervades the natural world including our inner nature.

Since the spring of 1993, Institute of Global Education, Department of Integrated Ecology instructors and associates have completed an informal study of over 4100 people, mostly aged 16-51, of differing occupations (Cohen, 1993a). Our object was to determine if we could observe the effects of separating people from nature by assigning inappropriate words and labels to a person's sensory inner nature. We did this by first asking the study participants:

"When did you first learn to know the color Green?

Participants responses fell into two main categories.

A. Some participants remembered when they learned to associate the word green with their green color sensation, thereby knowing green by its name or label. For example, "I remember that my parents told me that the name for the color of the grass and trees was green."

B. Some participants recognized that they naturally registered green (greenness) as a sense or sensation at birth or before: For example "Like many other species, I was biologically born knowing green. It is a God thing. I could naturally sense and distinguish the green grass from the blue sky even though at the time, I didn't know the names of their colors."

So we know green in two ways: by the biological, inborn natural color sense (sensitivity) to green (greenness) and by the word-symbol green which labels that sensitivity. However, consider the following findings and considerations of the study:

When Carol was an infant learning to talk, her father, an experimental psychologist, used her as an experiment. He purposely taught her that the name for the color green was orange and the name for orange was green. The word and the color bonded. Today she is 34 years old and she still gets confused when naming these colors. She still tends to call orange green and green orange. Carol often "thinks about" and "figures out" the correct terms for these colors rather than automatically knowing them. Sometimes she feels stupid and stressed for having to do so, sometimes she still mistakes one for the other. We found several participants who said they had similar experiences with color, and with other areas too, for example, left-handedness: "The teacher broke my left hand by hitting it with a ruler because I wrote with it." "Unfortunately, as a lefty, I did not learn to write left-handed—I learned right-handed, if you want to call it learning. Today, the only way I can communicate in writing without an interpreter is via typewritten characters." "I must wear a red glove on my left hand and a green one on my right while sailing in order to tell port from starboard." "Writing with my right hand stressed me; it resulted in me biting my fingernails."

Consider this scenario: A teacher tells her first grade class, "Today we are going to learn green" and a child says, "I don't need to learn that again. I've known green since before I was born." The teacher responds, "Can you read 'green'? Can you write 'green'? Can you spell it or tell me how many times it appears on this chart? If you can't, you are ignorant, illiterate, a failure, a problem for yourself and society." The color green, a vital natural part of the child, experiences itself as garbage, something unknown in nature, something that is rejected and unsupported. How can this part naturally find its identity? It senses abandonment and a child's natural self inherently knows abandonment to be death, for nothing survives without support in nature. So much for the child's security, self-esteem and self-confidence in this sensory area until his or her scholastic skills are achieved.

Hopefully, other intact ways of being support the child through this period, but many of them are under assault, too. In all too many young people we see violence, tranquilization and dependencies used to relieve the discomforting hole we dig ourselves into by not

learning to validate nature within and about us. Too often we call this process normal adolescence or rebellion against authority; too often our nature-blind eyes don't even see the hole.

Can we learn to feel good about ourselves as natural beings in a nature-separated society? As a control for this task, we first asked participants if they still had their "inner child" natural ability to quickly distinguish and identify blocks of ink colors that we painted on a separate page. Each person was able to do this but colorblind people reported that it was difficult to distinguish between the colors.

We then asked the same people if they were literate and could apply a name to each color. Everybody was able to apply some color name to each block of ink color.

We then asked each of our study participants to verbally call upon their inner nature, their inborn, non-language, natural sense of color, to express itself, to do its natural "inner child" 4-leg thing. The vehicle we used for this purpose is the list of color names found on the back cover of this book, not unlike the Strop Test. The words naming the colors were written in different colored inks (for example, the word "orange" was written in green ink). Participants were asked to quickly go down the color chart list and say aloud the ink colors, not the color names. For example, the first color is green, not orange. (*See this book's back cover for color copy*)

ORANGE written in green ink
RED in violet ink
BLUE in orange ink
BLACK in blue ink
BROWN in red ink
VIOLET in black ink
GREEN in green ink

When using this color chart, although practically every participant had no difficulty labeling the control blocks of ink colors, most participants had difficulty quickly identifying the same ink colors when they spelled out words. The overwhelming tendency was for participants' culturally trained sense of language to dominate and, out of habit, or "word addiction" read the colors as words rather than as colors.

We are not born thinking and communicating with words; we learn this skill. In addition, when doing this activity quickly, over 40% of the participants "deluded" in that they spoke a written color name aloud but actually believed they had said the ink color. For example, in the fifth item on the back cover color chart, Paul believed he read the ink color correctly even though he said the word "brown" while seeing the color red. If another person had had not been with him and caught the the error, Paul would not have known that he made it. It's similar to you, the reader, perhaps not noticing that the words "the" and "had" were doubled in the previous sentence until I now alert you to this fact. The difference is that Paul lost awareness of a vital sensory signal from his inner nature, not simply a typographical duplication.

Participants concluded: "My trained habitual dependency on using words overwhelmed my natural sensory inner child, an important, loving natural part of myself. I had trouble expressing my natural ability to recognize green in a non-language way." One participant offered: "I love nature yet I have a hard time loving myself. This helps explain why." Participants never experienced "difficulty," "tension," "conflict" or "stress" on the last word on the color chart, the word "Green" written in green ink. In all cases, "Green" written in green ink felt more sensible, relaxing, peaceful and attractive than did the other color words. "It feels like a refreshing oasis," says one participant.

Can we learn to feel good about ourselves as natural beings if we don't first meet the challenge of bringing into our awareness who we are as natural beings? This study suggests that our awareness, our consciousness, is overwhelmingly dominated by words that disconnect us from nature within and about us. We have to learn how to use language and reasoning to get past our stories, to find and validate our true colors.

Old-brain and new-brain thinking

From early in our lives, our formal and informal education excessively conditions us to bring the sensory world into our awareness by labeling it with language abstractions, words, symbols and images, and validating the reasonable cultural meanings of these abstractions. Usually two different natural sense groups lying in two different parts of the brain are at work when we "know" something natural like the color green, (Samples, 1976):

The Old-brain: Our natural sense of color lying in the large, anciently evolved "old-brain" enables us to experience color as an unlabeled, non-verbal sensation or feeling. The old-brain registers 4-leg non-language tensions, sensations, feelings and emotions. It makes up approximately 87% of the brain and is the home of 51 naturally pervasive sense groups, some of which I have already mentioned. Most of our old-brain sensitivities we inherit from and share with the plant and animal kingdoms, (Cohen, 1994, 1993; Murchie, 1978). These natural senses are facts as real as rocks, oceans and gravity; our desire to breathe is as much a property of air as is the wind. In multisensory concert natural sensitivities make the balanced "natural sense" that is nature's beauty, peace and wisdom, the web of life. In the natural environment natural sensitivities provide a non-language, interspecies attraction communion. This communion permits natural systems to act sensibly as a community, "to make common sense," "work by consensus," to organize, preserve and regenerate themselves responsibly, intelligently and diversely without producing garbage, war or insanity, (Cohen 1994). If assigning these powers to nature and the old brain seems invalid, consider this: The pervasive natural patterns that colonies of food-seeking bacteria form (in

the shape of the snail vortex, common snowflake, tree branches, and starfish chiral) result from how individual organisms in these bacterial communities communicate with each other and disseminate information throughout the colony. The behavior of these earliest forms of life shows that they change their behavior in response to changing environmental conditions, not through random genetic mutation. They cooperatively signal, calculate, network, regulate and control their community behavior, then their genes mutate and respond to environmental conditions. The patterns they produce are the same as those found in minerals, suggesting that the same process exists on molecular levels, (Lipkin, 1995).

The New-brain: Our two senses of language and reason combine in our small, more recently evolved, "new-brain," the neocortex. These two senses learn to know greenness as the culturally correct word or label (like the word "green") for sensory experiences. The new-brain makes up about 13% of the total brain. It 5-leg creates, experiences, validates and processes culturally trained symbolism: language, letters, words, numbers, drawings, logic, abstractions and stories. Society teaches us to mostly think and reason in new-brain symbols and stories, be they accurate or inaccurate, destructive or constructive, limited or wide-ranged.

Our new brain presently manages the world. Are we satisfied with the effects? Can we learn to do better?

Summary and discussion

From early in our lives, the ancient sense of color, lying in the old-brain, enables us to naturally register green color as a sensation. This sense experiences green directly as "greenness", as a non-language, unadulterated, unedited, unmediated sensation and feeling experience. The old brain brings to awareness how we naturally feel and is often called our inner nature, our inner self, or this sensory global wisdom is misnamed our inner child. When we operate from the old-brain, in Western culture we often say we are being too loving, emotional, sensitive, childlike, feelingful, intuitive, subjective, inexperienced, flaky, illiterate or over reactive. However, Carl Jung and many others note, "Our feelings are not only reasonable, they are as discriminating, logical and consistent as abstract thinking." Natural senses and feelings are the foundations of bio-logic, of nature's civilization which can best be unprejudicially measured by its long-term survival effects, by its ability to create an optimum of life and diversity without producing garbage, insanity or war; without civilization's violence, stress or pollution.

In the small more recently evolved new-brain, the neocortex, Western culture often trains the senses of language and reason to apply cultural words, labels or stories to the natural senses. We teach the new brain that it is reasonable to know greenness as the written or spoken word green, or verde (Spanish) or vert (French) or other words in different languages and cultures. We applaud it for doing so. When we operate from senses of language and reason we proudly say we are literate, cerebral, sensible, abstract, cognitive, reasonable, logical, educated or thoughtful.

Most of the study participants were unaware that a cause of their inability to express their inner nature is that the average American spends over 95% of his or her life indoors, isolated from nature. Studies indicate that we spend almost 18,000 critical developmental childhood hours in classrooms alone. Collectively, we spend less than one day per person per lifetime in tune with the non-languaged natural world. We live over 99.9% of our nature-estranged adult lives abstractly knowing the natural world through detached words and stories about

it rather than through intimate, non- verbal enjoyment of it. My observations outdoors tell me that our estrangement from nature restricts our natural sensory inheritance from growing and strengthening through natural connections with the natural world. This disconnects us from the wisdom, spirit and peace of nature and creation. Conversely, when I've sensuously connected people to natural areas, their problem solving abilities and harmonic relationships have increased dramatically, (Cohen, 1994b).

In America, the stressful anger, anxiety and sadness catalyzed by our overlooked or rejected natural feelings depress us. They fuel our problems at every level. We are not islands. As we remain estranged from the wisdom, spirit and unconditional love of the web of life in ourselves, others and natural areas, our negative personal, social and environmental indicators rise. Even outdoor education programs that fail to teach us how to daily validate and fulfill our inner nature's need and right to be connected, loved and nurtured by nature, do not resolve these problems, (Cohen 1993).

To reverse our troubles we must reconnect with nature. We must learn to effectively communicate with nature in order to know its ways and needs. To accomplish this we must either teach the natural world to speak English or learn to understand its non-verbal language. The latter course makes the most sense since we already know nature's sensory callings. We inherit them; they are our old-brain and its many distinct sensory signals.

Recommendations: the use of Nature-reconnection activities

The color chart activity is one of 124 *Well Mind, Well Earth* nature-connecting activities (an additional 24 key activities are in *Reconnecting With Nature*) used by counselors, educators and mental health workers to catalyze "green in green." These pioneering Applied Ecopsychology experiences counteract the adverse effects of the estrangement of our 53 natural senses from the natural world, (Goldman, 1993). In classrooms, counseling programs, environmental education, mental health facilities, nature interpretation and recovery work the activities help teach the new-brain the reasonableness of discovering, validating and respecting the old-brain and its sensory connections to nature's wisdom, to part of creation's higher power, (Cohen, 1993, 1994). The activities move participants. Even when participants learn the activities from our intercultural Internet email courses or our self-guiding training manuals, we see significant improvement in their self-esteem for they discover that nature's perfection outside themselves flourishes within them, (Cohen, 1994b). Nature-connecting lets the natural world teach us to revere nature in ourselves, others and the environment and we naturally refrain from hurting that which we hold sacred. This is the new frontier for counseling psychology. With over 70% of the nation suffering from stress, with environmental deterioration continuing and alarming over 85% of the public, counseling with nature holds a key to our destiny, (Cohen 1995).

References

Cohen, M. (1994a.) The Distinguished World Citizen Award: Responsible fulfillment and guidance from nature connections. Taproots, Fall 1994, Cortland, NY: Coalition for Education in the Out of Doors.

Cohen, M. (1994b.) Validations: The Experience of Connecting with Nature (Tech. Rep. No 21), Roche Harbor WA: World Peace University Press. Department of Integrated Ecology.

Cohen, M. (1993.) Integrated Ecology: The Process of Counseling with Nature. The Humanistic Psychologist, Vol. 21 No. 3 Washington, DC: American Psychological Association.

Cohen, M. (1993a.) Green in Green (Tech. Rep. No. 18) Roche Harbor WA: World Peace University. Department of Integrated Ecology.

Cohen, M. (1993b.) Counselling with Nature: Catalyzing Sensory Moments that Let Earth Nurture. Counselling Psychology Quarterly, Vol 6, No. 1, Abingdon Oxfordshire UK: Carfax Publishing.

Cohen, M. (1990.) Connecting With Nature: Creating Moments That Let Earth Teach. Portland, OR: World Peace University Press.

Knapp, C. (1988.) Creating Humane Climates Outdoors. Charleston, WV: ERIC/CRESS.

Goldman, D. (1993.) Psychology's New Interest In the World Beyond the Self. New York, NY: The New York Times.

Lipkin R, (1995.) Bacterial Chatter. Science News, Vol 147, No. 9 Washington DC: Science Service Inc.

Murchie, G. (1978.) Seven Mysteries of Life. Boston, Massachusetts: Houghton Mifflin.

Pearce, J. (1980.) Magical Child. New York, NY: Bantam.

Rivlin R., Gravelle, K. (1984.) Deciphering the Senses. New York, NY: Simon and Schuster.

Rovee-Collier C. (1992.) Infant Memory Shows The Power of Place, Developmental Psychology, March. Quoted in Science News, vol. 141 No. 16 p.244, Washington DC: Science Service.

Samples, B. (1976.) The Metaphoric Mind. Reading, MA: Addison-Wesley Publishing Co.

Sheppard, Paul (1984.) Nature and Madness. San Francisco, CA: Sierra Publications.

Spelke, E. (1992.) Infants Signal the Birth of Knowledge, Psychological Review, October, 1992 as quoted in Science News, November 14, 1992, Vol. 142 p. 325, Washington DC: Science Service.

Stevens, W. (1993.) Want a Room With a View? The New York Times, November 30, New York, NY: N.Y. Times.

Wynne-Edwards (1991.) Ecology Denies Darwinism. The Ecologist, May-June, Cornwall; England.

The author dedicates this article to Sunkyo Kwon whose devoted efforts improved its clarity and desirability.

Thoughtful Verbalization

These instructions are located on the last page of this book. Once you complete them, return to this page.

Optional:

Read Chapter 13 in *Reconnecting With Nature* for additional information about how negatives in nature are helpful attractions. (You need not do the activity there for this course).

Chapter Five

Webstring Intelligence

Symptoms of Intelligence

Below is a summary of observations and conclusions from people who have taken this course online and from Project NatureConnect's research, website and books. Do your think they serve as good examples of webstrings being intelligent?

Scientifically, it is clear that natural systems organize themselves with webstrings. Moment by moment natural systems are attracted to create additional strings and connections that increasingly weave, balance and repair the web of life.

Natural system organization is not done haphazardly, rather it forms from attractions to build mutually beneficial relationships in the next moment that support life.

Natural attraction organization produces nature's optimum of life, diversity, cooperation, balance and beauty.

The organization process is inclusive and caring enough to globally produce and sustain the web of life without creating garbage. Nothing is left out, unattached or unwanted, a condition of unconditional love.

Natural systems and nature-connected people don't display the runaway war, abusiveness, pollution and mental and environmental disorders that plague our lives.

Globally, webstrings are wise enough to edit the solar system and universe in order to maintain the conditions necessary for life to sustain itself on Earth.

Any person who could produce webstrings' results in a human population would be considered a supergenius.

Webstrings are intelligent enough not to separate from their wisdom. Rather, they are it, are conscious of it, and they share it freely to become more intelligent collectively.

Many problems of contemporary people arise because our estrangement from nature prejudiciously and addictively deprives our thinking from conscious connection with the attraction, nurturance and energies of webstrings.

Webstrings in people recognize nature is intelligent because our wellness and relationships improve when we genuinely reconnect to authentic nature.

Examples of Natural Intelligence in action:

Pinch yourself gently. Do you trust that you felt something? Now, pinch yourself too hard. Do you trust that a webstring sense (pain, reason or both) intelligently calls to you to stop pinching yourself that hard?

Each natural webstring sense and sensation, such as thirst, is a distinct intelligence. Thirst displays intelligence in that it knows to turn itself on, bring to our awareness that our body needs water, and to turn off when we have had enough water. In addition, thirst is wise enough to communicate with the senses of reason, smell, color, location and memory to determine if the water is fit to drink.

The Activity

Using the permission activity in Chapter 4, with a notepad and pencil, go to and obtain consent from an attractive natural area to visit it and enjoy its intelligence. Once you gain the area's permission, recognize that each natural attraction webstring you sense there is a basic intelligence. Try to identify that intelligence as follows:

A. Find a natural attraction.

B. Before you find another natural attraction, try to identify or imagine in the Web of Life what intelligent thing(s) this attraction is doing, or what intelligent role(s) it is playing.

C. Write down the attraction and the intelligence. If you can't identify the intelligence, see if you can find this webstring's intelligent value in yourself or in other people. (If you still can't identify the intelligence, later email your group members and ask them if they know what intelligence they think it might be and/or look it up in an encyclopedia.)

D. Repeat this activity a few times until you feel you have experienced and validated that webstrings act like (and therefore are) basic intelligences.

E. Personal experience: Think of a time or situation in the past when you have been aware of the intelligence(s) operating that you discovered in this activity. This could have taken place while you were at home, school, work or in a natural area.

F. Appreciation: Can you find some way to express appreciation to nature for the webstring intelligence it has given your life or shared with you here today?

Optionally complete this summary evaluation:
SUMMARY STATEMENT E: You are encouraged to do the following evaluation activity:webstring attraction

is an intelligence that people in industrial society seldom learn to celebrate and too often deny or abuse.

OPTIONAL: Either in your journal or on a piece of paper, record the SUMMARY letter above (E) along with the number on the continuum scale (below) that indicates the extent of your agreement with the Summary Statement.

1	2	3	4	5	6	7	8	9	10
disagree				partially agree					fully agree

Supportive Reading

Read and take the EcoSensory Perception Intelligence Test below as far as time permits before you tally your score on its last page. (You will score higher and learn more if you do all of its 70 statements.) As you do it, select the single statement you find that you would be most willing to sign your name to with respect to it best representing your thoughts and feelings in this Webstring Intelligence Activity. NOTE: The statements from "Project NatureConnect" are from Mike Cohen.

Save your IQ score for comparison purposes later.

ECO-SENSORY PERCEPTION
The EcoSensory Intelligence Test

INTRODUCTION
Many people are attracted to visit this Eco IQ webpage on our website because they have a hidden but high ecological IQ. Often they neither know how to validate this intelligence in them nor how to fully put it to work for themselves and society. Many of them have been slighted for sharing their intelligent thoughts and feelings about nature. Deep inside they sometimes consider themselves different or strange because of how they intuitively think and feel. The preface to this IQ test explores this phenomenon.

PREFACE

Intelligence True or False? You decide.

Most knowledgeable people consider Planet Earth to be an act of genius by the Universe and/or God. As mentioned previously, like a living organism, through natural attraction energies, Earth intelligently organizes itself to edit the light, heat and particle flow from the sun and cosmos. This makes possible an optimum of life to flourish in balance while sustaining an optimum of diversity and cooperation, too. The Earth community intelligently accomplishes this by recycling and regenerating substances and relationships without producing garbage or pollution. In Earth's natural systems, war, abusiveness, and insanity are virtually unknown. Seen from the moon, Earth is a marvelous, gigantic ball of wisdom, a glowing orchestra in the sky constantly performing a peaceful symphony of color and silence in motion. Some believe Earth is an intelligent cell or fertilized egg of the Universe.

Do you recognize that any person who could conceive and perform the functions of Earth or nature would be considered a super genius ten times over?

NON-INTELLIGENCE
Intelligence as most of us practice it is not fully intelligent because it is 5-leg out of synch with the 4-leg, life supportive creation and sustainability wisdom of our planetary home. The way we think deteriorates Earth and its ability to support life, including our lives. That is not intelligent. For example,

Two people producing 24 grandchildren is poor mathematics if you don't want to destructively overpopulate the planet.

Economic growth based on resource depletion is insane when the resource is your life support system. It is unethical and immoral.

Knowledgeably producing harmful chemical substances that poison the planet life system, including us, is stupid.

Our thinking is sick when we use fuels to the point that they increase the temperature of the living planet and give it a fever.

It is dumb to damage ecosystems and erode their habitats for they are and support life.

It is asinine to elect leaders who refuse to act intelligently with regard to helping Earth sustain its and our integrity.

It is stupid to learn to think and relate 99% of the time indoors, closeted from nature's supportive ways, yet believe we know how to manage the global life system. The de-structive results speak for themselves (Appendix B).

See Disconnected Intelligence http://www.ecopsych.com/alertiq11.html for additional examples and help on addressing them.

The Eco-Sensory IQ Test.

This is an opportunity to learn how much of your ability to think clearly has survived the abusive conquest of nature by our nature-estranged society. You may discover that you are a maverick genius in contemporary society and, if so, you can use this genius to your advantage while improving the quality of life.

Background:

The way most members of Western civilization think has resulted in altering the ability of Planet Earth to sustain life in balance. In the past 200 years our intelligence has devastated natural mineral, plant, animal and people populations as well as depleted and polluted the soil, water and air. With respect to the global life community, we are producing the same holocaust we inflicted on Native American and extinct biological populations. Worse still, we can't stop. As recent elections confirm, we want to increase our consumption of energy and goods at the expense of the natural world.

The profound stupidity and inhumanity of our relationship with Mother Nature so deeply pains our consciousness that we are psychologically in denial of our madness. To protectively hide our destructive effects from ourselves, we proudly call what we do "progress," "economic growth" and the "American way of life." Most people are intelligent enough to recognize that this way is too destructive in the long run, but we lack the level of consciousness needed to stop it. We partake in it every day. It is normal.

Nature supports, not destroys, itself in the long run. As part of nature, people are born with the natural intelligence to do likewise. Most cultures of the world have done this over the millennia. They learned to think with their natural intelligence while Western civilization thinks of ways to alter it.

Altered Intelligence

In 1974, after two months of being kidnapped and brainwashed by extremists, the consciousness and thinking of an American graduate student, Patti Hearst, transformed dramatically. From being an excellent scholar and constructive campus citizen at the University of California, Patti became an active, gun-slinging member of a group of militant murderers with a political agenda. Many times she could easily have escaped from them. She didn't simply because she had learned, under duress, to consider it intelligent to join the violence group in story, feelings and actions.

Ms. Hearst was finally arrested, prosecuted and jailed along with the gang. She was later forgiven because authorities determined that she had been brainwashed into doing what she did. She has not acted that way since.

As demonstrated by Ms. Hearst, brainwashing is a process that contaminates a person's intelligence and ability to think clearly. As mentioned in Chapter Two, things that define the brainwashing process include that it:

Takes an authoritarian and hierarchical stance.

Imposes a doctrine over person.

Restricts full awareness on the part of the learner.

Rewards a person for thinking a certain way and punishes them when they don't.

Uses an instructional mode to persuade.

Controls a person's time and, if possible, physical environment.

Creates a sense of powerlessness, covert fear, and dependency.

Suppresses much of a person's old behavior and attitudes.

Instills new behavior and attitudes.

Uses mystical manipulation.

Puts forth a closed system of logic.

Allows no real input or criticism.

The case has been made that with respect to intelligently living in balance with nature and Earth, people in contemporary society have been destructively brainwashed to fear, conquer and destroy nature against their better judgment. Like Ms. Hearst, we find ourselves unable to change without a radical form of assistance. Most of our destructive technologies, lifestyles and relationships reflect our anti-nature cultural training. We act as though our thoughts and acts are not causing life forms and systems to suffer along with ourselves.

During our 18 formative childhood years, our innate ability to think clearly with respect to living constructively with nature and people is far more brainwashed than was Patti Hearst during her mere two-month capture. Throughout childhood and most of our lives we are victims of:

Education that takes place indoors; it is required for twelve formative childhood years and strongly encouraged for an additional 4-6 years of higher education.

The doctrine of most science and religion that to survive we must conquer and subdue nature.

Learning to spend over 95% of our lives indoors.

Over 99.9% of our 5-leg thinking being disconnected from 4-leg sensory contact with the non-verbal process by which nature produces its balance and peace. We are 9-leg "in tune" with nature less than 12 hours/lifetime, on average.

Worshiping a God that lives in Heaven, not on Earth, spiritually detaches us from the environment. It leads us to believe humanity is divinely superior to all other forms of life and that creation lies elsewhere.

Rewards from high grades, approval and money for being good citizens of a society that is separated from nature delude us into thinking that it is intelligent for us, while disconnected from nature, to manage the world, grind nature into cultural resources, improve the land, and impose artificial systems on the natural, and that we can do so without being destructive.

Socialization and academics that hold suspect non-formal education, low grades, and low-technology relationships.

Exceptions to the rule:

Throughout the history of our civilization, some individuals have not completely fallen prey to our cultural brainwashing. Some, have somewhat survived it or, like Ms. Hearst, recovered from it. If you have read this far, chances are you may unknowingly be one of these people. These individuals display an exceptionally high ecological intelligence (IQ) and are sometimes acknowledged as "maverick" geniuses. The quality of their thinking is often admired, but it is seldom integrated by popular culture because society's basic quest is to overcome nature, not applaud its support.

NOTE: From books of quotations and the Internet, in an eight-hour period we collected the statements that appear on the IQ test below. There are a great many other statements that are similar; all of them are and have been accessible since their original publication. You can be sure that some of our leaders and the teachers and administrators of our education system were exposed to these statements during their education. That they may not include or emphasize these statements in most people's socialization further reflects our brainwashing against nature. For a fascinating look at this phenomenon and maverick genius in action, re-read Karen: Disconnecting From Nature in Chapter 2. (http://www.ecopsych.com/5grnchkaren.html)

Optionally complete this summary evaluation:

Summary Statement E:

Nature is intelligent. People are part of nature and vice versa. We inherit nature's intelligence; it is biologically and psychologically in us. Our civilization conditions us to abusively conquer nature in the environment and people thus producing many discontents. However, throughout history, in some people our natural intelligence has survived this abuse and expressed itself.

In your journal or on a piece of paper, record the SUMMARY letter (E) along with the number on the continuum scale below that indicates the extent of your agreement with the Summary Statement:

1   2   3   4   5   6   7   8   9   10
disagree   partially agree   fully agree

Record and retain your score.

If you find yourself in agreement with the statement, you are an excellent candidate for successfully completing the Eco IQ Test and increasing your intelligence, too.

Ecosensory IQ

To discover how much of your ecological intelligence is intact, take this Eco-Sensory IQ Test. It consists of 70 questions, but you can optionally get a general reading after the first 20 questions. You will, however, learn a great deal more by doing each of the additional questions as each comes from a different perspective.

The Test will help you support and put your natural genius to work for the benefit of yourself and the global life community. A special feature of this IQ test is that as you take it you will automatically increase your eco-intelligence.

This IQ Test results from the observation that:

-the anti-nature programming and prejudice we receive from our nature-disconnected society rewards us and produces our greatest troubles.

-the heart of our unsolvable problems is psychological.

-we are in denial.

-we deny that the rewards we receive for nature-disconnected thinking and relationships addict or program us to live out a misguided story that produces destructive side effects.

-we seldom understand that our society rewards us for learning: "To survive we must conquer, exploit and subdue nature within and around us."

The Eco IQ TEST

Purpose: Discover how much of your natural intelligence has survived the deadening impact of Western culture's conquest of nature.

Object: Learn if you are intelligent enough to recognize the psychological and spiritual importance of emotionality, passion and sensitivity in sustaining responsible personal and environmental relationships. This test is offered solely as an educational tool. The word ed-u-ca-tion comes from educare meaning "to draw out from within."

INSTRUCTIONS

1. Prepare an answer sheet of paper with the numbers 0-9, 10-19, 20-29, etc. written in 7 columns covering 70 questions.

2. Read, in order, the 70 quotes and statements on the following linked pages.

3. Note the length of time the message of some statements has been known to our society.

4. Recognize that the message of each statement that you understand exists somewhere within your cultural or natural heritage, otherwise you would not be able to understand it.

5. Signify on the indicator that accompanies each statement, the extent of agreement you think/feel/have for the statement. Place this number next to the question number on your answer sheet.

Here is a sample question and responder:
It is a fact of life that our senses, feelings and emotions are facts of life. They are as much a part of nature and our nature as is the land, sea and air. For example, the fact that we experience the sensation of thirst is as real and true as water itself.

What number represents your agreement with the statement ?

```
1     2     3     4     5     6     7     8     9     10
disagree        partially agree            fully agree
```

Final Instruction: Assign and record a number from 1 to 10, as above, to represent the extent of your agreement with each of the following 70 statements.

The Test

0. "Man is not himself only... He is all that he sees; all that flows to him from a thousand sources...He is the land, the lift of its mountain lines, the reach of its valleys."
    -Mary Austin

Write down the number that represents your agreement with the statement.

```
1     2     3     4     5     6     7     8     9     10
disagree        partially agree            fully agree
```

Write down your score to this question and all questions on your answer sheet, for use later on.

2. "There is one common flow, one common breathing, all things are in sympathy."
    -Hippocrates circa 450 B.C.

```
1     2     3     4     5     6     7     8     9     10
disagree        partially agree            fully agree
```

2. "When one tugs at a single thing in nature, he finds it attached to the rest of the world."
    -John Muir

```
1     2     3     4     5     6     7     8     9     10
disagree        partially agree            fully agree
```

3. "This earth which is spread out like a map around is but the lining of my inmost soul exposed."
    -Henry David Thoreau circa 1850

```
1     2     3     4     5     6     7     8     9     10
disagree        partially agree            fully agree
```

4. "The soul of man...is a portion or a copy of the soul of the Universe and is joined together on principles and in proportions corresponding to those which govern the Universe."
    -Plutarch circa 75 A.D.

```
1     2     3     4     5     6     7     8     9     10
disagree        partially agree            fully agree
```

5. "Wherever you may go, the least plant may bring you clear remembrance of the Creator."
    -St. Basil

```
1     2     3     4     5     6     7     8     9     10
disagree        partially agree            fully agree
```

6. "As I get older, I burrow more and more into the hills. The Great Spirit made them for us, for me. I want to blend with them, shrink into them, and finally disappear in them. All of nature is in us, all of us is in nature. That is as it should be."
    -Pete Catches, Sioux medicine man

```
1     2     3     4     5     6     7     8     9     10
disagree        partially agree            fully agree
```

7. "Nature is the unseen intelligence that loved us into living."
    -Elbert Hubbard

```
1     2     3     4     5     6     7     8     9     10
disagree        partially agree            fully agree
```

8. "Look at those cows and remember that the greatest scientists in the world have never discovered how to make grass into milk."
      -Michael Pupin

1	2	3	4	5	6	7	8	9	10
disagree			partially agree					fully agree	

9. "For what else is Nature but God and the Divine Reason that pervades the whole universe and all its parts."
      -Seneca the Younger circa 25 A.D.

1	2	3	4	5	6	7	8	9	10
disagree			partially agree					fully agree	

10. "Always think of the universe as one living organism, with a single substance, and a single soul."
      -Marcus Aurelius

1	2	3	4	5	6	7	8	9	10
disagree			partially agree					fully agree	

11. "Through the eons, as today, in building materials, life, and relationships nature, (with the exception of humanity,) has seldom used written or spoken words."
      -Project NatureConnect

1	2	3	4	5	6	7	8	9	10
disagree			partially agree					fully agree	

12. "The name that can be named is not the eternal name. The Nameless is the origin of Heaven and Earth."
      -Lao Tzu circa 600 B.C.

1	2	3	4	5	6	7	8	9	10
disagree			partially agree					fully agree	

13. "Nature does nothing uselessly."
      -Aristotle circa 350 B.C.

1	2	3	4	5	6	7	8	9	10
disagree			partially agree					fully agree	

14. "What we are looking for is what is looking."
      -St. Francis of Assisi

1	2	3	4	5	6	7	8	9	10
disagree			partially agree					fully agree	

15. "Human subtlety. . .will never devise an invention more beautiful, more simple or more direct that does nature, because in her inventions nothing is lacking, and nothing is superflous."
      -Leonardo da Vinci circa 1470

1	2	3	4	5	6	7	8	9	10

16. "Those things are better which are perfected by nature than those which are finished by art"
      -Cicero circa 1500 B.C.

1	2	3	4	5	6	7	8	9	10
disagree			partially agree					fully agree	

17. "What nature delivers to us is never stale. Because what nature creates has eternity in it."
      -Isaac Bashevis Singer

1	2	3	4	5	6	7	8	9	10
disagree			partially agree					fully agree	

18. "The natural world is the larger sacred community to which we belong. To be alienated from this community is to become destitute in all that makes us human. To damage this community is to diminish our own existence."
      -Thomas Berry

1	2	3	4	5	6	7	8	9	10
disagree			partially agree					fully agree	

19. "I believe in God, only I spell it Nature."
      -Frank Lloyd Wright

1	2	3	4	5	6	7	8	9	10
disagree			partially agree					fully agree	

20. "The art of medicine consists in amusing the patient while nature cures the disease."
      -Voltaire circa 1700

1	2	3	4	5	6	7	8	9	10
disagree			partially agree					fully agree	

21. "What greater grief than the loss of one's native land."
      -Euripides circa 450 B.C.

1	2	3	4	5	6	7	8	9	10
disagree			partially agree					fully agree	

22. "That which fills the universe I regard as my body and that which directs the universe I see as my own nature"
      Chuang-Tzu circa 370 B.C.

1	2	3	4	5	6	7	8	9	10
disagree			partially agree					fully agree	

23. "Man has created death."
      -William Butler Yeats

1	2	3	4	5	6	7	8	9	10
disagree			partially agree					fully agree	

24. "The purpose of life is to live in agreement with nature."

-Zen circa 520 BC

1   2   3   4   5   6   7   8   9   10
disagree   partially agree   fully agree

25. "If you would learn more, ask the cattle, seek information from the birds of the air, The creeping things of earth will give you lessons and the fishes of the sea will tell you all. Speak to the Earth and it will teach thee."

-The Bible, Job: 12, 7

1   2   3   4   5   6   7   8   9   10
disagree   partially agree   fully agree

26. "And the true order of going, or being led by another, to the things of love, is to begin from the beauties of earth."

-Plato circa 400 B.C.

1   2   3   4   5   6   7   8   9   10
disagree   partially agree   fully agree

27. "Never does nature say one thing and wisdom another."

-Jovenel

1   2   3   4   5   6   7   8   9   10
disagree   partially agree   fully agree

28. "The senses, being the explorers of the world, open the way to knowledge."

-Maria Montessori

1   2   3   4   5   6   7   8   9   10
disagree   partially agree   fully agree

29. "It is a fact of life that our senses, feelings and emotions are facts of life. They are as much a part of nature and our nature as is the land, sea and air. For example: the sensation of thirst is as real and true as water itself."

-Project NatureConnect

1   2   3   4   5   6   7   8   9   10
disagree   partially agree   fully agree

30. "You can't be suspicious of a tree, or accuse a bird or a squirrel of subversion or challenge the ideology of a violet."

-Hal Borland

1   2   3   4   5   6   7   8   9   10
disagree   partially agree   fully agree

31. "No two people —no mere father and mother—as I have often said, are enough to provide emotional security for a child. He needs to feel himself one in a world of kinfolk, persons of variety in age and temperament, and yet allied to himself by an indissoluble bond which he cannot break if he could, for nature has welded him into it before he was born."

-Pearl S. Buck

1   2   3   4   5   6   7   8   9   10
disagree   partially agree   fully agree

32. "Each natural sense is an intelligence. For example, it is intelligent for the sensation of thirst to turn on and attract us to water when we need water, or turn off when we have enough."

-Project NatureConnect

1   2   3   4   5   6   7   8   9   10
disagree   partially agree   fully agree

33. "We have repressed far more than our sexuality: our very organic nature is now unconscious to most of us, most of the time, and we have become shrunken into two dimensional social or cultural beings, aware of only five of the hundreds of senses that link us to the rich biological nature that underlies and nourishes these more symbolic and recent aspects of ourselves."

-Norman 0. Brown

1   2   3   4   5   6   7   8   9   10
disagree   partially agree   fully agree

34. "Every cell in your body is seeking fulfillment through joy, beauty, love and appreciation."

-Deepak Chopra

1   2   3   4   5   6   7   8   9   10
disagree   partially agree   fully agree

35. "Oh, what a catastrophe, what a maiming of love when it was made personal, merely personal feeling. This is what is the matter with us: we are bleeding at the roots because we are cut off from the earth and sun and stars. Love has become a grinning mockery because, poor blossom, we plucked it from its stem on the Tree of Life and expected it to keep on blooming in our civilized vase on the table."

-D. H. Lawrence

1   2   3   4   5   6   7   8   9   10
disagree   partially agree   fully agree

36. "A man who is in love declares that I and you are one and is prepared to behave as if it were a fact."
    -Sigmund Freud

    1   2   3   4   5   6   7   8   9   10
    disagree   partially agree   fully agree

37. "If you were to destroy in mankind the belief in immortality, not only love but every living force maintaining the life of the world would at once be dried up."
    -Fyodor Dostoevski circa 1850

    1   2   3   4   5   6   7   8   9   10
    disagree   partially agree   fully agree

38. "We belong to the ground. It is our power and we must stay close to it or maybe we will get lost."
    -Aborigine (Jennifer Isaacs)

    1   2   3   4   5   6   7   8   9   10
    disagree   partially agree   fully agree

39. "Climb the mountains and get their good tidings. Nature's peace will flow into you as sunshine flows into trees. The winds will blow their freshness into you, and the storms their energy, while cares will drop off like falling leaves."
    -John Muir

    1   2   3   4   5   6   7   8   9   10
    disagree   partially agree   fully agree

40. "A thing is right when it tends to preserve the integrity, stability and beauty of the biotic community. It is wrong when it tends to do otherwise."
    -Aldo Leopold

    1   2   3   4   5   6   7   8   9   10
    disagree   partially agree   fully agree

41. "Great things are done when men and mountains meet."
    -William Blake

    1   2   3   4   5   6   7   8   9   10
    disagree   partially agree   fully agree

42. "The world is not to be put in order, the world is order. It is for us to put ourselves in unison with this order."
    -Henry Miller

    1   2   3   4   5   6   7   8   9   10
    disagree   partially agree   fully agree

43. "Wildness can be a way of reassuring ourselves of our sanity as creatures, a part of the geography of hope."
    -Wallace Stegner

    1   2   3   4   5   6   7   8   9   10
    disagree   partially agree   fully agree

44. "A land ethic for tomorrow should be as honest as Thoreau's Walden, and as comprehensive as the sensitive science of ecology. It should stress the oneness of our resources and the live-and-help-live logic of the great chain of life."
    -Stewart Udall

    1   2   3   4   5   6   7   8   9   10
    disagree   partially agree   fully agree

45. "Nature knows no indecencies; man invents them."
    -Mark Twain

    1   2   3   4   5   6   7   8   9   10
    disagree   partially agree   fully agree

46. "I would feel more optimistic about a bright future for man if he spent less time proving that he can outwit Nature and more time tasting her sweetness and respecting her seniority."
    -E. B. White

    1   2   3   4   5   6   7   8   9   10
    disagree   partially agree   fully agree

47. "This is how a human being can change: there's a worm addicted to eating grape leaves. Suddenly, he wakes up, call it grace, whatever, something wakes him, and he's no longer a worm. He's the entire vineyard, and the orchard too, the fruit, the trunks, a growing wisdom and joy that doesn't need to devour."
    -Jedaluddin Rumi , 1207-1273

    1   2   3   4   5   6   7   8   9   10
    disagree   partially agree   fully agree

48. "The interior landscape responds to the character and subtlety of the exterior landscape; the shape of the individual mind is affected by the land as it is by genes."
    -Barry Lopez

    1   2   3   4   5   6   7   8   9   10
            disagree   partially agree
                                    fully agree

49. "Wind over the lake: the image of inner truth."
    -I Ching circa 1200 B.C.

    1   2   3   4   5   6   7   8   9   10
    disagree   partially agree   fully agree

50. "Remember, your mind is not your own. It is a gift from nature. It is imperative to use it positively, constructively. To do otherwise, to use it for worry, anger or negativity is to abuse the mighty gift."
    - Hua Ching Ni, Taoist Master

    1   2   3   4   5   6   7   8   9   10
    disagree   partially agree   fully agree

51. With regard to domestication, "The human relationship to the natural world was gradually changed from one of respect for and participation in its elliptical wholeness, to one of detachment, management, control and finally domination."

-Chellis Glendinning

1   2   3   4   5   6   7   8   9   10
disagree   partially agree   fully agree

52. "Insanity is a perfectly rational adjustment to an insane world."

-R. D. Laing

1   2   3   4   5   6   7   8   9   10
disagree   partially agree   fully agree

53. "Except during the nine months before he draws his first breath, no man manages his affairs as well as a tree does."

-George Bernard Shaw

1   2   3   4   5   6   7   8   9   10
disagree   partially agree   fully agree

54. "Most of us have become Ecozombies, desensitized, environmental deadheads. On average, society conditions us to spend over 95% of our time and 99.9% of our thinking disconnected from nature. Nature's extreme absence in our lives leaves us abandoned and wanting. We feel we never have enough. We greedily, destructively, consume and can't stop. Nature's loss in our psyche produces a hurt, hungering, void within us that often bullies us into our dilemmas."

-Project NatureConnect

1   2   3   4   5   6   7   8   9   10
disagree   partially agree   fully agree

55. "A human being is part of a whole, called by us the 'Universe,' a part limited in time and space. He experiences himself, his thoughts and feelings, as something separated from the rest —a kind of optical delusion of his consciousness. This delusion is a kind of prison for us, restricting us to our personal desires and to affection for a few persons nearest us. Our task must be to free ourselves from this prison by widening our circles of compassion to embrace all living creatures and the whole of nature in its beauty."

-Albert Einstein

1   2   3   4   5   6   7   8   9   10
disagree   partially agree   fully agree

56. "Until mankind can extend the circle of his compassion to include all living things, he will never, himself, know peace."

- Albert Schweitzer, Nobel Peace Prize, 1950

1   2   3   4   5   6   7   8   9   10
disagree   partially agree   fully agree

57. "There is an ecological unconscious that can be drawn on to restore people to harmony with the natural world, a bond between our species and the planet as tenacious as the sexual instincts Freud found in the psyche."

-Theodore Roszak

1   2   3   4   5   6   7   8   9   10
disagree   partially agree   fully agree

58. "This is what you shall do: Love the earth and sun and the animals"

-Walt Whitman

1   2   3   4   5   6   7   8   9   10
disagree   partially agree   fully agree

59. "In a democracy, in order to learn to unashamedly love nature and reach our hopes and ideals, we need a readily available psychological process that reverses our anti-nature programming and heightens our innate ability to feel and validate natural attractions. We must learn that we seldom own our senses and feelings; we share them with natural systems."

-Project NatureConnect

1   2   3   4   5   6   7   8   9   10
disagree   partially agree   fully agree

60. "In the woods we return to reason and faith. There I feel that nothing can befall me in life—no disgrace, no calamity (leaving me my eyes), which nature cannot repair. Standing on the bare ground—my head bathed by the blithe air and uplifted into infinite space —all mean egotism vanishes. I become a transparent eyeball; I am nothing, I see all; the currents of the Universal Being circulate through me; I am a part or particle of God."

-Ralph Waldo Emerson circa 1860

1   2   3   4   5   6   7   8   9   10
disagree   partially agree   fully agree

61. "One touch of nature makes the whole world kin."

-William Shakespeare circa 1580

1   2   3   4   5   6   7   8   9   10
disagree   partially agree   fully agree

62. "Now I see the secret of the making of the best persons. It is to grow in the open air and to eat and sleep with the earth."

-Walt Whitman

1	2	3	4	5	6	7	8	9	10
disagree				partially agree				fully agree	

63. "Scientific research is based on the idea that everything that takes place is determined by laws of nature, and therefore this holds for the action of people."

-Albert Einstein

1	2	3	4	5	6	7	8	9	10
disagree				partially agree				fully agree	

64. "We must engage in a process of natural systems thinking, one that scientifically reconnects nature's supportive intelligence with our contemporary mentality. This enables us to help nature and ourselves in concert recover from our society's abusiveness. The process transforms our abusiveness into mutually supportive relationships."

-Project NatureConnect

1	2	3	4	5	6	7	8	9	10
disagree				partially agree				fully agree	

65. " From the masses to the masses'
The most Revolutionary consciousness is to be found
Among the most ruthlessly exploited classes:
Animals, trees, water, air, grasses."

-Gary Snyder

1	2	3	4	5	6	7	8	9	10
disagree				partially agree				fully agree	

66. "As we gain satisfaction from artificial substitutes for nature we forget that there is no known substitute for Nature, the real thing and its eons of intelligent, life supportive, experience. Each substitute we create falls short of nature's balanced perfection, thus producing our pollution, garbage and relationship conflicts."

-Project NatureConnect

1	2	3	4	5	6	7	8	9	10
disagree				partially agree				fully agree	

67. "It is difficult to get people to understand something when their salary depends upon them not understanding it."

-Upton Sinclair

1	2	3	4	5	6	7	8	9	10
disagree				partially agree				fully agree	

68. "Given the abundance of nature forms, it is important to go straight to nature."

-Leonardo Da Vinci

1	2	3	4	5	6	7	8	9	10
disagree				partially agree				fully agree	

69. "The major problems in the world are the result of the difference between how nature works and the way people think.." .

-Gregory Bateson.

1	2	3	4	5	6	7	8	9	10
disagree				partially agree				fully agree	

A-B-C: The Three Key Eco-Sensory Intelligence Questions

A. "We cannot win this battle to save species and environments without forging an emotional bond between ourselves and nature as well - for we will not fight to save what we do not love."

-Stephen Jay Gould

1	2	3	4	5	6	7	8	9	10
disagree				partially agree				fully agree	

B. "Apathy is the greatest evil of all."

- Helen Keller

1	2	3	4	5	6	7	8	9	10
disagree				partially agree				fully agree	

C. "When we are conscious of them, our natural attraction bonds (webstrings) enable our thinking to safely and intelligently dissolve the apathy and fear that keep us in denial and produce our unsolvable personal and environmental problems."

-Project NatureConnect

1	2	3	4	5	6	7	8	9	10
disagree				partially agree				fully agree	

Your Objective Score

In our nature disconnected lives, part of our true nature is missing. We work, play, think and dream halfheartedly. If you have a high Eco IQ, are you satisfied that you are engaged in using it to its best advantage for yourself and Earth? As in A, above, are you, to your full potential, involved in a process that helps people feelingly enjoy our inherent emotional bonds with nature and each other? These bonds are Nature's voice, natural attraction loves that directly connect us, in balance, to people and the environment.

D. What score do you think Mother Nature would give you with respect to you, in reality, rejuvenating these bonds in yourself and others?

1   2   3   4   5   6   7   8   9   10.
disengaged   partially engaged   fully engaged

How high can any person's D score be if they are involved with, or support contemporary 5-leg thinking as described by Pulitzer Prize winner Maureen Dowd at http://www.ecopsych.com/alertiq11.

ECO-SENSORY IQ DETERMINATION
INSTRUCTIONS
1. To obtain your RAW SCORE, on your answer sheet, total the number of statements you responded to and divide that into your total score.

2. Because it is not intelligent to not use your Eco IQ to its best advantage, multiply your score in "D" above with your page score total Raw Score. This is your ADJUSTED SCORE.

3. Add a percentage sign to your adjusted score. That percentage represents the percentage of your inherent ecosensory intelligence that you presently use to think and build relationships. It is your ECO-SENSORY IQ.

The Bewilderment Factor
Be-wil-der-ed: to detrimentally be separated from wilderness.

As previously mentioned, during 99.9% of our "normal" lives our mentality is closeted from nature. This deeply teaches our thinking not to be in tune with the natural environment. Like a fish removed from water, our psyche emotionally gasps to survive. With respect to living in balance, we become isolated and feel bewildered. For this reason most people believe the statement below is FALSE even though it is TRUE. Do you think it is FALSE?

( ) TRUE   ( ) FALSE: Because our psychological disconnection from nature produces unsolvable problems, genuinely reconnecting our psyche with nature helps us restore our psyche and solve these problems.

Are you bewildered? It is not intelligent to ecologically know the right thing to do and then not do it. This is very bewildering when you are immersed in a society where knowledgeably acting destructively to nature is the norm. It leads you think your D score is much higher than it would be if the global life community determined it.

C. Thoughtful Verbalization
These instructions are located on the last page of this book. Once you complete them, return to this page.

Optional:
For an example of webstring intelligence in action, read Chapter 2 of *Reconnecting With Nature*.

Students in IGE Certificate of Degree programs may from this point forward submit their Student Cooperative Application forms to the Institute office. The form is located at http://www.ecopsych.com/iupscoopapplication.html.

Chapter Six

The Creation of Inspiration

The Secrets-of-Natural Attractions Trail
A hands-on challenge for educators, leaders, counselors and students.

Reading time: 15 minutes.

SUGGESTION: For best results, follow the Trail to its completion without interruption, then repeat it and explore its links and references.

Background
Material that appears on this Trail and its Internet links is drawn from articles that have been professionally reviewed and published in

> The Journal of Humanistic Psychology
> Journal of Environmental Education
> Interpsych Journal of Mental Health
> The Trumpeter
> Counselling Psychology Quarterly
> Clearing Magazine
> Outdoor Communicator
> Nature Study
> International Journal of Humanities and Peace
> Cooperative Learning
> Journal of the Oregon Counseling Association
> Between the Species
> Proceedings: North American Association for Environmental Education
> U.S. Department of Education Educational Resources Information Center
> Greenwich University Journal of Science and Technology

NOTE: To keep the integrity of this Trail intact, we have included a few statements that the book has already covered. By repeating them here, the Trail remains a complete activity you can learn from and offer in and of itself.

TRAIL START:
Consider this intelligence test question regarding mathematical aptitude:

"If you count a dog's tail as one of its legs, how many legs does a dog have?"

"Five," of course, is the answer. Intelligent people say "five" because it's valid in mathematical systems and thinking. However, our sense of reason only recognizes five as correct until we additionally validate what we know from our, or other people's, contact with a real dog. Then, many of our multitude of natural senses come into play: senses of sight, touch, motion, color, texture, language, sound, smell, consciousness, community, trust, contrast, and love. They each help our sense of reason make more sense and recognize that a tail is different than a leg; a dog has four legs, not five.

> "Aristotle thought there were eight legs on a fly and wrote it down. For centuries scholars were content to quote his authority. Apparently, not one of them was curious enough to impale a fly and count its six legs."
> **- Stuart Chase**

Most scientists recognize that just as our arm is attracted or "loves" to be attached to our body, all people are biologically, psychologically and spiritually part of, and thereby attached to nature. We each hold a basic love of nature's "resources," sunshine, food, water, soil, air, in common with each other and all of nature.

However, we live very nature-disconnected lives.

Our thinking has very little genuine 4-leg contact with authentic nature. We desperately need this contact if we are to reasonably and sensibly combine 4-leg and 5-leg knowledge. The contact enables us to produce balanced 9-leg thinking and relationships that help us harmoniously co-create with the natural systems within and around us.

This trail is a 9-leg tool that helps you reach this goal.

Introduction
Although we are part of nature, nature does not suffer our disorders. We don't find uncontrolled garbage, war, loneliness, pollution, crime, abusiveness and mental illness in intact natural areas or natural people. As contemporary people, we have bonded to a destructive way of life, yet we are still part of nature.

How does nature sustain life and avoid producing our problems?

As part of nature, don't we inherit this intelligent gift and then learn to disregard it?

Discover these secrets by doing this unusual nature trail. Learn how to let nature help you build and teach sound personal, social and environmental relationships.

This trail visits rewarding natural areas that flourish in the environment and in hidden natural valleys of your mind. To gain some rewarding insights, try to be open to letting nature help you recycle the destructive ways that Western civilization has taught us to think and relate.

The hidden valleys of our mentality do not register in our consciousness because mountains of anti-nature socialization don't train us to respect or value their communications to us. This weakens and injures them so they no longer have the energy or desire necessary to register.

An important phenomenon

As you read these words you register them and their significance. At this moment, however, you probably neither notice nor register the air that sits between you and the words on this page until these words bring it to your attention.

As in this example, too often, the value of air lies hidden from your immediate consciousness.

Can we afford to continue to overlook air and its importance to our lives and all of life?

Does air have a language that speaks to us and all of nature?

Why, historically, has the quality of the science we learn increased while the quality of air decreased?

This trail reverses that dilemma. It helps you scientifically discover a language that enables us to learn from air about our important relationship with it and nature.

Station 1: A gift to you from nature.

In unspoiled nature, clean, fresh air prevails. It is a global phenomenon, a product of, by and from nature's self-organizing, mutually supportive relationships between sunshine and rain and millions of different plant, animal, and "mineral" species in the soil and atmosphere. You and I are members of humanity, one of those species.

We too often forget that when we inhale fresh air, we receive a gift. Air is a nurturing present to our lives from nature's global community. Air supports our ability to live. Let's not overlook that.

NOTE: The spaces below offer thinking and feeling time between trail stops. When they appear, identify what feels attractive to you from the preceding trail stop. Write down what was attractive. What you write will often be a valuable 9-leg way of knowing that we will use later.

What do you find attractive in the Station above?

Station 2: Your gift to nature.

Do you recognize that when you exhale your breath, Earth breathes you? You breathe out carbon dioxide and water vapor into the air. They are food and water that nurture the plant, animal and mineral world.

Your breath helps to sustain all other forms of life. It is one of your gifts to them. Let's not overlook that.

Notice how you feel right now as you breathe air normally. Would you feel better if you were breathing pure, sunshine-clean, rain-washed air? Why?

What do you find attractive in the Station above?

Station 3: The gift of life.

In earlier times, the word for air was "psyche." Psyche also means spirit and mind.

Breathing air is called respiration, originally meaning "re-spiriting."

The word inspiration means "bringing air/spirit in."

The word expiration means "letting air/spirit leave."

Psychological can mean "logic of the spirit."

Atmosphere comes from the ancient word for soul.

What do you find attractive in the Station above?

Station 4: Disconnect from nature.

For demonstration purposes here, please exhale and then hold your breath for a few moments. Do this now. It is a 4-leg contact activity. While holding your breath, read on:

You have stopped breathing and are now disconnected from air and nature in this regard. Notice how a sensation is developing in you, a natural feeling attraction, a consciousness of air, a webstring of the web of life to air that increasingly communicates with a 4-leg message that urges you to breathe again.

The desire/attraction for things to connect with atmospheric air has been part of nature for 400 million years. That's when plants introduced oxygen in the atmosphere. The natural attraction for oxygen in water and minerals has been around for over three billion years.

Like air itself, the natural attraction for air is of, by and from nature. Scientists did not invent this attraction. It is a form of communication that could be considered nature's attraction language that we inherit. That sense is nature feelingly urging you, "asking you," to reconnect with the atmosphere and the natural world (Cohen, 1995). Do you trust this natural attraction feeling and what it is telling you to do?

Continue to hold your breath. Don't breathe until you absolutely have to.

What do you find attractive in the Station above?

Station 5: Nature wants you alive and connected to it.

Here is a secret of nature: Your sensory desire to breathe is a natural attraction love to reconnect with nature. Your love of air, and it of you, insists that you breathe, even if you choose not to. The 4-leg feeling says, "Participate in the natural community that sustains you. Share and enjoy its physical and sensory gifts," (Adler, 1995.)

Even if you faint from lack of air, your natural attraction to air will revive and rejuvenate you by making you breathe again. That is nature's loving 4-leg intelligence and voice, Natural Attraction, in action. That desire to breathe is a way nature works and communicates. Nature needs and wants you to help sustain the global community so, intelligently, it reconnects you. It also does the same thing for each member of the web of life.

Through natural attraction senses, sensitivities, and sensations, nature feelingly speaks. It tells you its desire for you to participate in life. You belong.

What do you find attractive in the Station above?

Station 6: Connecting with natural life feels good.

Begin to breathe normally again if you have not already done so.

Note that when you reconnect with air by breathing, nature rewards you. It gives you an attractive, satisfying, enjoyable 4-leg natural sensation. Nature "invented" that attractive, fulfilling sensation. It is a form of communication. Through this natural reward nature expresses its appreciation for your supportive participation. Without using words, the sensation thanks you for reconnecting. It thanks you for your natural gifts of carbon dioxide and water vapor to the global community. They could not survive without this gift from you.

Do you trust or celebrate this rewarding feeling of thanks from nature and the ancient life relationship it brings to mind? It is a 4-leg communication and connection with all of life. It is with you all your life. Doesn't it deserve your respect, your attention, your trust?

It is 4-leg reasonable for us and the environment to breathe together, to communicate, to cooperatively connect. That mutually beneficial "love" relationship

helps support and sustain all of life. That's why it is intelligent, right and feels good, why it has been called "spirit."

Nature biologically and psychologically created good feelings to contact, connect with, and reward sensuous forms of life for heeding and fulfilling their natural attraction senses (webstrings).

What do you find attractive in the Station above?

Station 7: Words are your destiny.

The 5-leg words of Section 4 on this nature trail asked you to stop breathing. Their story message had the power to disconnect you from your natural attraction to nature.

When you sentiently ignored your connection to nature and disconnected, that is, stopped breathing, you became uncomfortable. Then nature sensuously 4-leg signaled you that some vital connection was missing. It told you to follow that attraction and fulfill it by breathing. Isn't that a form of intelligence? Were you frightened, hurt or thankful for that sense and its reasonable message?

What do you find attractive in the Station above?

Station 8: Natural sensations and feelings guide you.

By Station 6 it was not this trail's 5-leg words and story that led you to reconnect by breathing. It was a 4-leg natural attraction, your feelingful attraction to breathe that did this. Nature itself intelligently, feelingly, contacted and guided you in a good way, without using words.

When you sentiently listened to nature's attraction "voice" and reconnected, you felt comfortable and safe.

Naturally and safely feeling good can come from being directly connected to nature through natural attractions, (Logan, 1995). It is very 9-leg important to keep this in mind. It's a secret of how nature produces its perfection through its Natural Attraction "language."

Thinking with 9-legs tells us that connective attraction sensations and feelings are nature's way, an intelligent essence of how nature reaches and nurtures us. How often do you seek and trust fulfilling experiences in nature?

What do you find attractive in the Station above?

Station 9: Nature has no words.

Here's a 5-leg story we often overlook: The natural world is a non-verbal community. It does not use words to communicate. It does not know itself or its members by a name or label. It is non-literate. Nature knows and relates to itself in 4-leg ways.

Like all of nature the desire to breathe has no name. We sense that air exists and we feel our attraction to breathe, however, even though both have no word labels. That's how infants know to breathe when disconnected. That's how your "inner child" or "inner nature" knows it, too, (Cohen, 1995).

Can you learn to 9-leg trust these words and the breathing experience you just had? When you fulfill your natural attraction for air by breathing, nature within and about you, without using words, rewards you by giving you good feelings. Isn't that a form of intelligence?

Doesn't air communicate and make sense by creating a reasonable attraction sensation? Do you trust that this is nature's way? If so, you can trust thoughtful sensory connections with attractions in nature to intelligently help you guide and support your daily life in many ways.

What do you find attractive in the Station above?

Station 10: Nature is multisensory.

Here is another vital secret of nature that is seldom taught in our society. In addition to the sense of desiring to breathe, nature has similarly created and contains at  least 52 other distinct, intelligent, natural attraction 4-leg sensitivities, (Cohen, 1997b). Each of them is like a voice of nature, a strand of the web of life found in some form throughout the global community, (Cohen, 2000). The life wisdom in each strand can produce good feelings in us when we sense the attraction strand.

As with your desire to breathe, in conjunction with natural areas, each of our other natural attractions also feelingly, responsibly communicates with you and guides your relationship with the environment, (Bower, 1999).

Nature also does this on some natural attraction level with every other member of the web of life including minerals. Natural Attractions are nature's language and essence.

In sentient, non-verbal 4-leg ways, you may learn to hear nature's voice, reconnect with nature, enjoy its balance, 5-leg validate its wisdom and feel 9-leg good.

The 53 natural senses that help you accomplish this include senses of sight, sound and smell; gravity, reason and temperature; nurturing, community and trust; empathy, belonging and place; thirst, hunger and motion; compassion, touch and taste, (Cohen, 1995A). Each of these senses offers you enjoyable, trustable feeling signals that blend into a common sense when you connect with nature through them. This includes your connections with human nature, the nature of natural systems in people, too.

What do you find attractive in the Station above?

Station 11: The wisdom of natural attraction sensations.

We don't exclusively own our natural attraction webstring senses and sensitivities. Rather, they are a voice that we share with every species and mineral. They attract the natural community, the web of life, to beneficially flow through us and us through it. This is another secret of nature: every five to seven years every molecule in our body becomes part of the environment and is replaced by a similar molecule from the environment. We become it; it become us. That makes Earth like our other body, our second mother.

Natural Attraction senses wisely balance us personally by balancing themselves and each other. For example, the natural attraction of thirst knows just how much water we need so it regulates us by turning itself on and off appropriately. And although you may be thirsty, without being told verbally, you probably won't drink water that looks bad or has the wrong smell, taste, temperature, color or texture. These additional Natural Attraction senses modify your thirst.

The blending of 53 Natural Attraction sensations is the wisdom of the senses and natural attraction sensitivities. It is nature's story of the eons as told in its sensory language to us and via other forms of attraction to the non-sensuous world.

Natural Attractions in atomic particles, molecules, materials, gases, land, sea and air, and the solar system hold our world together. Our sense of reason recognizes that these natural attractions are real facts of life for if these things were not held together by attractions, they would fall apart and they don't. For this reason, what we call "things" are actually natural attraction relationships manifesting themselves.

What do you find attractive in the Station above?

Station 12: It is your choice.

We are given the natural ability to reason—it is one of our natural attraction senses we share with the global life community. It is an attractive thing to do. The sense of reason enables us to rationally choose or not choose to feel good responsibly and intelligently. We inherently know how to heed and consider nature's voice, our natural attraction senses, our contact with genuine nature. The good feelings they produce guide us.

Although this type of "literacy" is rarely taught or applauded in contemporary society, it is also true that contemporary society is stupidly polluting and destroying the natural systems that support it and does not seem able to stop. That is not natural. It is a way to describe a cancer. A cancer overruns and destroys, rather than cooperatively lives in balance with, its environment.

What do you find attractive in the Station above?

Station 13: You belong.

On a personal level, in nature, as demonstrated by breathing, we get good feelings by directly giving and gaining support from the global community. In that

community, every member, including you, knows that it is very important. In some way, every member is naturally attractive, loved, and included. That is how and why nature does not produce garbage.

On a macro level everything in nature is needed. Nothing natural is thrown away. Alive or "dead," each natural being is naturally attractive, wanted and belongs. That is the reason runaway pollution, abusiveness, violence, loneliness, war and mental illness are virtually unknown in nature. It is why it is reasonable to gain good feelings by becoming fluent in Natural Attractions and thereby consciously reconnect with nature. It is also why some people believe that nature is a good example of unconditional love in action. On a macro level, nature leaves nothing out; everything is attractive, belongs and is wanted.

SUMMARY: Reconnecting with nature by becoming literate in Natural Attraction is a vital, intelligent and responsible way to safely gain fulfillment. By activating multiple natural attraction senses, the reconnecting process helps our sense of reason rebuild

our personal relationships as well as our society, economics, and the environment. It helps our thinking establish a communion and partnership with nature. Being reasonable, it recognizes that our thinking is our destiny.

What do you find attractive in the Station above?

Station 14: Nature pulls things together.

Here is another well kept secret of nature: At every level, the global life community is built upon many mutually beneficial but vastly different Natural Attraction callings and relationships. This process is so effective that the greater the creativity, diversity, and differences of each individual community member, the stronger the whole community becomes. It is as if each diverse part of nature knows something special about life so that collectively the web of life is an intercommunicating super intelligence, attraction or love, a global brain. Our inner nature inherits and trusts this natural attraction, cooperative, wisdom. As with air, it biologically and emotionally enjoys, encourages and operates from it. Our inner self always expects to be loved and supported by natural attractions simply because that is nature's way.

What do you find attractive in the Station above?

Station 15: Effects of disconnecting.

The value of our natural attraction loves and their intelligence is often hidden from our awareness by cultural 5-leg stories that tell us love is not scientific or objective; we should avoid, disconnect from, or conquer nature within and around us. Doing this often gains us money, approval and status. The purpose of science has long been to conquer nature. The economics of consumerism drives us to convert nature into cultural objects. Even in our Bible, God tells humanity to subdue Earth and dominate it. But is all this reasonable considering its destructive effects?

We live over 95% of our lives indoors; 99.9% of our thinking consists of verbal, not sensory, Natural Attraction, consciousness. That de-energizes our awareness of Natural Attractions. In our extremely nature-separated, indoor world our stories make it practically taboo to sensuously reconnect with and trust nature. We learn (read: "are brainwashed") instead to dance to misleading, nature-conquering, labels, stories and acts. Salaries, high grades and prestige reward us for doing this dance. However, the dance further separates us from nature's balance, intelligence and fulfillment, thereby promoting many runaway personal, social and environmental disorders.

What do you find attractive in the Station above?

Station 16: You are in charge of how you feel.

Just as when you inhaled air, you always have the option to safely feel comfortable by reconnecting with nature through Natural Attractions. You can do this even when a story within or around you stresses you by telling you to do otherwise.

An important example: once you complete this nature trail, do the first part of it again. When you come to Station 4, you now know the 5-leg story there will tell you not to breathe. You also know that heeding that story will disconnect you from nature and produce uncomfortable 4-leg suffocation feelings. This time, think with nature. Choose not to pay attention to that disconnecting story at Station 4. Seek permission from nature and your body to stop breathing. If you don't obtain their consent, i.e., it does not feel attractive to stop, then don't stop breathing. Instead choose to pay attention to what Natural Attractions tell you, what naturally feels safe, attractive and worthwhile to you as part of the global life community. Be 9-leg responsible by choosing to breathe in connective consent with the Natural Attraction voice of your body and your planetary mother, Earth. Cooperate with nature by sustaining your natural integrity, good feelings and the Earth community. Help your sense of reason heed the natural logic of the psyche.

SUMMARY: When we ignore or divert our natural attractions to nature, we lose contact with the voice and intelligence in nature that knows how to sustain and regenerate us as responsible citizens of the global life community that lies within and around us.

What do you find attractive in the Station above?

Station 17: Non-verbal learning, relating and knowing.

Reminder: The natural world produces its beauty, peace and balance through non-verbal attraction relationships and callings. You can personally learn to choose to reconnect to this sensory form of "higher power." It fulfills you, relieves stress and helps recovery from social and medical problems. You can easily teach others how to reconnect with it, too.

This interpretative nature trail contains only one nature-reconnecting activity. There are an additional 128 published activities you can do and teach at your convenience. Each further reconnects you with nature

and empowers you to think and relate in responsible ways that feel good.

Each activity helps you seek consent, think more reasonably and make sense in 53 natural sensory ways, building friendships in the process, (Cohen, 1993) Online, you can take courses or obtain Certification or BS, MS or Ph.D. degrees and scholarships in this Natural Systems Thinking Process (NSTP). You learn how to  do it and share it with other people and learn from their experiences, too. This is important because without contact and support, in our nature-disconnected society, our nature connections often don't have enough energy to remain in our thinking and we revert to destructive ways. NSTP enables you to prevent this from happening.

As we strengthen our natural attraction senses, they become more alive in our consciousness. We begin to safely think with nature's intelligence, in a way that is more feeling, sensible and sensitive to people and the environment. This helps us feel more alive and make sense of our lives. For this reason, many educators, counselors and leaders advocate and use nature-reconnecting activities. It is why every form of education, counseling and healing works better when it is in contact with attractions in nature. It is why we bring flowers to sick people and pets increase our wellness and sanity.

What do you find attractive in the Station above?

Station 18: What have you learned here?

This nature-reconnecting trail is a structured 9-leg educational tool. It attempts to teach you that you inherit from nature at least 53 natural webstring attraction senses and feelings. Like the sense of respiration, they are sensible natural 4-leg communications that non-verbally but responsibly enable you to connect your 5-leg thinking to nature's intelligence because they are an essence of that intelligence. In our nature-disconnected way of life this often sounds very strange, foreign or foolish. However, when connected to nature, like breathing, our natural attractions not only feel good, they wisely 9-leg sustain and balance our thinking, psyche and spirit, just as they balance the natural world. This is significant because our thinking is our destiny.

When we fulfill our Natural Attractions to breathe clean air, drink pure water and eat uncontaminated food, we enjoy worthwhile, healthy satisfactions. Similarly, safely reconnecting with nature through our many other natural sensory attractions is also fulfilling, healthy and responsible. It is what every other species on Earth does. Natural people(s) do it, too. NSTP reconnecting lets nature help us recycle our destructive ways of thinking and relating.

The word consensus means "to feel with many senses together." Because nature-centered communities think by consensus while in contact with nature, they don't produce our runway personal, social and environmental problems, (Bower, 1995.)

What do you find attractive in the Station above?

Station 19: Something to think about.

Reminder, nature consists of 4-leg, non-verbal, webstring attraction relationships, but we learn to mostly think and communicate in the 5-leg abstract of words and stories. Abstracts are shortcuts that often subdivide and replace the whole of life. That separation subdivides our thinking from nature's perfections and leads us to produce our many problems.

We need to listen to our natural senses and feelings to discover how nature works. To live and relate more harmoniously it makes sense to reconnect with nature and seek its consent as part of the way we think.

Have you ever noticed that our inherent natural intelligence, loves and values are often lost to nature-conquering images, stories and labels that demean them. For example, in uncomplimentary ways, our natural attraction senses are often called *subjective, unscientific, environmentalist, imagination, fuzzy thinking, immature, crazy, non-academic, flaky, childish, tree hugging, unimportant, spiritual, foolish, nostalgia, fantasy,*  *unreasonable, touchy-feely, drives, needs,* or *instincts.*

Consider this: Isn't our sensory natural attraction to air just as vital and real as air itself? Just as air is a scientific fact, isn't the sensation of our natural love to breathe air an equally scientific fact? Isn't it polluted thinking, bad science and limited consciousness to prejudicially value material facts while devaluing sensory facts?

Trust your experiences. You can think, learn and know using more than just verbal language and "five senses." You can learn to think and speak in 53 multisensory, Natural Attraction ways with nature in

people and places, relate more responsibly, and feel better too.

What do you find attractive in the Station above?

Station 20: No need to stop now.

This trail contains one activity that helps you think and feel with nature. You can continue learning that process. An additional 127 activities are found in the self-guiding training books *Einstein's World, Reconnecting With Nature* and *Well Mind, Well Earth.* An optional, online email course accompanies each of these books along with optional professional or academic independent study credit and distance learning certification and degree programs. A good introduction to the books and courses is available through links at www.ecopsych.com.

You may safely, anonymously chat and share attractive nature-connecting experiences with others at our workshops and/or by joining our discussion list. You can request the assistance of a Project NatureConnect guide to share doing the activities with you.

What do you find attractive in the Station above?

Station 21: Your conclusion?

Researchers suggest that nature consists of resonant attraction connections between natural things, (Wald, 1985, Langer, 1995.) The deteriorating state of Earth and people signals that we and the environment are at risk. Our thinking is excessively separated from nature within and around us. We must consciously reunite it with natural systems. Doing nature-reconnecting activities helps make this happen. They offer an urgently needed service and vast economic benefits.

Interestingly, the word for breathing and sharing spirit together is "conspire." Shouldn't we learn how to conspire to support life and our lives on Earth rather than dance on the deck of our sinking ship?

What do you find attractive in the Station above?

Station 22: An extra reward.

You can do this nature-reconnecting activity and build some lasting, rewarding relationships.

Part 1: Go to the most attractive natural plant, animal, mineral or place that you can conveniently find. A "weed," potted plant or aquarium will do if a park or sanctuary is not available. Go to nature in reality, not to a story, artifact, picture, video, visualization, spirit, memory or other likeness of nature. With respect to nature and its balanced eons of life experience, there is no substitute for the real thing.

Be sure not to get too close to any natural area or thing that may irritate, hurt or be unhealthy for you. In nature, that is not attractive.

Part 2: Find an immediate natural attraction(s) for you at this natural site and for ten minutes get to know them non-verbally. Erase labels or other mental chatter that accompany them or prevent it from occurring by repeating the words "natural attraction" as you do this  activity. With your eyes closed become aware of it or them through some of your other inherent natural attraction callings, senses and feelings, senses such these 28 of the 53 that our natural systems can register:

sight   touch   taste   smell   sound companionship   motion   nurturing community   trust   empathy   belonging   place reason   peace   texture   gravity   consciousness beauty   color   pleasure   appreciation   form respiration   temperature   distance.

Keep the experience nameless so that it remains in nature's sensory attraction voice.

Then repeat this experience with your eyes open.

Part 3: Now translate into 9-leg English from Natural Attraction. In a total of 400 words or less, write:

a) What happened.

b) What you sense, think and feel from doing this activity.

c) Why you think the activity led you to feel as you do.

ONLINE COURSE PARTICIPANTS
Send Part 3 to your course member Interact Group.

Anybody can send their paragraphs to the NatureConnect Discussion List (http://www.ecospych.com/list.html) along with a note asking people there to share, enjoy and respond to your submission by telling you what they may have learned from it, of how it affected them when they read it. You will make 9-leg contact with a group of people who are unified by the connections with nature that they hold in common.

You may also send your paragraphs to anybody else you think might appreciate them. Ask them to respond.

Your nature-connected thoughts and feelings may connect you with the Natural Attractions of others, and vice versa, especially as a letter to a local news editor. This process is a good way to build or strengthen relationships on-line or in your community and family.

For educational purposes only, we reserve the right to post your entry to our newsletter readers anonymously, or with your name if you so choose.

If learning to master and use the process of reconnecting with nature is of interest to you, the best possible way to proceed is by taking a short Orientation Course online. You can optionally transfer it into your academic or professional training curriculum. You can use it as part of our cooperatively run, low cost, degree program, too.

Another activity. If you want to do more with the written results you obtained on the trail stops above, do this activity:

1. Read through your notes that you wrote from the box attractions on the Trail or repeat the Trail and this time make Attraction notes. Select the most attractive things you found and make a list of them.

2. Obtain permission from a natural area to visit it and learn from it. Instructions for doing this are found in the Global Wellness and Unity activity (Chapter 4)

3. Once you have gained the area's consent, read one of your Attractions and see if you can find an example of this Attraction taking place in the natural area you are visiting.

4. Note if some Attraction in the area comes to your attention with respect to the attraction you shared with it. Then repeat this process with other attractions you located "on the Trail." Share this experience with others and discover what they find attractive about it.

* * * * *

Return to the beginning of this Nature Trail and do it again. You'll find its just as interesting and worthwhile as the first time. Like the air you may still be overlooking as you read these words, there's lots to learn.

References
Adler, B. (1995.) Providing the data to protect biodiversity. Science News Vol. 148, No. 21 p. 326 Washington DC: Science Service Inc,

Bower, B. (1995.) Return of the group. Science News, Vol. 148, No. 21 p. 328. Washington DC, Science Service Inc.

Bower, B. (1999.) Simple Minds, Smart Choices. Science News, Vol. 155, No. 22 p. 348. Washington DC: Science Service Inc.

Cohen, M.J.(2000.) Nature Connected Psychology: The Natural Systems Thinking Process, Greenwich Journal of

Science and Technology, Volume 1, Number 1, June 2000. Norfolk Island, Australia: Greenwich University, http://www.ecopsych.com/natpsych.html

Cohen, M. J. (1997.) Well Mind, Well Earth: 109 environmentally sensitive activities for stress management, spirit and self-esteem. PO Box 1605, Friday Harbor, WA, Project NatureConnect.

Cohen, M. J. (1997b.) Reconnecting With Nature: Finding wellness through restoring your bond with the Earth. (P.O. Box 1605, Friday Harbor WA,) Corvallis OR, Ecopress.

Cohen, M. J. (1995.) Counseling and Nature: The greening of psychotherapy. Interpsych News. Internet, http://www.ecopsych.com/~nature/counseling.html

Langer, W. (1995.) Watching a young star eat. Science News, Vol. 148, No. 21 p. 334. Washington DC: Science Service Inc.

Logan, R. (1995.) Healing Ourselves and the World Through Applied Ecopsychology. Common Future Magazine, Corvallis, OR. http://www.ecopsych.com/theory.html

Wald, G. (1985.) in Cohen, M. J. Proceedings: Is the Earth a Living Organism? Sharon, CT: National Audubon Society.

Optionally complete this summary evaluation:

SUMMARY STATEMENT F: In our society, our thinking has become destructively dependent on nature disconnecting words and stories.

Either in your journal, or on a piece of paper, record the SUMMARY letter code (F) along with the number on the continuum scale below that indicates the extent of your agreement with the summary statement:

1	2	3	4	5	6	7	8	9	10
disagree				partially agree				fully agree	

Record and retain your score.

Supportive Reading

A Lesson In Belonging
Michael J. Cohen

Indigenous Elders and healers are deeply rooted in their spiritual ways and tribal protocol. For this reason, a conflicting mixture of trepidation and honor filled me when I accepted an invitation to participate in the Belonging to Mother Earth Indigenous People's Conference in October, 1998. The purpose for this gathering of nature connected spiritual people from remote parts of the world was to help them teach their wisdom and healing powers to the 600 members of the public in attendance. My role was to show them and the attendees how to use the Natural Systems Thinking Process as a means to close the destructive gap that exists between people of different cultures and that separates modern humanity from nature, too.

Although most people acknowledge that we are psychologically bonded to a way of thinking that produces the noxious personal and environmental effects of our schisms, few have the motivation to risk their emotional safety to produce greater interspecies and intercultural connectedness. My goal was to introduce an Earth connected interaction process that dependably, without pain, reconnected communities, as of old. This proved to be highly successful for those who were open to the process. However, it was my expertise as a traditional musician that identified where we have to go and how we may get there.

Many of the attending shamans and medicine people use music as part of their rituals. Their music and dance were performed, intact, as evening programs throughout the week. As did the others, I, too, volunteered my services as a veteran Anglo American folk song artist. They turned me down. "I was not an indigenous person," they said. Many members of the gathering disagreed with this decision and urged me to make efforts to correct it. "If we are here to heal the Earth in a good way, we must accept contributions from all members of the Earth community, including citizens of Western society," they argued. With this  rationale, I made further efforts to be included in the program. Finally its producer, a member of the Sioux Nation, somehow included me by the third evening of the five-day conference.

The challenge for the world, the conference and every citizen of Earth became obvious in the evenings that followed. The performers had their special time needs to properly present their sacred art, yet they also knew time was limited and other participants needed to be accommodated. A discomforting form of chaos followed. While performers would be on stage explaining to the audience the time pressure, and preaching how their heart-felt Earth rituals produced trust and unity, they necessarily ran well over their allotted time on-stage thereby eliminating the participation of others and causing mistrust, irritation and disunity. The producer pleaded helplessness; it would be unconscionable for him to interrupt anybody's sacred presentation. He held a meeting of all the performers the following day. They pledged to each other and him to present their programs within a time frame they consented to. Within eight hours they again broke their pledges by surpassing their consensual time allotments in order to meet the spiritual parameters of their performance. The trust and unity they were dedicated to building became a sham, yet the delighted audience was never aware of the situation.

On the final evening, the producer solved the problem by prohibiting ceremonial performances. Instead, he requested that music only be presented in celebration of this moment: of the conference and its amazing participants. He personally orchestrated the evening and performers; minute by minute, nobody was left out, all belonged. A special spirit of elation bound together by music and dance came into being and we created a unifying occasion of extraordinary proportions. The drums beat together from the Congo, rain forests and Siberia for most of the night.

The producer had become a catalyst that helped this unifying spiritual moment occur. He acted out the same role that is played by the Natural Systems Thinking Process when it is used in our daily lives. The Process introduces Earth's web of life, the interconnected animal, plant and mineral kingdom, into our consciousness and immediate relationships. Like the producer, and as throughout the eons, the web embraces all. It becomes the story to heed for living in the moment. This orchestrates individual and global unity without producing garbage; nothing is left out. When engaged in the process, everything senses it belongs.

Thoughtful Verbalization
These instructions are located on the last page of this book. Once you complete them, continue with the course.

Chapter Seven

Webstring Self-Discovery

The Experience

This is a two-section reconnecting activity you can do to help your new brain discover and validate your connections with the web of life within and around you.

SECTION 1: Go to an attractive plant, animal, mineral or place in a natural area. Try not to impose on it. As per Chapter 4, thankfully ask for its permission to become involved with it. Gain its consent to help you with this activity.

Do the following activity once you are sure the natural thing you selected continues to give you some sort of comfortable, attractive good feeling. Be sure that you like this natural attraction.

Write down what thing or webstring in this area you like and why. Make this a simple response as follows:

I like (am attracted to, or love) this (1) _____ (plant, animal, mineral, place, thing, sensation)
because it (2)_____. (Complete this sentence fully. State why you like (or love) the natural attraction and enter that reason in (2). Notice that you have produced a webstring connected statement.)

Copy the "because (2)" statement you wrote above and be ready to use it elsewhere. Then go to the end of this chapter and continue the activity there in SECTION 2. Upon its completion, you will be instructed to return here to do the short Supportive Reading below.

B. Supportive Reading

This Self-Discovery activity can serve as an indicator. People who find value in it show that they trust their non-verbal self and attractions to some extent. That is key in living in balance with nature within and around us. Non-verbal attraction relationships are an essence of the natural world and its eons of creation and sustainability.

As mentioned earlier, since we produce artificial substitutes for parts of nature we have lost, we, too often, forget that there is no known substitute for nature, the real thing and its intelligent, life supportive, non-literate ways. Each substitute we create falls short of nature's perfection, thus producing pollution, garbage and relationship disorders. Wildlife flees our insensitivity as do people. We feel lonely. We accurately sense that we don't belong. In this Self-Discovery activity we choose to risk making 4-leg contact with nature and then 5-leg translate it into a 9-leg statement. I say "risk" because many folks who do these activities want to do them in private. They feel foolish or ashamed about what other people will think if they are seen hugging a tree or seeking consent from an attractive cloud to ask it an important question. We do not have these inhibitions as children; we learned them from being rejected for these behaviors and we now want to protect ourselves from having these past rejections activated into consciousness or from being rejected again by a stranger or neighbor. Too much of our lives are spent protecting or dancing to this nature disconnection hurt we subconsciously carry.

Some environmentally enlightened friends of Dr. Cohen own land that lies next to a national park. Recently, he tried to convince them not to clear cut their parcel for the big dollars to be made in second home building. The glazed look on their faces indicated his suggestion did not register. Missing in their mentality were  the webstrings necessary to modify their action.

The outlooks of Cohen's friends remind us of a man who was pinned in the wreckage of a train. Only his upper torso was visible. During his rescue he said he felt OK; he even joked with his rescuers. Then he died. When they freed his body, they found his legs had been amputated. Traumatic shock to many webstrings had prevented him from being aware of his demise.

Cohen's clear cutting friends, with respect to their relationship with nature, were similarly in traumatic shock. So are most members of industrial society. In far too many of us, that glazed look not only appears with respect to our abuse of the environment, it also appears with respect to our abuse of substances and each other.

We have earlier called attention to the phenomenon that nature does not display our runaway problems. Biologically and psychologically, every human being is to nature as our leg is to our body, or our toe is to our hand. We are born of, and consist of the least 53 natural sensory relationship webstring attractions that pervade the natural world. Our troubles result from socialization that educates us to think differently than how nature's webstring attractions work.

Unlike members of nature-centered cultures, at birth we are physically and emotionally "amputated" from the environment. Our traumatic separation desensitizes us to natural life, including the nature of our children, each other and our inner nature. We uncontrollably violate the world with the anger and frustration from our lack of natural fulfillment and wisdom and the subconscious hurt we feel and protect from further irritation. Often, to our cost, we emotionally attach, addict to or depend on persons or substances that fulfill our wanting, nature-disconnected senses. With respect to nature, we live in a state of Traumatic Psychological Shock (TPS). It pollutes healthy reasoning, environments and budgets. It is reversed by nurturing and restoring our 53 natural senses back to wellness and contact with Earth. We have lost conscious sensory contact with our living planet and community. How many of us can stand up before a group of strangers or neighbors and unashamedly say we fully love Planet Earth or nature without getting repercussions?

Our study of 4237 participants shows that psychologically, our excessive indoor upbringing makes us indoor addicts. Our earth-separated New-Brain literacy overpowers our natural thinking processes. Through TPS, it subdues eons of natural beauty, balance and profound Old-Brain sensitivities. Nature-assaulting stories flood our consciousness, overriding, rather than

integrating, the web of life's intelligent contribution. Invasiveness and abusiveness often become our destiny. We live with, and act out, their stress and discomfort. We learn to shrug our shoulders and say, "That's life." Our nature-conquering society stops us from learning that "That's life within our Earth-disconnected cultural cage, socialization and thinking." In contrast, a student with a high Eco IQ did a nature-connecting activity on the Introductory Course. Consider the following repeatable, teachable, discovery that resulted. What might Earth and our interpersonal relationships be like if many people learned to do and teach these activities?

Participant A:

"As I continued this special forest activity, I found myself attracted to the various songs of the birds and then gradually to the various stones and nuts and shells in the path. I would stop in the path, pick up the stone, admire its beauty and then feel

clearly called to return it to its appropriate place. So often other times I have felt I needed to put it in my pocket and carry it home. Now, through the activity, I had a real sense of appreciating each rock, each shell, each leaf in its place for the time I was there. I felt suddenly freed from the need to possess something. I had a growing sense of letting things be and to just be still and glory in the fullness of the moment. As I allowed myself to connect, appreciate, thank and move on with so much of what surrounded me, I felt a letting go into being present. In this transformation, I began to feel I was part of the scene more, not my other self that needed to possess. I learned that I do not need to possess something to have the joy of it."

Participant B:

"Your earlier questioning of the work place sounds so familiar but we have our cultural story that tells us we need to maintain in our present society. I find daily that I am changing things and getting back to more basic life choices. I think each little one counts. These changes feel so good. I find that I want less matcrial things these days."

Visit the Survey of Participants (Prerequisite Section, Page 31). It shows that the Natural Systems Thinking Process inexpensively reverses TPS. It strengthens creativity, critical thinking and self-esteem. Environmental literacy, citizenship, and learning abilities increase while apathy and "extravagant clear cutting" wane. Test results affirm observations that the process reduces our abuse of Earth and people as well as substance abuse, depression, sleeplessness, anger and loneliness. The Process promotes local and global citizenship, the environment and the economy. Our spirit soars and natural areas gain added value.

SECTION 2
(continued from SECTION 1)

Be sure you have completed Section 1 before doing this section.

Instructions:

Place the phrase "I like (or love) myself because" in front of (2), the "because " clause of the sentence that you just wrote in SECTION 1.

I like (or love) myself (myself is substituted for the part 1 attraction) because (2)_____. Now read the sentence including the new prefix: "I like (or love) myself because"_____(2) aloud. Read it to others, if possible. Sometimes it is a metaphor for what you and your attraction hold in common. Search for that attraction.

How does the whole sentence feel? Does it describe part of you? For example: "I like the tree because it is beautiful and strong," becomes "I like myself because I am beautiful and strong." You will find that relationship somewhere in the statement you produce. Here's why you should trust it:

You are a seamless continuation of nature and the web of life. This revised sentence "tricks" your nature disconnected reason and language senses to become more conscious of the natural systems in you. Can you validate that the changed sentence: "I like (or love) myself because (2)_____" describes some aspect of yourself, your inner child or nature. How do you feel about yourself in this light? Does it feel right? You can be absolutely sure that some part of you is described by this sentence. That part is the webstring in you that found the webstring in nature attractive in the first place.

If reading the sentence makes you feel uncomfortable, search your life for at least one incident, example or dream relating to the sentence that feels right or accurate. Perhaps you can imagine or create one, if necessary. You might ask a friend to help you find this part of yourself. Friends usually can see past your self-doubts.

Your sentence may be a metaphor. Try to find examples of parts of yourself that accurately match this metaphor. Remember that sometimes you have been taught to deny them because they are your nature and, like a weed, nature is to be conquered, not supported. For this reason, many people have trouble admitting shamelessly they are beautiful, strong, worthy, etc.

Additional activities in the Project NatureConnect courses and books will help you reconnect discomforting parts of you with nature and let nature nurture them so that they feel comfortable to you.

You will become more immune to nature desensitized people and they will become more respectful of you.

When you are with other people, you can do this same activity with their inner nature. You can also reverse the activity. Find some natural part of yourself that you like or love and see if you can discover and speak to that part of you in another person or a natural area. This also helps build relationships.

To find NSTP friends, send this activity to a person as a unique greeting card or gift via the internet at http://www.ecopsych.com/naturelov30greet.html. It is worth your while to visit this site. Use it as a tool in your work or relationships. Send it to people and discover their response to it. Then connect to the webstrings in them that attract you.

Optionally complete this summary evaluation:
SUMMARY G: It is reasonable to unashamedly have our senses of reason, language and consciousness validate our hidden webstring connections with nature and enjoy the responsible rewards this whole brain connection produces.

Either in your journal, or on a piece of paper, record the SUMMARY letter code (G) along with the number on the continuum scale below that indicates the extent of your agreement with the Summary Statement:

1	2	3	4	5	6	7	8	9	10
disagree				partially agree			fully agree		

Record and retain your score.

Thoughtful Verbalization

These instructions are located on the last page of this book. Once you complete them, return to this page.

Optional:

Read Chapter 6 in *Reconnecting With Nature* for additional information about the relationship of words to webstrings. (You need not do the activity there for this course).

Chapter Eight

Summary Activities

Discover if you have the ability to benefit from making webstrings more vibrant in your thinking and relationships. Try this simple two-part activity:

Rationale:

The web of life can be seen, in story, as a webstring common ground that has an integrity of its own, even though it is produced by, and in turn supports, a wide diversity of plants, animals, minerals and webstrings. It is similar to luke warm water resulting from a mixture of very hot and very cold water. No matter its temperature, however, hot, medium, or cold, water is water; that is an integrity held in common.

Do this temperature-webstring activity:

1. Get three bowls. Place hot water in one, cold water in the second, and medium temperature water in the third. The hot and cold water should not reach the range of being painful.

2. Connect with diversity. Place one hand in the cold water, the other hand in the hot water and leave them there for a minute or more. Then plunge both hands into the medium temperature water at the same time.

What happens during the plunge? Usually the temperature webstring in the cold hand register the luke warm water as hot while the other hand finds the water cold. How do you explain this with respect to webstrings and bonding to environments and stories? What role does the webstring of time play? Would the effect be the same if your hands were only in the hot and cold water for two seconds?

Let us now apply this phenomenon to how we know nature and webstrings:

The Mind in Nature Activity:

Study the image for a few moments. If you want to view it in color, look at the back cover of this book. This pottery design was made almost 1000 years ago by a Mimbres person in the American Southwest. What do you think he or she had in mind with this drawing?

Part of you full well knows the answer. Biologically, this Mimbres person was identical to you;0 you could have had children together. This is similar to the medium temperature water.

The biological part of you, natural systems in you, operates through webstrings and may understand the nature-connected pottery design. However, today, we and Earth are in hot water. We have ignited a flaming assault on most natural things to the point that we call their integrity and the web of life a "resource." Nature is the place we too often dump our garbage. Along with the environment, the webstring part of you has also been burnt, subdued and deteriorated by contemporary ways. No longer in your awareness, many webstrings now lie buried alive, smothered within you, overlaid by the sizzling conquer-nature technological and material way of thinking that excessively produces our nature separated indoor ways.

On average, over 99.9% of our lifetime is spent thinking and living in our "hot" nature-separated life-styles, consciously disconnected from webstrings. Through the hot story of contemporary ways of knowing, although we are biologically and psychologically born in nature's supportive mild water, you mostly know yourself and the world as hot. However, it is nature's mild way of knowing and relating that creates and sustains the natural world's diverse balance and beauty, including pure water.

Archeologists report that Mimbres thinking was not in contact with the horse, gun or metal for Contemporary Thinking had not yet come to America. Mimbres people, and those who preceded them, evidently knew little of the way we, today, meet the callings of survival. Foreign to Mimbres were the "hot " background of our familiar cultural objects such as electric power, indoor plumbing, cars, air conditioners, airplanes, radio, TV, computers, shopping malls, photography, newspapers, pencils, books, etc. There was no telephone, no written language, no metal. Without them, they knew and touched the supportive, warm womb of nature.

Today, when we ask contemporary people to draw a picture of what is in their head, be they Native Americans or not, the picture usually contains money, conflict, cultural loves, technologies, sex, tranquilizers and professional skills. Rarely does the picture look like the Mimbres drawing. However, those of us who have had even one good experience in nature know the difference between how it feels to have our psyche in nature versus the stress of a shopping mall, school, workplace, or, too often, family.

Perhaps the pottery design reflects what we have forgotten due to our separation from long-term conscious contact with webstrings in nature. A millennium ago, this ancient person seems to depict that our being, psyche and nature are identical. Deep within us we have the inherent biological ability to creatively think and relate with the natural balance and beauty of webstrings. This is significant because that way of thinking does and did not produce the stress and problems of modern life that deteriorate the wellness of people and the environment.

To see the results of the nature-disconnected "hot" way we are taught to think while estranged from contact with nature's mild reality, see Appendix B.

We can choose to be sensible. We can let our webstring of reason help us enjoy the integrity and benefits of our inherent natural way of knowing and thereby improve our relationships with self, society and the environment. To this end, try this activity:

ACTIVITY

1. Look at the Mimbres Pottery Design on the back cover of this book.

2. Go to a natural area that attracts you: backyard, park or sanctuary.

3. Gain consent from this area to help you draw a picture of your webstring way of knowing, as of old.

4. Locate immediate attractions in this natural area: shapes, sounds, odors, colors, motions, feelings that you like. Each is a webstring. Try doing this with your eyes closed, too. Each time you find a webstring attraction, in your imagination, replace the bird in the Mimbres design with that natural attraction, for example, webstrings energized by a leaf, brook, tree, flower, star, mountain or the wind. Draw in webstrings of gravity, temperature, nurturing, trust, beauty.

5. Notice that in this activity nature itself is helping you locate and register in your awareness your webstring attraction connections. Through this and 124 other nature-reconnecting activities, webstrings can become alive and well in your psyche. You can rely on them to trigger good feelings and help your thinking and relationships come into balance.

6. People often lastingly feel more relaxed, centered and grounded upon completing this activity. When they share the experience, they find it builds unifying webstring relationships with people and places in new ways. That is one of the special qualities of mild water; it is comfortable to hot or cold alike.

7. Write a paragraph or two about what was attractive to you in doing this activity.

8. Optionally send a self-addressed envelope and a dollar bill for obtaining your small, lapel button that is a picture of the Mimbres design. (Webstring Button, P.O. Box 1605, Friday Harbor, WA 98250)

9. Wear the button for 3 days as a lapel button at work, school and home. Report back to your Interact group (if you taking the course online) what kind of responses you received from doing it and whether it helped you and others gain more benefits from webstrings.

You may occasionally pin the button to your sleeve, and use it to repeat the activity and gain its benefits whenever you want. You can look at the button and thereby help your webstring of time revive some of the webstrings you enjoyed during the activity. You can pin the button on your shirt as a conversation piece to encourage others to better know you and your webstring connections with nature.

10. Acts are facts. If you are in the online Orientation Course, obtaining and experimenting with the button is a 9-leg act generated by your webstring of reason. It also signifies that you have completed the course core material and may now proceed to the Evaluation portion of the program.

A letter received:

"I received my beautiful webstring button in the mail this weekend. It couldn't have arrived at a more perfect time. Tomorrow is the two year anniversary of the death of John Denver. Everyone (internationally) is wearing a green ribbon this week in his memory. In particular, for what he did for the environment. I attached the ribbon to my clothes this morning by using by webstrings button. It's beautiful. And what a compliment to each other. I've already been asked many times today what it means. It's a great way to open the door to nature/ environment/connectedness in a non-threatening way. It also serves as a reminder to myself. I find myself getting 'high strung' (webstring irritated, I hate the word stressed) during the day. I need to have a visual reminder of what is REALLY important."

- **Teresa**

Summary of Techniques

"If you count a wolf's tail as one of its legs, how many legs does a wolf have?"

A distinct breach in consciousness exists between 4-leg and 5-leg (Old and New-Brain) thinking. No matter the excellence of 5-leg thinking, it alone can not and will not breach this gap because discussion is verbal and nature is a non-verbal phenomenon with a proven, long established integrity of its own. It is 5-leg arrogance to believe the New Brain will find a perfection greater that nature's. To the contrary, today's invention often becomes tomorrow's unsolvable problem.

To be known, nature must be known on its own non-verbal, sensory terms and then translated. It is not about to globally start learning to communicate using the words of English or any other language.

The 4-leg versus 5-leg breach remains until 5-leg folks do the NSTP activities and meld words and thinking into webstrings that unify. It is, too often, a waste of time to explain the value of reconnecting with nature to people who will not do the activities in full. We have found no shortcut for them that does not usually produce another breach of some kind at a later date.

REVIEW:

To operate properly, NSTP requires that each of the following operants be used as each addresses some aspect of our disconnection from nature:

1) CONTACT: Let Natural Attractions lead you. Make a safe, non-verbal, sensory (Old Brain), contact with an attractive, natural area or thing. Call one or more senses that were energized in this activity "webstring attraction energies" and note how doing this felt.

2) CONSENT: Sensitively, through attraction time, obtain permission from a natural area to visit it, be it a wilderness or aquarium, (as per Chapter Four).

3) FEEL: Recognize that contact with natural attractions feels good. Thank the Natural Attraction you found and the webstring(s) involved for the valuable feelings and information they have provided.

4) TRUST: Trust the thoughts and feelings arising from the contact.

5) VALIDATE: Write, in reasonable language (New-Brain), your thoughts and feelings from the Old-Brain experience to produce 9-leg communication and reflection.

6) READ aloud what you wrote. Note that your translation is intelligent, enjoyable and honest.

7) SHARE your nature-connected story with other consenting people, personally or via the Internet. Encourage them to let you know what they may have found attractive in your message to them and continue this relationship with them as long as it feels attractive.

8) OBSERVE that you now feel less stressed, that your nature-connected story builds supportive contacts and closer relationships with people and the environment.

9) ACT to stop your discomfort from abusive or exploitative relationships with nature or your inner nature. Insist on receiving and giving permission to relate before interacting.

10) RECOGNIZE that you own this nature-reconnecting activity; you may repeatedly use and teach it to benefit yourself, others and the environment.

11) IDENTIFY what reasonable things you will put into the trustable, uncontaminated thought and feeling room you have built into your psyche.

12) WRITE one or two keywords that convey what important thing you learned from this assignment.

13) WRITE one or more complete, single, short, power sentence "quotes" that convey a significant contribution that this assignment makes to improving relationships.

14) ENJOY a minimum of one night's sleep (integrating dream time) before doing the next activity.

15) REVIEW (optional) your Eco IQ, and NSTP Knowledge scores. Summarize and change the scores on those that may have increased or strengthened due to this activity or other growth experiences.

16) REMEMBER that you learn this material much better by teaching it.

Summary of Process Basics:

Below are nine basics of the Natural Systems Thinking Process that help people solve the personal, social and environmental problems that result from the difference between the disconnected way we learn to think and how nature works. Please share how you would you edit, add to or modify them.

Rationale:

The heart of our unsolvable problems is psychological. We are in denial. We deny that we are addicted to a story that says for us to live we must conquer, exploit and subdue nature, including our inherent human nature. Every other part of nature survives in balance through attractions that unite, build and sustain consensual, mutually supportive relationships. NSTP enables us to think and act this way by identifying and addressing our denial and addiction.

1. Nature can be seen as a unifying attraction process that organizes, preserves and regenerates itself to produce an optimum of life, diversity and balanced cooperation without producing garbage, madness or death as we know it. Nature's way of expressing love prohibits the pollution, abusiveness and stress that deteriorate life.

2. We are born part of and attached to nature but learn to spend 99.9% of our conscious time and thought detached/disconnected from nature. Our psyche is dismembered from its origins. It silently suffers its profound loss of contact with its nurturing sensory and sensibility roots in nature's ways and intelligence. However, any word or incident that reminds us of our psychological dismemberment breaks the silence. It triggers the emotional pain of it into consciousness and we feel it. As reflected by the state of the world, indoors or outdoors, our mentality is often guarded, stressed, ill, wanting and destructive due to our painful deficiency of nature's peace, wisdom and beauty.

3. When we provide material, social or financial rewards for nature-disconnecting stories and technologies, we become psychologically bonded to them and their destructive effects. Things that experience these effects suffer.

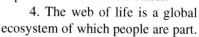

4. The web of life is a global ecosystem of which people are part. To be part of a system one must in some way be in communication with the system. The Natural Systems Thinking Process enables a person to restore their inherent 53-sense ability to consciously register, enjoy, and respond to communication with nature. It accomplishes this by helping us bring into our awareness the webstring attraction loves that we share with the web of life and make sensory contact with them in nature, backyard or back country.

5. People experience webstrings as sensory attractions; uncomfortable sensations are webstrings attracting us to find and follow additional webstrings.

6. Attractiveness is conscious of itself. When people think in consent and connection with webstrings they experience an attractive global consciousness that leads to unity at every level of endeavor.

7. There is an age old purpose and non-verbal process that sustains nature's web of life and its members, including people. That attractive purpose and process is to support life in balance. In this regard there are no known substitutes for the real thing. People must connect with genuine nature or suffer from the imperfections of the substitutes we create for it.

Since in this model there is no substitute for the real thing, if a person is not in conscious connection with webstring attractions, they are probably playing God in some way without the wisdom to do so.

8. Because we are nature renegades, to reconnect with nature, relationships must be entered by gaining consent and measured by their long term effects on local and global life in balance.

9. To reverse our imbalance and its discontents, repeated, thoughtful, shared, consensual, sensory contacts with webstring attractions in natural areas reconnect our thinking with nature's ways. This produces more sensitive and responsible personal, social and environmental relationships. A person can learn to trust and use these nature connected experiences to help produce unity and balance.

Supportive Reading

Visit the NSTP Free Course on the Internet at http://www.ecopsych.com/giftpersonal.html It is a gift to you that you can give to others and also acts as an excellent review and summary of this book and course. As you do it, note what material that it covers feels familiar or unfamiliar and work on these areas in additional online courses we offer. You can use this free course as a resource and make it available to people who want to know more about NSTP.

Optionally complete this summary evaluation:
SUMMARY H:
The Natural Systems Thinking Process gives us a practical means to resolve conflict and restore integrity on personal and environmental levels.

Either in your journal, or on a piece of paper, record the SUMMARY letter code (H) along with the number on the continuum scale below that indicates the extent of your agreement with the Summary Statement:

1   2   3   4   5   6   7   8   9   10
disagree   partially agree   fully agree
Record and retain your score.

Your Total Score:

You may determine your Nature Reconnection Fulfillment Aptitude by adding up the scores of SECTIONS A-H; then multiplying the sum by 12.5. Make that number a percentage or a decimal number. It indicates your potential for enjoying the rewards of balanced personal and global thinking through the use of the Natural Systems Thinking Process. Repeat the activities offered in this Orientation Course and see if your score rises and how that helps you feel and relate. You may continue to increase your score and potential through the additional courses, materials and degree programs offered by Project NatureConnect.

Thoughtful Verbalization

Instructions are located on the last page of this book.

Chapter Nine

Evaluation

The following activities can help you find additional global ecology citizenship insights and understandings. They involve you in evaluating and communicating your 9-leg experiences on this course. Areas in gray apply only to those on the email course.

ONLINE COURSE PARTICIPANTS

CREDIT REMINDER: An Optional 1-credit that is transferable to any school where appropriate, is available from the Portland State University Extended Studies program once you have completed this course and its evaluation online with an Interact group and approved facilitator. Follow links to the Orientation Course at www.ecopsych.com or email <nature@interisland.net> if you want to take the course for credit and get consent to do so or call 360-378-6313.

INTRODUCTORY COURSE REMINDER The Introductory Course, ECO 501, online that follows this Orientation Course will be starting shortly so sign up now if you want to take it soon. Contact: nature@interisland.net.

Evaluation Activity One: REQUIRED

A. Please write a short one-paragraph statement that conveys what you know and feel to be the attractive value of this course for yourself and others. Share the statement with your Interact group.

Evaluation Activity Two: REQUIRED

Write an attractive title and 30-word description for an introductory Applied Ecopsychology workshop that you could present.

Submit it to your Interact Group members and consider and incorporate improvement suggestions from them into your workshop title and description.

Evaluation Activity Three: REQUIRED

Write a 3-page scholarly paper about your participation in this course in a manner that integrates, validates and contributes important concepts and ideas to the profession or general field of learning with nature and/or nature-connected psychology.

Identify what to you are the most important parts of this course including things you have placed in the protected box in your mentality.

You may demonstrate your growth by comparing your "before" and "after" scores on the questions in the Course Description Section of this book (Pages 20-22).

Quote some of the dialogue from your Interact Group to show how the course helps people, including yourself, become involved with ways of thinking and relating that benefit Earth and us. Use before and after question scores from the Course Description section for this purpose as well.

If you have done other reading that applies to the work in this course, use it as references.

Submit the paper to your Interact group. Add their reactions to it on a separate page. Have them suggest a grade for it and for your work on the course.

Evaluation Activity Four: REQUIRED

Evaluation Form

Your name:
Your email address:

Write a paragraph or two describing the value of the Natural Systems Thinking Process in helping the environment and people who suffer the effects of the disconnection of their webstrings from nature, then please write answers to the following questions and email them to nature@interisland.net.

1) Write a phrase that best describes why you took the course.
2) Did you complete the course?
If you did not complete the course, please explain why.

3) How did you initially find out about the course?

4) Were your expectations of the course met? Explain briefly.

5) What did you like most about the course?

6) What did you like least about the course?

7) What was the most important thing you learned from the course?

8) Has the course made a difference in the quality of your life? Explain briefly.

9) If your group had a facilitator, did he/she meet your expectations?

10) If your group had a facilitator, can you suggest ways in which the facilitator might have better assisted your learning process on the course?

11) How can the course be improved?

12) Describe the value of the course in 25 words or less?

13) Do you know where on the Internet we would find folks who would like to take the course?

COURSE COMPLETION NOTE: Your schedule of implementing the Evaluation and Action activities beyond this point depends upon how you plan to use the course. It may help you in the required sections 1-4 above. You may optionally do these additional evaluation activities for further personal growth and experience. You can use these activities in evaluating additional courses for extra credit in this course.

Evaluation Activity Five: (optional)

Those of you who used the SUMMARY OPTION STATEMENTS in the chapters may find them beneficial in evaluating your growth and development in future courses and web visits by applying the statements after completing new material or courses. You might do them again now and see if your completion of the course has changed you score on them.

Evaluation Activity Six: (optional):

Visit this book's Course Description on Pages 20-21. Respond again to the questions there and compare your results this time with those from when you first started.

Re-use the NSTP Important Values, Page 21, in the Course Description section. It is often useful to have a means to measure how far you have progressed or grown in an area of interest that is new to you. For this reason, with reference to the course material, you may

optionally measure changes in your knowledge of it by applying the Growth Measurement Indicator now and compare it to the results you obtained with it at the beginning of the course. You may also use it now for the first time and again, at the end of additional courses you take, or if you do this course again. It may also be helpful in determining and/or validating what you've learned and to discover new directions and areas for further learning and growth.

Evaluation Activity Seven: (optional)

Work with your Interact group to create a shared set of evaluation and grade criteria that critically measure a student's growth and expertise in this course.

Help group members apply these standards to themselves and present their self-evaluation and grade to the Interact group.

Help Interact members consent to modify their grade and evaluation based on input from the group until a consensus for their grade is reached by all.

Help involve your Interact group in assisting others to modify their grades and evaluations by consent.

Evaluation Activity Eight: (optional)

Write an attractive 5-word maximum title and 15-word encapsulation of the course that a student could submit as an Internet link to the course and/or themselves on the Internet.

Submit your titles and descriptions to your Interact group.

Help other Interact group members improve their titles and descriptions so they work well and have them help you in return.

Select, submit, and have your Internet link incorporated into 5 appropriate websites of your choice on the Internet. Check first to see if a link at these sites already exists.

Evaluation Activity Nine (optional)

Based on the readings and learning from the activities, design a final test for the course consisting of at least 10 true / false questions and 10 multiple choice questions.

Ask some members of in your Interact group to take the test; add to it or help improve it.

Thoughtful Verbalization

These instructions are located on the last page of this book.

Course End.

Introduction to the Co-Authors

People who had natural attractions to develop this book

The material in this introductory book and course, since 1994, has come from the natural attractions, questions and comments of its faculty and students as they engaged in and facilitated online courses based on Michael J. Cohen's book *Reconnecting With Nature* and *Well Mind, Well Earth*. Each of these individuals has become an expert in this work and co-author of this book. Each centers a part of his/her personal and professional life around the healing, educating and counseling with nature benefits of the Natural Systems Thinking Process. Updates of co-author contact information is available at http://www.ecopsych.com/coauthors.html

Carol Biggs, M.S., Alaska
Greenwich University
Founded Alaska Nature Connection and Counselor Without Walls. Educates and counsels with nature through individual and group addiction recovery sessions, writes edible and medicinal plant field guides and teaches classes in nature writing and photographic art.
aknature@alaska.net

Mark Brody, Ed.D., Pennsylvania
Temple University
A school psychologist who sees the need for the most important education: living in peace on earth and peace with earth, which are teachings for him to share.
Markbrody@aol.com

J. Christina Brittain M.A., Washington State
Concordia University
Ecopsychologist and originator/teacher of Nature Visioning, which unites deep relaxation, natural attraction energies, and sensate visioning into a process that guides people to harmonious balance for enhanced wellness in three essential life areas: work, relationship, and creativity.
Email: *BeyondTheBounds@aol.com*

Brigett Hurley-Camarena, B.A., Arizona
Arizona State University
A professional member of the Arizona Counselors Association, Brigett works as Spiritual Counselor with families and women on the issues of abandonment and separation through healing and community. She supports the Hispanic people in Whole Life Guiding Principles for success. *CamarenaB@aol.com*

Susan Chernak McElroy, B.A., Idaho
Americus University
Internationally recognized teacher and storyteller, and the author of several books including New York Times bestseller, *Animals as Teachers and Healers,* and national bestseller, *Animals as Guides for the Soul.* She explores the psycho-spiritual healing potential in our relationships with animals and wild nature.
www.susanchernakmcelroy.com
SusanChernak@aol.com

Kurtland Davies Ph.D., Washington State,
Greenwich University
A counselor who does consultation and training for mental health, educational, travel and corporate organizations using methods that develop healthy individuals and organizations through reconnection to nature.
kurt.gaia.davies@mindspring.com

Gaia Davies, M.S.W., Washington State
University of Connecticut
A clinical therapist who does consultation and training for mental health, educational, travel and corporate organizations using methods that develop healthy individuals and organizations through reconnection to nature.
kurt.gaia.davies@mindspring.com

Sarah Anne Edwards, LCMSW,
California
Kansas Universtiy
Author of the ecopsychological novel
Sitting with the Enemy, she directs the Pine Mountain Institute, providing continuing education programs for professionals in ecopsychology and healing practices of nature-based cultures.
PineMountainInstitute.com

Gerry Eitner, B.S., Virginia
SUNY Buffalo
Gerry is a counselor working with people to help identify their highest capacities. She has founded a nonprofit organization, www.themastersgroup.org, that creates projects focusing on children and peace.
gerryei@aol.com

Andrew E. Fister, Kentucky
Currently working with friends and teachers to develop a process for children incorporating NSTP with music and creative writing. Actively involved in community development practicing and sharing the NSTP as the model of relationship for sustainable community.
aefister@ juno.com

David R. Givers, M.S., Minnesota
North Dakota State University
Science, engineering and mathematics research infrastructure development programs administrator for the North Dakota University System.
drgivers@i29.net

Jan Goldfield, Ph.D
University of Chicago
Psychologist, retired, ornamental garden pond builder, current. I use NSTP to originally help my clients and me determine the style and feel of their landscape design. It brings the life of the client to the garden and the life of the garden to the client.
pondlady@aol.com

Peggy Garrigues-Cortelyou, M.Div., Michigan
Wesley Theological Seminary
Founder and facilitator of EarthSong Seminars— offering workshops, retreats, and consultations on strengthening our healing connections with nature through our senses and our spirits.
pgarrigues@voyager.net

Gretchen Grani, M.S. California
University of Pennsylvania
Regional planner, Ecopsychologist and Stay-at-Home Mom currently working children.
gretchen@greenminds.com

Gary Leroy Hoover, Ph. D.
Seoul, South Korea
Commonwealth Open University
Professor of ESL/Freshman English at Chung Ang University, and researcher of and developer of individualized educational programs, specializing in the developing the Progressive/Regressive Forming and Establishing Developmental Model.
phdhoover@yahoo.com

Jane Anne Jeffries, M.A., California
California State University at Los Angeles
Bilingual teacher [English/Spanish] who presents Upper Elementary Curriculum to Latino children in an understandable manner. Nature is the core of our study using the Natural Systems Thinking Process (NSTP).
Jeffries41@aol.com

Mardi Jones, Ph.D., Western Washington State
Greenwich University
Environmental educator, writer and counselor who has pioneered the use of NSTP in her private practice.
seagrace@sos.net

Dr. Janet LeValley, Washington State and Sri Lanka
California Institute of Integral Studies
Professor of Psychology and Sociology, American National College, Sri Lanka; Director, Center for Energy Medicine, Akamai University, Hawaii; Hypnotherapist; Crosscultural Photographer/Ethnographer researching trance and transpersonal identity issues in healing.
drjanet@levalley.net

Charles M. McClintock, B.A., Missouri
Missouri Southern College
Holistic health practitioner specializing in Polarity Therapy and eco-psychology.
nature@sbcglobal.net

J. Marc McGinnes, J.D., California
Environmental lawyer, legal ecologist and faculty of the Environmental Studies Program of the University of California, Santa Barbara. Recipient of the UCSB Alumni Association Outstanding Teacher Award and leader in fields of environmental education, law, and conflict resolution.
mcginnes@envst.ucsb.edu

Marie McLean, M.A., Toronto, Canada
Concordia University
Doctoral student; 'Science of Intuition and Applied
Ecopsychology currently an elementary school
teacher, specializing in Kindergarten.
lucidliving@acncanada.net

Kaisa Naskali, M.Ed., Nova Scotia
Institute for Studies in Education, Toronto
Doctoral student writing a dissertation on Ecopersonal
Intelligence and Wisdom: developing a personal
relationship with our natural earthly home and all
family members.
KaisaN@aol.com

Maria Odum, M.S., Virginia
Fordham University
Traditional Usui Reiki Master and Aura-Soma
Practitioner offering private sessions and classes
involving energywork and color with NSTP as an
integral aspect of the client's/student's therapeutic
process.
allahaull@mindspring.com

Dave Paulsen, B.A., Washington State
Eastern Washington University
Executive Director of Attraction Retreat, a non-profit
organization for educating and counseling with nature
using NSTP. Faculty member in the graduate
Department of Applied Ecopsychology of the
Institute of Global Education.
dave@reststop.net

B. James Rowe Ph.D., Costa Rica
Greenwich University
Executive Director, Costa Rica Rainforest Outward
Bound School. Blends Outward Bound experience-rich
adventures with the Natural Systems Thinking
Process. Develops courses for youth and adults that
function as a deep soul exploration.
jimrowesurf@hotmail.com

Cyrus Rhode Jr., M.P.A., Mississippi
University of West Florida
35-year employment with the Naval Oceanographic
Office as an oceanographer specializing in the physical
and dynamical aspects of the coastal marine
environment and interrelated human activities.
rhodec@navo.navy.mil

F. Richard Schneider, Ph.D., Oregon

Clayton University
Educator, poet, and administrator, founder and director
of the Institute of Global Education and World Peace
University.
frs35@yahoo.com

John Scull, Ph.D., British Columbia
Retired clinical psychologist and adjunct associate
professor of Psychology at the Univerisy of Victoria. A
student of NSTP since 1998, he has extensive experience
in Psychology, International Development, and
Education.
jscull@island.net

Kacy Sigl, B.Ed, Augsburg, Germany/Bellingham, WA.
University of British Columbia.
Wellness, walking and nature games workshop leader.
kacysigl@yahoo.com

Steve Smith, R.N., B.A., Alabama
University of Alabama,
Member of the Institute of Noetic Sciences
Stewardship Committee who coordinates the
Birmingham IONS Community Group. He pioneered
and moderates several ecopsychology listserves and uses
NSTP to enhance his work in biofield energy and
develops courses in it.
sasmith@wellspring.net

Theresa Sweeney, Ph.D., Florida
Greenwich University
Ecopsychologist and mental health counselor who
pioneered a fun, innovative approach to self-discovery
and wellness by combining art therapy with eco-therapy
to help clients find their authentic selves.
keleka@stis.net

Janet Thomas, Washington State
Editor, writer, and administrator active in sustainability
and green politics, author of *The Battle in Seattle*
(Fulcrum).
jthomas@rockisland.com

Teresa Votlucka, R.N., M.S., Florida
Miami Institute of Psychology
Registered Nurse-Doctoral Student specializing in
combining the physical/psychological with our inner/
outer Nature of oneness, our true healing path of love
with no limits.
StressStrategist@aol.com

Allison Weeks, M.S., Washington State
University of Southern Alabama
Doctoral candidate, teacher and administrator of school and workshop training center programs that use and teach NSTP in retreats, sustainable community development, workshops and political and social movements.
allison@reststop.net

Cheri Wells, M.S., C.P.C., Arizona
Western Washington University
Substance Abuse and Violence Prevention Counselor at Tuba City Primary School on the Navajo Reservation who specializes in counseling/teaching young children non-violent life skills.
JCWELLSFLAGAZ@aol.com

APPENDICES

Appendix A

Exploring Self-evidence

Nature builds its perfection nonverbally. It and Earth have been sustained in balance by wordless relationships throughout the eons.

As part of nature, people inherit nature's way of knowing. It provides us with sensory, non-verbal, knowledge arising from self-evidence, from our senses and feelings registering the world and our relationship to it.

In our conquest of nature, we learn to think and communicate in nature-disconnected, verbal stories and labels 99.9% of the time. We lose the ability to think with the profound self-evidence that produces things like the Declaration of Independence's "We hold these truths to be self-evident."

Below is an simple activity that will help you experience self-evidence and its value. It may also help you become aware of an additional way to know yourself.

The Natural Systems Thinking Process (NSTP) helps people think and build reasonable relationships using self-evidence. If you find the activity below presents conflicts or discomfort, you should carefully evaluate whether NSTP will be of good service to your education and goals.

ACTIVITY
Exploring Self-Evidence
1. Using your best thinking and attention, have one finger touch a material object and become aware of what sensation is consciously registering in you by doing this. For example, touch a desk or a tree and be aware of what you feel with eyes open and then closed.

(SUGGESTION: Also touch a loose part of the clothing you are wearing so that your body beneath it does not feel you touching it.)

2. Repeat doing this but this time touch some natural part of your body. Become aware of what new sensations are consciously registering in you by doing this. For example, touch your ankle and be aware of what your finger and your ankle feel with eyes open and then closed.

(SUGGESTION: Also touch the same, as in 1 above, loose part of the clothing you are wearing hard enough so that your body beneath it does feel you touching it.)

3. Can you recognize that a major difference exists between 1 and 2 above. You might want to repeat them several times.

In 1, you felt something in one way, via your finger.

In 2, you feelingly sensed two things, what your finger sensed and also what the part of you that you touched sensed when you touched it. For example, your finger could feel your ankle while your ankle could feel your finger.

4. Can you recognize that even if you could not talk or think in verbal language, you would still be able to register 1 and 2 in some distinctly different way? That the sensations themselves communicated some sensible knowledge?

5. Can you recognize that the ability to apply the concept of "1" and "2" to your experience further helps you register it? Numerical or verbal abstracting adds to our ability to register the environment. It does not, however, accurately replace it. In people, math and words can be part, but not all, of the whole.

6. Can you conclude from this sensory self-evidence activity that self-evidence produces worthwhile knowledge? That one way to distinguish yourself from your surroundings is that when you touch yourself, as 2 above, you sense two things and when you touch your surroundings as 1 above, you sense one thing.

Can you distinguish that there is a sensory difference between experience "1" and "2"? Does this bring to mind the value or significance of sensory, non-verbal self-evidence?

ADDENDA: A helpful self-evidence activity is found in the online free course Integrity 101 located at http://www.ecopsych.com/integrity101.htm

NSTP and Self-Evidence
NSTP is based on using the same kind of scientific process and critical thinking that occurs in the self-evidence activity above. NSTP expands this exploratory "touching" process by including an additional 52 of our inherent natural senses as part of the process. Touch is but one of them. Each of these additional 52 senses is a fact as real and true as the sense or sensation of touch. In addition, to help offset our

psychological estrangement from nature, rather than learning indoors, NSTP asks you to thoughtfully choose to sense and explore the attractions that you discover while in contact with a genuine natural area, backyard or back country.

By enabling you to restore authentic sensory nature connections in your awareness, NSTP helps your introduce self-evidence from nature into your thinking, relating and community.

An Objective

Discovering and using self-evidence in our thinking and actions has value. It enables us to consciously choose to relate through Earth-connected, passionate, interpersonal and transpersonal reasoning. This locally and globally unifies rather than disconnects us from ourselves, each other and all of life.

Because people are part of nature, touching the natural world can, in time, be experienced similarly to touching our ankle. For this reason, NSTP offers an important contribution to producing and sustaining peace within yourself and internationally. After all, our finger rarely conflicts, exploits or is at war with our ankle. More often it supports it, like scratching it when it itches.

Self-evidence is also intelligently self-regulating and self-organizing. For example, if you are attracted to a light and move towards it, other self-evidence will signal when the light may have become dangerously too bright or hot for your welfare.

Self-evidence also helps us become more passionate about Earth and thereby be more motivated to contribute to the wellness of global life. It helps us overcome our consciousness being distorted by hurtful stories.

Our challenge is to differentiate our world of 5-leg stories that we become attached to, with the sensory, non-verbal, self-evidence 4-leg world of nature that we can personally register.

The most efficient and effective way to learn to use and teach the NSTP is by taking a short, online Orientation Course along with this book.

Nature connected psychology is based on Self-Evidence, a missing link in how we learn to think. Its definition is: to validate what we sense and feel. It critically applies our sense of reason to what we sense and feel while in consensual contact with attractions in nature. It compares these findings to our cultural attachments and their effects.

By *nature*, we mean the non-literate, unadulterated, biological and psychological attraction process that has existed for eons before and during humanity's arrival.

Natural attraction energy is the essence of most systems and things including the solar system. It makes total sense that anything that is held together, from atomic particles to materials to weather systems, is held together by natural attractions in balance. Otherwise these things would fall, or be pulled, apart and not exist. Similarly, things or energies in motion are simply following natural attractions in order to fulfill these attractions.

By *culture* we mean humanity's abstract, literate, thinking process, its stories, artifacts and effects.

Validity of Evidence:

"At root, ecology is an erotic attitude of closeness, relatedness and care. We have made it into a rational/activist project and lost sight of its heart."

-Thomas Moore

The Natural Systems Thinking Process is super objective in that it welcomes all evidence. It includes sensuous information from non-verbal, transpersonal connections rather than dismiss this evidence as subjective, unscientific, spiritual, psychotic or fuzzy thinking. NSTP enables us to choose to think and relate like nature works. For decades, it has been taught and accredited in more than 58 Universities and published extensively.

Self-Evidence often consists of Natural Attraction sensations and feelings in natural areas that, to help insure our survival, nature registers in our consciousness. Although prejudiciously overlooked, Self-Evidence is valid because it is:

REASONABLE: Mathematics, Archimedes' abstract "Mechanical Theorems," is considered to be pure rational fact. However, the self-evident fact that humanity inherently senses, feels and learns from Natural Attractions is more ancient, true and universal. For example, the sense of taste: When a natural substance is sweet, it is attractive, often edible and digestible; it rewardingly satisfies our sense of hunger so, in time, our sense of reason may validate the substance as food and allow us to eat it again. The sense of temperature: If the heat from a fire burns a person, he or she may learn to trust that sensation and be attracted to use their sense of reason or fear and keep a safe distance from the fire.

AVAILABLE: For survival, humanity is endowed by nature to continually register attraction sensations and feelings on conscious and subconscious levels.

TRUSTABLE: For example, if people pinch themselves they register and trust that they feel something. They trust they will feel something again if they pinch themselves again.

REPEATABLE: For example, if people pinch themselves many times over a period of time, they feel something every time. Other people demonstrate the same attribute.

GLOBAL: For example, humanity throughout the world senses and feels as well as trusts that the ability to sense and feel exists in themselves and others.

TIMELESS: Records show, and we commonly reason that humanity, past, present and future, contains and will contain the ability to sense and feel.

PREDICTABLE: No matter where humanity goes, if people are conscious, they will sense or feel attractions. Consciousness itself is an attractive sensation or feeling.

DIVERSE: There are at least 53 distinct natural attraction sensations and feelings humanity can register and thereby know the world.

EDUCATIONAL: Sensations and feelings provide humanity with a wide range of survival information.

VALUABLE: Sensations and feelings enhance survival potentials as well as help establish a strong sense of self. "I feel, therefore, I am," is as true, significant and important as "I think, therefore, I am."

HONEST: Sensations and feelings always offer us excellent information about the state of our being.

WIDE-RANGED: Sensations and feelings help humanity register the many attraction sensitivities displayed throughout nature by the plant, animal and mineral kingdoms.

DEMONSTRABLE: Humanity can often register what other members of humanity are sensing and feeling.

INDEPENDENT: Humanity can register and reason with attraction sensations and feeling that lie outside the accepted or destructive operants and dogmas of their culture or society.

SPIRITUAL: Natural sensations and feelings enable people to register and relate to nature-connected aspects of spirit and soul that, to our loss, some parts of society omit.

ATTRACTIVE: Humanity embraces and seeks sensation; it is attractive; we normally never desire to give up our ability to sense and feel.

INTELLIGENT: The natural world achieves its perfections by relating through nonverbal attraction sensitivities, many of which register as sensations and feelings in humanity and add to our ability to make intelligent decisions.

FREE: Sensations and feelings are of, by and from nature; no culture or individual lays claim to inventing or owning them or legally restricting their availability.

SELF-REGULATING: Sensations and feelings help regulate and guide each other. For example if a person is attracted to pinch themselves too hard, another sense or senses (sense of pain, sense of reason, or both) attract him or her to stop pinching too hard.

Self Evident Thinking:

Our self-evident, non-verbal way of knowing and thinking makes up the 4-leg, large, anciently-evolved Old-Brain, sometimes called the horse brain. In humanity, the Old-Brain registers non-literate tensions, sensations, feelings and emotions. It makes up approximately 90% of our mentality and is the home of at least 52 different sense groups. It enables us to sensuously experience nature as nature operates and knows itself.

The remaining 10% of our mentality, the 5-leg, more recently evolved Cerebral Neocortex or New Brain, consists of a bonding of the senses of verbal language, consciousness and reason to produce and act out abstract stories, be they accurate or inaccurate, constructive or destructive, connective or disconnected.

For additional information about the 53 natural senses see Chapter 5 of *Reconnecting With Nature*.

Appendix B

State of the Earth

Earth Day Plus Thirty as Seen by the Earth

By Donella Meadows
April 22, 2000.

If, in the thirty Earth Day celebrations we have held since 1970, the human population and economy have become any more respectful of the Earth, the Earth hasn't noticed.

The planet is not impressed by fancy speeches. Leonardo DiCaprio interviewing Bill Clinton about global warming is not an Earth-shaking event. The Earth has no way of registering good intentions or future inventions or high hopes. It doesn't even pay attention to dollars, which are, from a planet's point of view, just a charming human invention. Planets measure only physical things...energies and materials and their flows into and out of the changing populations of living creatures.

What the Earth sees is that on the first Earth Day in 1970 there were 3.7 billion of those hyperactive critters called humans, and now there are over 6 billion.

Back in 1970 those humans drew from the Earth's crust 46 million barrels of oil every day-now they draw 78 million.

Natural gas extraction has nearly tripled in thirty years, from 34 trillion cubic feet per year to 95 trillion. We mined 2.2 billion metric tons in 1970; this year we'll mine about 3.8 billion. The planet feels this fossil fuel use in many ways, as the fuels are extracted (and spilled) and shipped (and spilled) and refined (generating toxics) and burned into numerous pollutants, including carbon dioxide, which traps outgoing energy and warms things up. Despite global conferences and brave promises, what the Earth notices is that human carbon emissions have increased from 3.9 million metric tons in 1970 to an estimated 6.4 million this year.

You would think that an unimaginably huge thing like a planet would not notice the one degree (Fahrenheit) warming it has experienced since 1970. But on the scale of a whole planet, one degree is a big deal, especially since it is not spread evenly. The poles have warmed more than the equator, the winters more than the summers, the nights more than the days. That means that temperature DIFFERENCES from one place to another have been changing much more than the average temperature has changed. Temperature differences are what make winds blow, rains rain and ocean currents flow.

All creatures, including humans, are exquisitely attuned to the weather. All creatures, including us, are noticing weather weirdness and trying to adjust, by moving, by fruiting earlier or migrating later, by building up whatever protections are possible against flood and drought. The Earth is reacting to weather changes, too, shrinking glaciers splitting off nation-sized chunks of Antarctic ice sheet, enhancing the cycles we call El Nino and La Nina.

"Earth Day, Shmearth Day," the planet must be thinking as its fever mounts. "Are you folks ever going to take me seriously?"

Since the first Earth Day our global vehicle population has swelled from 246 to 730 million. Air traffic has gone up by a factor of six. The rate at which we grind up trees to make paper has doubled (to 200 million metric tons per year). We coax from the soil, with the help of strange chemicals, 2.25 times as much wheat, 2.5 times as much corn, 2.2 times as much rice, almost twice as much sugar, almost four times as many soybeans as we did thirty years ago. We pull from the oceans almost twice as much fish.

With the fish we can see clearly how the planet behaves, when we push it too far. It does not feel sorry for us; it just follows its own rules. Fish become harder and harder to find. If they are caught before they're old enough to reproduce, if their nursery habitat is destroyed, if we scoop up not only the cod, but the capelin upon which the cod feeds, the fish may never come back. The Earth does not care that we didn't mean it, that we promise not to do it again, that we make nice gestures every Earth Day.

We have among us die-hard optimists who will berate me for not reporting the good news since the last Earth Day. There is plenty of it, but it is mostly measured in human terms, not Earth terms. Average human life expectancy has risen since 1970 from 58 to 66 years. Gross world product has more than doubled, from 16 to 39 trillion dollars. Recycling has increased, but so has trash generation, so the Earth receives more garbage than ever before. Wind and solar power generation have soared, but so have coal-fired, gas-fired and nuclear generation.

In human terms there has been breathtaking progress. In 1970 there weren't any cell phones or video players. There was no Internet; there were no dot-coms. Nor was anyone infected with AIDS, of course, nor did we have to worry about genetic engineering. Global spending on advertising was only one-third of what it is now (in inflation-corrected dollars). Third-World debt was one-eighth of what it is now.

Whether you call any of that progress, it is all beneath the notice of the Earth. What the Earth sees is that its species are vanishing at a rate it hasn't seen in 65 million years. That 40 percent of its agricultural soils have been degraded. That half its forests have disappeared and half its wetlands have been filled or drained, and that despite Earth Day, all these trends are accelerating.

Earth Day is beginning to remind me of Mother's Day, a commercial occasion upon which you buy flowers for the person who, every other day of the year, cleans up after you. Guilt-assuaging. Trivializing. Actually dangerous. All mothers have their breaking points. Mother Earth does not soften hers with patience or forgiveness or sentimentality.

Donella Meadows was an adjunct professor at Dartmouth College and director of the Sustainability Institute <www.sustainer.org> in Hartland, Vermont. She died in 2001.

Intergovernmental Panel on Climate Change Report July, 2001

3,000 scientists involved in the Intergovernmental Panel on Climate Change have given their unqualified backing to the argument that global warming is taking place and at a much faster rate than was expected. The Panel established by the United Nations and the World Meteorological Organisation stated that temperatures were rising more quickly than at any time in the past 1,000 years. Experts are warning that this will put millions of people at risk with a future of floods, droughts and landslides if predictions are correct. Poorer countries will be the most vulnerable if temperatures rise as predicted by the end of the century. Plants and animals will disappear and many developing countries that depend more heavily on water and agriculture for survival will suffer.

Strong evidence depicts that over the past 540 years human activities such as the burning of fossil fuels has speeded up the global warming process. The IPCC report said that the concentration of carbon dioxide in the atmosphere is now at its highest for 400,000 years. Politicians from more than 150 countries meet in Germany next week to try to salvage the Kyoto agreement.

The United Nations Millennium Forum Declaration reports:

The statistics shift slightly from year to year and from report to report but they are, nevertheless, always shocking to our unzombified sense of humanity.

Some 840 million people remain malnourished.

1.3 billion do not have access to clean water.

One in seven children of primary school age is out of school.

An estimated 1.5 billion people subsist on less than one US dollar per day.

Some 2.8 billion subsist on less than two dollars a day.

As of the most recent count, there were some 35 armed conflicts raging in the world.

The weapons and the disagreements that could lead to worldwide war of horrific destruction still exist.

Nature Journal: International Consortium of Scientists Report

October, 2001: A shocking and groundbreaking new scientific study by an international consortium of scientists has concluded that humanity's assault on the environment has left many ecosystems - from coral reefs and tropical forests to lakes and coastal waters - in such a fragile state that the slightest disturbance, from a dry spell to a fire or flood, may push them into a catastrophic collapse. The study, published in the prestigious journal, NATURE, found that human impacts on many of the world's ecosystems could cause them to abruptly shift with little or no warning from their apparently stable natural condition to very different, diminished conditions far less able to support diversity of life, including human. "Models have predicted this, but only in recent years has enough evidence accumulated to tell us that resilience of many important ecosystems has become undermined to the point that even the slightest disturbance can make them collapse," said Marten Scheffer, an ecologist at the University of Wageningen in the Netherlands and lead author of the study.

Conventional scientific and conservation thinking has been that ecosystems such as lakes, oceans, coral reefs, woodlands or deserts respond slowly and steadily to climate change, nutrient pollution, habitat degradation and other human environmental impacts. But the new study shatters this paradigm, finding instead that, after decades of continuous change imposed by human activity, many of the world's natural ecosystems are now susceptible to sudden catastrophic change. In dramatic contrast to conventional environmental thinking, the investigators paint a picture of unexpectedly sudden, drastic switches of state, from lush, lake-dotted forests teeming with plants and animals to scorching, parched deserts devoid of all but the hardiest of lifeforms, for example. "In approaching questions about deforestation or endangered species or global climate change, we work on the premise that an ounce of pollution equals an ounce of damage," said co-author Jonathan Foley, a University of Wisconsin-Madison climatologist and director of the Center for Sustainability and the Global Environment at the Institute for Environmental Studies at UW-Madison. "It turns out that assumption is entirely incorrect. Ecosystems may go on for years exposed to pollution or climate changes without showing any change at all and then suddenly they may flip into an entirely different condition, with little warning or none at all."

"The idea that nature can suddenly flip from one kind of condition to another is sobering," said Foley, who said that such changes can be irreversible. "For hundreds of years, we've been taught to think in very linear ways; we like to think of nature as being simple. But now we know that we can't count on ecosystems to act in nice simple ways."

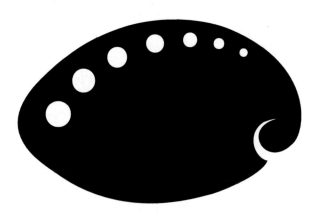

UN paints grim global picture "Global Environment Outlook 2000"

Time is running out for ecology, report warns; new threat is found.

It is too late to halt global warming and time is quickly running out to prevent other potential environmental catastrophes, the UN's environment agency said in a major report yesterday.

"Global Environment Outlook 2000" offers a gloomy view of the planet's condition on the eve of the next millennium. It points to new threats, such as increased levels of nitrogen in the water supply, that the world has not yet tackled.

"The gains made by better management and technology are still being outpaced by the environmental impacts of population and economic growth. We are on an unsustainable course," Klaus Toepfer, head of the United Nations Environment Program, said at the launch of the report in Nairobi.

The report says emissions of greenhouse gases that cause global warming have quadrupled since the 1950s, and that "binding" targets to reduce emissions, agreed by governments at the summit last year in Kyoto, Japan, may not be met.

The rate at which humans are destroying the environment is accelerating, often because of excessive consumption by the rich, and to the detriment of the poor.

About 20 percent of the world's population lack access to safe drinking water, and 50 percent have no access to a sanitation system. This state of affairs will deteriorate as the world's population, set to reach 6 billion next month, will increase by 50 percent in the next 50 years.

Eighty percent of the world's original forest cover has been cleared or degraded, and logging and mining projects threaten 39 percent of what forest remains.

A quarter of mammal species are at risk of extinction, while more than half the world's coral reefs are threatened by human activity.

There were 850 contributors to the report, which took two and a half years to compile, and which highlights some lesser-known environmental problems.

Disasters such as hurricanes and forest fires are increasing in frequency and severity, and have killed 3 million people in the past three decades. Armed conflicts and refugee flows are causing greater damage to the environment than ever before.

There is also mounting evidence that humans are seriously destabilizing the global nitrogen balance. Huge amounts of nitrogen are being deposited on land and in water through intensive agriculture and the burning of fossil fuels.

Eventually, this problem could make fresh-water supplies unfit for human consumption, the report says.

"The full extent of the damage is only now becoming apparent as we begin to piece together a comprehensive overview of the extremely complex, interconnected web that is our life support system," said Toepfer, a former German environment minister.

Much of the damage is irreparable, but through a huge mobilization of resources and political will, much can be done to prevent further destruction, the report says.

A long-term target of a 90 percent reduction in the consumption of raw materials in industrialized countries may seem far-fetched, but without it hundreds of millions of people will be condemned to a life of suffering, the report concludes.

More Results of Disconnection

From B.F. Skinner, 1971: "In trying to solve the terrifying problems that face us in the world today, we naturally turn to the things we do best. We play from strength, and our strength is science and technology. To contain a population explosion we look for better methods of birth control. Threatened by a nuclear holocaust, we build bigger deterrent forces and anti-ballistic-missile systems. We try to stave off world famine with new foods and better ways of growing them. Improved sanitation and medicine will, we hope, control disease, better housing and transportation will solve the problems of the ghettos, and new ways of reducing or disposing of waste will stop the pollution of the environment. We can point to remarkable achievements in all these fields, and it is not surprising that we should try to extend them. But things grow steadily worse and it is disheartening to find that technology itself is increasingly at fault. Sanitation and medicine have made the problems of population more acute, war has acquired a new horror with the invention of nuclear weapons, and

the affluent pursuit of happiness is largely responsible for pollution. As Darlington has said, 'Every new source from which man has increased his power on the Earth has been used to diminish the prospects of his successors. All his progress has been made at the expense of damage to his environment which he cannot repair and could not forsee.'"

Summary of Reports from the Union of Concerned Scientists

Human culture now has the potential to inflict irreversible damage on the environment and on its life sustaining systems and resources. Already, critical stress suffered by our environment is clearly manifest in the air, water, and soil, our climate, and plant and animal species. Should this deterioration be allowed to continue, we can expect to alter the living world to the extent that it will be unable to sustain life as we know it.

Indiscriminate dumping of toxic, nuclear, and biomedical waste and environmental disasters of enormous scale have begun to cut deep scars into the Earth's ecosystem and disrupt its delicate ecological balance. Global warming, thought to be resulting from increased levels of carbon dioxide in the atmosphere from fossil fuel use and from deforestation, may have the potential to alter climate on a massive scale. Air pollution near ground level and acid precipitation, and stratospheric ozone depletion causing enhanced ultra-violet radiation at the earth's surface, are causing widespread injury to human and animal populations, forests and crops. Our remaining rainforests and many wild forest regions, essential to worldwide ecological balance, are slated for clear cutting due to poor management policies.

Uncontrolled exploitation of depletable ground water supplies have endangered food production and other essential human systems and heavy demands for surface waters have resulted in serious shortages in many countries. Pollution of rivers, lakes and ground water has further limited the supply of potable water. Destructive pressure on the oceans is severe. Rivers carrying heavy burdens of eroded soil into the seas also contain toxic industrial, municipal, agricultural, and livestock waste. With the marine catch at or above the maximum sustainable yield, some fisheries are already showing signs of collapse.

Soil productivity is on the decline and per capita food production in many parts of the world is decreasing as a result of destructive agriculture and animal husbandry practices. Already, more than ten percent of the earth's vegetated surface has been degraded, an area larger than India and China combined.

Over one third of the valuable topsoil used to grow the grains that feed much of the world has blown or washed away. This desertification, caused by overgrazing domestic animals and by over-cultivation, salinization, and deforestation, has already impacted over 35 percent of the land surface of the Earth, (United Nations Environmental Program). Desertification has caused many millions to abandon the land, lacking the bare essentials of survival, they have migrated to urban slums, where all that awaits them are meager government relief packages and poverty wages.

We are fast approaching many of the Earth's limits; its ability to provide for growing numbers of people, to provide food and energy, and to absorb wastes and destructive effluent. Current economic practices which damage the environment, in both developed and underdeveloped nations, cannot be continued without the risk that vital global systems will be damaged beyond repair.

No more than a few decades remain before the chance to avert the threats we now confront will be lost and the prospects for humanity immeasurably diminished. We must begin to bring environmentally damaging activities under control to restore and protect the integrity of the earth's ecosystems. The greatest peril is to become trapped in spirals of environmental decline, poverty, and unrest, leading to worldwide social, economic and environmental collapse from which we may be unable to recover.

The Human Condition

If we could shrink the Earth's population to a village of precisely 100 people, with all the existing human ratios remaining the same, it would look something like the following.
There would be:
57 Asians
21 Europeans
14 from the Western Hemisphere, both north and south
8 would be Africans
52 would be female
48 would be male
70 would be non-white; 30 would be white
70 would be non-Christian; 30 would be Christian
89 would be heterosexual; 11 would be homosexual
6 people would possess 59% of the entire world's wealth and all 6 would be from the United States
80 would live in substandard housing
70 would be unable to read
50 would suffer from malnutrition
1 would be near death
1 would be near birth
1 would have a college education
1 would own a computer.

If you have food in the refrigerator, clothes on your back, a roof overhead and a place to sleep, you are richer than 75% of this world.

If you woke up this morning with more health than illness, you are more blessed than the million who will not survive this week.

If you have money in the bank, in your wallet, and spare change in a dish someplace, you are among the top 8% of the world's wealthy.

If you can attend a church meeting without fear of harassment, arrest, torture, or death, you are more blessed than three billion people in the world.

If you have never experienced the danger of battle, the loneliness of imprisonment, the agony of torture, or the pangs of starvation, you are ahead of 500 million people in the world,

Appendix C

Prerequisite Course Instructions

Much of the course instruction information in this section pertains to the course that is given online. The reader is cordially invited to take the Internet course in conjunction with reading this book as it offers many advantages. It is especially helpful because it connects you by email with an Interact study group consisting of diverse individuals from different countries and cultures. You learn as much from them as you do the book as their email responses to the activities become your textbook. While one person may be connecting with a maple tree in New Brunswick, another may be connecting with a penguin in Antarctica.

These instructions are designed to provide insights to help you do and teach this program anywhere. The online course is also an Orientation Course and prerequisite for other courses and IGE's degree programs. To take the online Orientation course as you read the book, visit www.ecopsych.com/orient.html for details.

You have connected to this Instruction Page because you received a letter or invitation from the Institute of Global Education to visit here with respect to the online Orientation Course you signed up for via the Internet. You may have already received the tentative starting date and the names and addresses of some or all of the participants in your section of the course. If not, you will receive them when they are complete.

If you will not be participating on the section of the course you are assigned, please let the staff know immediately so arrangements can be made for the course to continue without you. Another section of this course may start in about two weeks. Perhaps you can join it or others that follow. Again, be sure to contact the staff if you will not be participating in this section of the course and tell them what you would like to do.

You will be given 4-6 days to familiarize yourself with the instructions below (more when possible.)

Please recognize that each of us, and the experiences we share, become an important "real life textbook" for this course. To participate effectively, be sure you have submitted your application and made payment arrangements, sent for books, buttons, etc. where applicable as described below, and have your email and web contact program in good working order.

The following information and instructions is based on your familiarity with the contents of a short article "The Natural Systems Thinking Process: How restoring our inherent 53 sense way of knowing corrects destructive personal and environmental relationships." This article is the Introduction to this book. You may skip any parts of the instructions you may have already read on the web site as long as you know how to apply them.

NOTE: To obtain a helpful overview of the Internet course, please read the nine short "pages" of instructions that follow, starting with Page One.

Page 1 Instructions
("Page" refers to a page on the course Internet site)

SECTION 1 - COURSE MECHANICS AND GOALS
What is the general course topic?
The course topic is
Educating, Counseling and Healing with Nature: Nature connecting activities for wellness, spirit and deeper learning.

How is the course taught?
The course is taught via readings in books (optional) and on the Internet; activities you do in local natural areas; email that is used to receive and send instructions; and by sharing experiences and responding to emails received.

How many hours of work does the course require?
The Orientation Course is based on 8-10 hours minimum of participation in email/course work and reading with an additional 20-30 hours of activities, email corresponding and organization.

What is the best way to learn the course material?
Retention and application of the course material may be as high as 85% or more by "teaching" the course (co-facilitating it) after completing it. This opportunity is usually available and is a requirement of the Introductory Course (ECO 501) if you are in the IGE Cooperative Degree or Certificate program.

Do I have to take the course before I can facilitate it or intern in it?

This is highly recommended and a responsible thing to do, but it is not always required of students with previous training that gave them the expertise to facilitate/intern on the course. Their expertise is determined by their passing with honors a short 25-question Leadership Compatibility Examination designed by previous course students and guides.

Who are the course participants?

Course particpants are usually people who have strong interests in improving personal and environmental relationships and making them sustainable. They often have had many years of experience in their professions or social roles and know they must help solve our "unsolvable" problems because they feel help is needed. They want to learn how they can best contribute. Many desire to support and nurture the natural spirit or other aspects of themselves that have survived society's conquest of nature, the nature-connected parts of their integrity that refuse to be disrespectful of Earth's ecosystems, locally and globally.

Page 2 Instructions

What is it like being on the course once it has started?

Below is an example of what the course looks like when it is running smoothly. The challenge here is to make this description a reality by painstakingly following the guidelines and instructions on these Internet pages.

Preparation: "Carol, an online course member has done her preparatory "homework." She read the introductory course and web site material, submitted her application to the course, and received a course participation confirmation. She ordered her optional *Reconnecting With Nature* book, completed the required prerequisite activities and her self-introduction, and set up a group mailing list from the addresses sent to her by the course organizer. Then she carefully read the instructions you are reading now.

The specific dates for her course were made for the convenience of all, then send and receive dates for email assignments were set. Group guidance roles were offered to participants, the co-facilitator was identified, and the email addresses were checked to verify that they worked properly.

Attitude: "Enthusiastic" is the way Carol feels about the course. She knows what is important in it to her because she read through the prerequisite material to identify areas of interest and results that others found important for them. She also tried some of the activities with friends and knows they work well for her. They

help her thinking to reasonably cooperate with nature's intelligence, balance and beauty by safely connecting with it. She recognizes that with respect to nature's eons of balanced relationship building experience, there is no known substitute for the real thing. Substitutes often pollute or deteriorate naturally balanced relationships.

Schedule: Carol reads her course instructions online from an Internet "base camp" web page, which tells her what activity she and her email partners who live in many different countries will do in their local park, backyard, or even with a terrarium on the scheduled day. In general, her group has been doing two activities a week. Their schedule is posted at their Internet "Base Camp" web page where they were directed when the course began.

Role of attractions: Carol begins each activity by seeking what is most attractive to her at the moment in a local natural area. Unexpectedly, she becomes aware that the delicate sparkle of a water droplet on a fern attracts her. She does additional activities that reinforce this nature-connected sensation and she becomes aware of other things that come to mind from the total experience. They include other times she has felt nature's joy and meaning as well as her past disconnection from it, what caused it and the effects of the loss. She discovers that the droplet being attractive to her was not an accident. It was subconsciously attractive to parts of her that sought the fulfillment of the balanced tenacity,  brightness and refreshment it provided. Contact with the droplet brought these hidden parts of her into her conscious awareness.

Written material: Carol then reads, or has already read online, (and optionally in her *Reconnecting With Nature* book,) material which helps her understand and model various aspects of the activity she has just done and how she might apply them to improve and further enjoy her daily relationships with people and the environment.

Guidelines and process: Carol closely follows the seven-step guidelines that come with the activity instructions. At some convenient time on the date for the completion of the activity and readings, Carol goes on-line and shares her thoughts, feelings and reactions from her nature-connecting experience with her 7-person Interact group. She also downloads, reads, and later reacts to the attractions she finds and things she has learned in all the emails she received from the group by the due date. They become the course textbook. They convey her group member's experiences in nature with the same activity and readings she just did. Later she reads their reactions to the description of her experiences with the activity.

Unity: Carol finds the course process enjoyable and educational. She feels relieved that participants hold something important in common, are supportive, and are not bogged down in "flaming" arguments about differing viewpoints, ideologies, religions, politics, etc. Carol feels alive, spirited, and sustained by her email partners' genuine responses as well as the group's rejuvenating reconnections to nature.

Value and self-empowerment: Her day brighter and energized, Carol looks forward to applying the learning she gained from the activity to connect more deeply with the people and natural places that attract her. As these relationships gain new value for her, she becomes aware of an often-unrecognized natural worth in herself and others along with greater values in natural areas. She gains new confidence from doing the activity and knowing its effects. She owns it, can teach it, and is rewarded by it at will.

Why does the process work? The course work sounds and feels simple to Carol, and explaining how and why it works to others challenges her intellect and spirit in fun ways. The process and its effects are so steeped in nature's balanced ways that for Carol and others they are, like nature's perfection, beyond words. To be known and understood, the process must be experienced first-hand. To our loss, in our nature-disconnected society, nature-centered thinking is often suspect.

What guidelines help the course organize itself?

Below are the guidelines and instructions that Carol and her Interact group members followed to help them make the course operate in ways that optimize their learning and enhance their rewards from taking the course together.

Page 3 Instructions

What is the major task in the course? The major task in the course is to help participants meet the obligations and challenges that can prevent it from operating smoothly and accomplishing its goal. The instructions on these pages help course participants get the most from the course. The instructions have been compiled from the questions and situations that have arisen since the inception of this course in 1993.

What challenges does the course present? It may be helpful to know that the adverse situations below have occurred during the seven years that the course has operated:

-improperly completing an application http://www.rockisland.com/~process/5grnchapplic.html
-electronic email failure
-not studying the instructions carefully
-incorrect email addresses
-Internet overcrowding, making web or mail pages inaccessible for a period of time
-some members' newness to computers
-computer breakdowns
-personal life complications
-necessary schedule changes
-misunderstanding the instructions or a point made in the email
-going off topic on an tangent that becomes controversial
-not paying attention to the instructions and not helping others do likewise
-sending requests for credit to the wrong place or at the wrong time

How have past participants met the course challenges?

The group and its members have meet the challenges listed above by:
-being extra familiar with the course operating instructions so that they are able to help others be guided by them
-being supportive and sharing their expertise
-being patient so folks have time to cope with difficulties
-seeking, obtaining and giving permission to make room for extenuating circumstances
-being their word. Making the words they convey accurately coincide with their actions on the course and vice versa

Is the course always successful?

The course process has operated successfully since its inception. However, some groups have coped with more challenges than others.

If questions arise, who do I contact?

If questions arise, you should write the whole group for answers, not just the facilitators. This way, the group may learn from your questions and/or help answer them. Once you learn the answers, share them with others, when appropriate. Reminder: The mailing addresses of the group have been, or will be, sent to you once it is established.

What and why are the two course starting dates?

Usually the course has the two starting dates identified below. They are sent to you by email once the 3-6 course participants have completed their registration.

1. First date: The day you personally start to complete your work on the prerequisite activities located at http://www.rockisland.com/~process/5grnchdprerqust.html and check your email contact list to see if it's working This period is usually a minimum of Wednesday or Thursday through the following Sunday.

Participants are encouraged to start earlier on these activities when convenient.

2. Second date: The first official posting date for the course is usually a Sunday or Monday morning at which time you send your introductions and prerequisite reactions to the "All Participants" mailing address list. Please do not send them before these days as they can unnecessarily influence others before personal contacts are established and thereby reduce your chances of getting the most from the course yourself.

Page 4 Instructions

Where can I find a course application form?

An application form link is at http://www.rockisland.com/~process/5grnchapplic.html.

Do I need to buy extra course credit if I am in an IGE Degree or Certificate Program?

If you are in an IGE Degree Program or Certificate Program, credit for the completed course will automatically be provided to you by Institute of Global Education (IGE) once you officially enroll in it.

How do I sign up for course credit from Portland State University?

Once you have completed this one-two credit course and received your grade, you may arrange and pay for optional Portland State University credit at $42/credit (3/3/03). At the same time, you will complete a hard copy of the credit application and mail it with the appropriate credit fee via postal mail to

Project NatureConnect, P.O. Box 1605, Friday Harbor, WA 98250.

PLEASE NOTE: You do not need PSU credits if you are only going to use this course with IGE as in Page 2 above. PSU credit is for transferring this course to a degree program or professional situation that is unaffiliated with IGE, or for other training or professional credit purposes.

What aspects of the course are covered in the Course Organization Letter I will receive?

You will receive an email with updated course information. It will cover some of the following items:

1. Interact Group name _____(you can change the unofficial name by mutual consent of all participants after the course convenes.)

2. How do I contact the other course participants to share activities and results with them?

You contact other participants through the Interact Group Participants Mailing List.

You will be asked to make a group mailing list from the names and addresses on it, so save this email until you do. You can put the group list together and mail it out asking the other participants to respond to it and see if it is reaching all the participants in the group. Note that there may be participants added or subtracted from list by the Sunday starting date.

Can I share the names of the people taking the course with others outside our Interact group?

Very important! The course is controversial in some religious, political and anti-environmental circles, which at times, has subjected participants to harassment, such as spam and discomforting letters. Email addresses, therefore, should be kept in strict confidence to avoid unpleasant complications from "outsiders." If any question arises about giving out email addresses to non-course participants, check with the group before acting.

How do the course participants help organize and lead the course? Guide support roles in the group will be offered, identified and described as below. If you are not comfortable with the role you are offered, write the course organizer and facilitator to replace you in your role.

How does the course organize itself?

In nature, the purpose of life is to support life, which is accomplished by members of the global life community following their natural attractions as they occur. For this reason, the course Interact group attempts to think and self-organize like nature and ecosystems work. For the group to function and meet its psychological global citizenship goals this way, the roles described below are fulfilled by group participants who are attracted to their assigned roles. The group may decide to share all roles or individuals may specialize in one type of support. Often, participants learn how to best provide this kind of community support by providing it.

*Do the course guides need special skills?

For the most part, the groups are self-sustaining because each participant is born with all the natural attributes needed to complete and teach the course.

How is self-governance achieved?

The group support roles make each course participants part of a group facilitating team, which eliminates the necessity for a co-facilitator for the group, even though one is usually assigned for training purposes and to offer assistance based on past experiences with the course.

Upon successful completion of the course, participants are invited to help further the program by co-facilitating new groups as a way of sharing the knowledge you have gained in this course. This is part of the process of self-organization and higher learning. The most effective and potent way to learn the material in this course is by teaching it to others.

Page 5 Instructions

How do I find out if I have a guide role assigned to me?

By Saturday morning preceding the course start date, you will be assigned, with your consent, a role. Please let the course organizer know if you are not attracted to the role assigned to you. You can also ask others in the group to trade roles with you. you can also tell the group facilitator or other group members that you have preference for a particular role where you think you can best contribute. (You are welcome to repeat the course free in a different role, or in other courses that follow. All of the courses use the same process.)

The roles and assignments are as follows:

A: Group Consciousness and Communication Supporter: This person helps participants get online and in communication by helping develop a group email address list. A test letter is sent to all participants. Each participant forwards the letter to all other participants to verify that everyone is connected by email. The "GCC person" also monitors the course time schedule to be sure it is working as planned or needs to be modified by group consent. Those with experience in creating group mailing list can be most helpful to less experienced participants.

B. Participation Supporter: On the agreed upon due dates for sharing activity experiences, the "PS person" notes whether all participants have sent their activity responses to the group or made other arrangements. If a participant is missing, the "PS Person" informs the group and tries to help the missing participant get his/her response posted

C. Agenda Supporter: We all carry a tendency to get into side issues, stories and experiences that may take so much time and energy that they enervate or dissolve the group. We also have a tendency to want to teach what we think we know. If side conversations arise, the "AS Person" helps participants return to the group goal of helping each other connect more deeply with nature by sharing what has been learned.

D. Coordination Supporter: The "CS Person" steps in when help is needed by other support people or this person may also offer help in areas wehre they have special expertise. This is an excellent growing opportunity for those who want to learn how to facilitate groups. If you want to play this role, let the organizer or facilitator know and they will refer you to some articles and Chapter readings in *Reconnecting With Nature* that will provide guidelines. At times, a co-facilitator will help the group with this; at other times, the group coordinates and learns how to facilitate by doing.

SECTION 2: COURSE TIME SCHEDULE

How long does the course take?

The course can be completed, with pressure, in two days, however such a short timeframe is minimally effective in improving personal and environmental relationships. Many relationships are based on conditioned thinking and relating habits that take time to change, as past rewards are relinquished for greater, more reasonable satisfactions.

Why is so short a course so long?

If participants want the course to go into sufficient depth to let their experiences improve their relationships, sleep time is necessary. An essence of NSTP is that participants have at least one night's, and  preferably two night's sleep between activities, which makes the course last a minimum of 8 days. The course operates best when participatns do and share two activities a week over 4-5 weeks.

Can the duration of the course be adjusted?

By consensus, participants can agree to make the course go faster or slower depending on the number of days between assignments. Two to five days between activities works best. Seven days tends to lose important course momentum unless the group is very interactive during those days.

Is it easy to modify the course duration?

It is usually time-consuming and difficult to change the course posting dates to the convenience of all.

Page 6 Instructions

SECTION 3: INTERACT GROUP PROTOCOL

Is the course based on both day-by-day and long-term commitments?

Since course participants learn from and through each other, each participant should conscientiously fulfill his/her commitment to participate once the commitment is made. In addition, each participant should commit to giving and seeking support to and from other course participants regarding their course experiences, thoughts and feelings.

How do course participants actually study themselves and each other?

One thing participants study in the course is how each of them relates to the natural world in nature, others and themselves. To have this work, particpants should commit to what they are doing and going to do and keep the commitments. If a participant finds that a commitment cannot be kept, he/she must ask the group for permission to change the commitment. For example, if the assignment for Day 3 is to read Article 6 and the participant will be away on Day 3, he/she should email this information to the other participants and commit to completing the activity by Day 4. This promotes trust and integrity and demonstrates caring about the effects we have on nature in others.

Why does the course insist that participants learn to make conscious sensory contact with and in natural areas?

Perhaps you have already run across the following mathematical question on an intelligence test: "If you count a wolf's tail as one of its legs, how many legs does a wolf have?"

"Five," of course, is the answer. Intelligent people say "Five." People who don't say "Five" will probably not get the job because the question addresses a person's mathematical-logical ability. However, reason only recognizes Five as correct until we validate what we believe to be true from contact with a real wolf. Then, many of our other natural senses come into play, such as sight, touch, motion, color, texture, language, sound, consciousness, fear, contrast and love. Each of these natural senses help our sense of reason recognize that a tail is different than a leg and that a wolf ordinarily has four legs, not five.

Does the course support all kinds of learning and ways of knowing?

Although all people are biologically and psychologically part of nature, contemporary people mostly learn and are habitually conditioned or addicted to know nature from 5-leg, out-of-touch, "as if" stories about nature. Often, we cling to our stories in the belief that our survival or well-being now, or in the hereafter, demand that we act from them. The course is psychologically unique in that it offers additional sensory experiences with nature on a 4-leg basis.

Why does the course focus on nature-connected learning?

Many course participants have a great deal of 5-leg "as if" knowledge and intelligence that accumulated from and continues to mold their nature-disconnected, contemporary world. In addition, many participants do not "walk their talk." For example, they might make exceptions to the rule and say "a wolf has four legs," while also acting on the belief that "the only good wolf is a dead wolf." Genuine contact with attractive things about  wolves that can be observed in a wolf pack can help change that idea and the notion that a wolf's tail counts as one leg. After all, every wolf is intelligent enough to know that its tail is not one of its legs. We can appreciate wolves more when we realize they relate to each other cooperatively and lovingly and that there is no record of wolves attacking humans.

How does the course help participants undo destructive relationships?

Too often without realizing it, we have been taught to dance to the drumbeat of "as if" messages that produce destructive thoughts and relationships and that are seldom found in natural systems. The deteriorating state of ecosystems and people suggest that we must improve the "as if" drumbeat of the way we learn to think about and relate to the natural world and its people. The course addresses this problem through developing respect and 4-leg contact with "genuine" nature and with people as part of nature. We then learn to think and relate based on our 4-leg experiences rather than misleading 5-leg stories.

Aren't many of our 5-leg stories deeply ingrained and unchangeable?

Some of us are very attached to our "as if" way of knowing the world and are very attached to teaching or preaching it as well. Participants should try not to influence other course participants with conditioned or favorite ways of knowing, such as personal religion, politicals, vocational/academic training, factual knowledge, race, subculture, etc. Instead, if it is attractive, help the group members discover if or how past stories compare with the new learning from conscious sensory contact with natural areas through course activities and other participants.

Is the course atmosphere safe?

Each participant's commitment to refrain from bringing the group into their old stories helps establish good will and trust that allows group email relationships to form safely. If a participant has any questions or doubts his/her ability or desire to relate on the course this way, explore the self-evidence activity in Appendix A, Page 111. Most people find it a useful and helpful tool here and for application elsewhere, as well.

Page 7 Instructions

SECTION 4: FULFILLING REWARDS

Who teaches the course?

Although past course participants help instruct/ facilitate this course, nature and Earth teach it. Dr. Cohen may instruct by involving participants in nature-connecting activities and discoveries that enable them to let Earth connections register their intelligent ways in current awareness and thinking. Particpants accomplish this by doing course activities, sharing with others through the Interact group, learning from others' responses to questions that are asked, from participants' emails, and from Dr. Cohen's occasional email postings.

What is the course purpose?

The course purpose is to learn how to locally sustain a life-long relationship with the intelligence and joy of Earth and the web of life, both of which are alive in every neighborhood, every neighbor and everyone.

How does the course reward participants? Through grades?

"If the day and the night are such that you greet them with joy, and life emits a fragrance, like flowers and sweet scented herbs-and is more elastic, starry, and immortal-that is your success."
- Henry David Thoreau

The greatest rewards and education that particpants get from the course do not come from others or course grades. They come from relating through natural attractions to other course participants and to attraction gifts in the natural world. Dr. Cohen tries to read all the postings and participate as much as possible. He also makes himself available as time permits and enjoys telephone conversations initiated by students. The telephone number is 1-360-378-6313, PST.

SECTION 5: POSTING EXPERIENCES

Isn't having a good experience enough? Why verbalize it and post it by email?

To fully benefit from the email portion of the course, participants should freely share the attraction, thoughts and feelings they get from the activities and readings with others in their group. In this way, everyone can learn from each other by reading and reacting to attractions in all of the Interact postings, which helps 4-leg knowledge integrate with 5-leg thinking.

Recognize that the amount of learning that each participant will gain partially depends on email correspondence between all of the participants. The course is not effective without the open exchange of everyone's global attraction experiences. Keep in mind, too, that the course is part of a degree program for some participants and they are depending on other students to expand their learning.

Do course participants ever get together?

The Interact groups attempt to emulate nature's ways by offering as much diversity and consensus as possible within the participants. If someone is interested in personally getting together with other course members, work it out and/or let the course organizer and facilitators know if help is needed.

SECTION 6: WE ARE THE TEXTBOOK

How does the course include and integrate participants' past experiences?

Rather than learn from the deeply-conditioned, nature-conquest, thinking and history of Western civilization, this course recognizes that we are it, that we carry, think and relate with and through it. We each have been and become what we call civilized. (It is worth noting here that Thoreau called nature "A civilization other than our own.") For this reason, on the course we learn from our experiences in the civilizing process in conjunction with unadulterated contact with unadulterated nature in the environment, others and our present selves. To accomplish this, try to share the "now" of your life, including your immediate experiences, thoughts and feelings while on the course because now is not fantasy. The immediate moment is a 4-leg way of knowing, one where Earth and we exist and relate equally.

Why does the course focus on immediate experiences?

We best know, trust and learn from our own experiences; they are essential truths of our lives. The immediate moment is the only time we can gather 4-leg self-evidence and the course attempts to make its participants aware of this by practicing it. Make efforts to consciously respect, validate and be thankful for your experiences, your thoughts and your feelings while involved with nature and this course. If you can't trust them, what can you trust?

Why do you say the course is a science?

Because it uses critical thinking and empirical logic applied to evidence. It is unique, however, in that much of the evidence it collects is obvious and easily obtainable. In its quest to conquer and manage nature, most 5-leg sciences overlook the 4-leg obvious or demean it as being subjective, touchy-feely, fuzzy thinking. However, this "evidence" holds natural systems locally and globally in balance and is an essence of nature's perfection.

How does the course focus on immediate experiences?

By using the "gaining permission" attraction process, Interact group participants enjoyably organize and maintain themselves and grow. We accomplish this by staying in the immediate natural attractions of each moment and sharing what's happening in the activities, chapters and email. Experiences in the moment tend to produce 4-leg knowledge, not inaccurate 5-leg stories. Seek immediate natural attractions. Try to refrain from bringing in stories or references outside of your immediate personal experiences, as they tend to take you out of the moment and into cultural cubbyholes that, as in our history, may trigger arguments and disunity. If these stories are part of you, own them; they are there as you in the immediate moment along with nature and your Interact group. If, for example, some author's or institution's dogma has made a statement somewhere and you feel and believe it, share that part of you as you, not as "Dr. Archibald says" or "Calmocrucians believe," etc. Stories that share thoughts and feelings about, or from moments connected with, nature hold something special in common. They unify rather than disconnect relationships because that's how nature works.

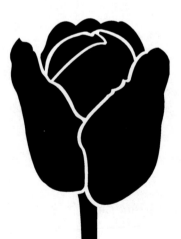

Please keep in mind that many of the stories and beliefs we are attached to come from a different knowledge base, time, place, way of life, technological power, ecological and social literacy and old problems that contribute to today's troubles. Try to be open-minded. Try to discover if what seemed appropriate then is appropriate now.

What is the significance of immediate experiences with nature?

Being born into a nature-disconnected culture is like any animal, plant or mineral growing in a barrel full of disconnected pollutant. The pollutant attaches, coats and sticks to everything, and contaminates it. We often addict to knowing nature in and around us through polluted glasses and stories that we cherish or addict to, yet they block us from nature and its intelligence. When we put energies into knowing and teaching through such stories, we too often pass up opportunities to let nature teach us about itself in its non-verbal, sensuous, 4-leg ways. They only exist in the immediate moment and often tell a different story since nature is not nature-disconnected.

You can always change and grow from the present, especially if you know who and where you are in the present. Stories that share thoughts and feelings about your nature-connected moments hold something very special in common with other people and other life forms. They are best found in present moment experiences in nature rather than stories about them alone.

Page 8 Instructions
SECTION 7: RESPONDING TO ATTRACTIONS

If the course is largely self-organizing, what holds it together?

Attractions. You will find it attractive and rewarding to read all the email and respond to what attracts you. Because of the number of participants, please keep your messages brief...a few paragraphs is enough. Share thoughts, feelings and reactions that are important to you, especially if you want input on them or want somebody else to know them. If you appreciate that somebody is sharing him or herself with you, let them know if it's attractive or important to you. If it is attractive, tell them what you have learned from what they have shared.

If you want to help others by facilitating the course, or you want credit for a degree program, save the course postings to reference in the future.

SECTION 8: SUSTAINING TRUST

Since nature is uneducated and non-literate, why should I trust what it teaches me on the course?

This course is trustable because it uses words to connect the language-reason (5-leg) part of your mentality to the non-verbal (4-leg) rest of the web of life that is part of nature in the natural world, others and yourself. The words in the email, training manuals, and the people who produce them are only trustable if the information they present accurately conveys what is happening, will happen or has happened.

How can I help the course be trustable?

In our world of words, it is our responsibility to accurately and honestly convey our actual experiences, senses and feelings if we are to know the joys and rewards of trust and community. Help build trust. Make an effort to have what you share honestly describe the attractions you sense, think and feel while doing the activities. In this way the course helps us learn to be our word.

Does the course produce unsafe dependencies upon its members?

It is hoped that participants will not drop out of the sessions once they start because Interact members depend on sharing experiences to learn and to complete the course. Each participant has consented to be on the course, and has consented to share their experiences with each other. We are all part of nature and deserve the respect given to attraction relationships with nature in the environment and each other.

SECTION 9: POSTING TO YOUR INTERACT GROUP

Are their any special "best ways" to exchange email information among course members?

Here are some important hints:

A) Send Interact group postings via email only; do NOT send attachments to emails as they may contain viruses. Use lower case as UPPER CASE IS HARDER TO READ AND COMES ACROSS AS SHOUTING.

B) When you post to your Interact group, briefly indicate the subject and/or person you are responding to, i.e., UCSB OSPREY GROUP, PART 1A, Sue's response to Jan C.

This connecting with nature course is designed to help discover the participant's relationship with nature

based on the truths of his/her conscious, sensory contacts with the natural world. For this reason, try and focus communications on:

1) sharing personal experiences -attractive sensations, feelings, reactions when doing the activities.

2) sharing parts of the readings that are attractive to nature-connected thinking and feeling and that help validate activity experiences

3) Note: Unless you request otherwise, we may anonymously archive and distribute Interact group postings through the NatureConnect List, PNC newsletters, or other communications that unify the natural world and people. These distributions also help others become familiar with the benefits of reconnecting with nature. People who make this discovery are thankful for others' contributions to their experience.

4) The web has further instructions on doing assignments and hints on sharing thoughts, feelings and experiences with other participants via the Interact groups.

D) Participants who are not taking the course for credit through the IGE degree or Certificate Program can find more information in the course syllabus at http://www.ecopsych.com/eco500.html

What does the "Base camp" web page look like? How does it operate?

A sample "Base Camp" web page is located at Appendix F. If you have questions, ask other course participants for help.

Before the course begins, participants should read the following letter:

June 4, 1995
Dear Mike,

Having finally completed the *Reconnecting With Nature* course, I consider it very valuable to me and I'm glad I did it. As you know, I had to do it twice because some of the eight participants in my first Interact group had little respect for each other's needs with regard to taking the course. Even though they had good intentions, they knew that some of us were taking the course for credit or needed it for professional or personal reasons, yet they did not hold up to their end of the bargain very well–

some, not at all. Some did not keep up with assignments, so it became difficult to continue because I did not receive reactions to my postings to the group, or their assignments were so late that they made things confusing. Two people just quit the course without saying anything, and one did not follow the guidelines and quoted authors all the time instead of sharing what happened when he did the activities, if he ever did them.

Isn't there some way that you can screen those who say they want to take the course so that those that take it keep their participation commitment to the group? I think it was right for Erica, Dan and me to decide to start over with a new group. The second course was terrific, we all learned a lot and had a great time. We still write each other and Morgan actually visited me. I'm really happy things worked out for the best. Actually, I might have had to postpone my graduation if the course did not work out.

It seems to me that you should emphasize that on the course, as in nature, each individual depends upon the cooperation of the others to sustain the email group community. Our lives are usually so disconnected and out of our control that we often lose sight of the importance of what we can contribute and how much we gain from doing it. Also it might be better if the groups were smaller. Our second group of six worked well.

Thanks for offering the course. I'm looking forward to helping guide the next group and taking the second part of the program. Perhaps I'll send the new group a copy of this letter so they have some idea of what is needed to make the course work well.

In Friendship,
Ricki Forbes

SECTION 10: SUMMARY

How would you summarize the intent of the Orientation Course?

The object of the course is to let nature touch us with its sensory,"non-literate," 4-leg communications that we can translate into 5-leg stories that accurately show us how nature works. This beneficially influences the stories by which we now know the natural world of which we are part and that's the point of the course.

Our greatest challenge is to respect and support nature in the Earth, others, and ourselves. Global warming suggests that the way we have learned to think is giving the Earth a fever. When you feel you trust these words in the present moment, you are ready to proceed with the Assignment schedule.

REMINDER TO COURSE PARTICIPANTS:

A place has been saved for you on the next Orientation course.

Please do the following:

1) Confirm you want to participate by sending your application by email to nature@interisland.net. In addition, send a hard copy of the application and $35.00 and by regular mail to IGE, P.O. Box 1605, Friday Harbor, WA. 98250.

2) Become familiar with the Preparation and "Base Camp" web pages you will receive when the addresses are sent to you.

(3) Optionally, order the RWN book. With your payment, include a SASE for your button if you have not elected to receive it with the book.

You will receive an email list of other participants shortly before the course starts.

Enjoy the fun and strength the forthcoming weeks will bring.

Are you familiar with the answers to these questions? If so, you are ready to participate in the course. Answers are in the previous text on the website pages indicated.

Website Page One

What is the general course topic?
How is the course taught?
How many hours of work does the course entail?
What is the best way to learn the course material?
Do I have to take the course before I can facilitate it or intern in it?
Who are the course participants?

Page Two

Preparation and Overview
Attitude
Schedule
Role of attractions
Written material
Guidelines and process
Unity
Value and self-empowerment
Why the process works
What guidelines help the course organize itself?

Page Three

What is the major task on the course?

What challenges does the course present?

How have past participants met the course challenges?

Is the course always successful?

If questions arise, whom do I contact?

What and why are there two course starting dates?

Page Four

Where can I find a course application form?

Do I need to buy extra course credit if I am in an IGE Degree or Certificate Program?

How do I sign up for course credit from Portland State University?

What aspects of the course are covered in the Course Organization Letter I will receive?

How do I contact the other course members to share activities and results with them?

Can I let other people know who is taking the course with me in my study group?

How do the course participants help organize and lead the course?

How does the course organize itself?

Do the course guides need special skills?

How is self-governance achieved?

Page Five

How do I find out if I have a guide role offered to me?

What are the four main guide roles?

How long does the course take?

Why is so short a course so long?

Can the duration of the course be adjusted?

Is it easy to modify the course duration?

Page Six

Is the course based on day-by-day as well as long term commitments?

How do course participants actually study themselves and each other?

Why does the course insist that participants learn to make conscious sensory contact with and in natural areas?

Does the course support all kinds of learning and ways of knowing?

Why is nature connected learning the course focus?

How does the course help us undo our destructive relationships?

Aren't many of our 5-leg stories deeply ingrained and unchangeable?

Is the course atmosphere safe?

Page Seven

Who teaches the course?

What is the course purpose?

How does the course reward its members? Through grades?

Isn't having a good experience enough? Why verbalize it and post it by email?

Do course participants ever get together?

How does the course include and integrate participants past experiences?

Why does the course focus on immediate experiences?

How does the course focus on immediate experiences?

What makes immediate experiences so important?

What is the significance of immediate experiences with nature?

Page Eight

If the course is largely self-organizing, what holds it together?

Since nature is uneducated and non-literate, why should I trust what I learn from it on the course?

How can I help the course be trustable?

Does the course produce unsafe dependencies upon its members?

Are there any special "best ways" to exchange email information amongst course members?

Page Nine

How would you summarize the intent of the Orientation Course?

Appendix D

Substantiation of the Natural System Thinking Process

Why a nature-connected psychology helps people overcome their addiction to thinking and relating irresponsibly.

Mardi Jones with Michael J. Cohen

PART ONE

We as a society are in denial. We deny that the most destructive parts of contemporary thinking result from our psychological addiction to rewards from nature-disconnected stories and technologies. This addictive disconnection separates us from nature's purity and benefits (Brown, 1992; Bower, 2000; Carin, 2001; Cohen, 2002c; Frumkin, 2001; Greenway, 1995; Taylors, 2000; Wiley, 1994). It contaminates our thinking and our relationships with natural systems within and around us.

Indisputably, nature recycles and purifies itself. We are part of nature and, as a surgically reattached arm demonstrates, Nature regenerates our wholeness when we are correctly connected to it. Since 1990 a readily available nature-connecting psychology program has existed that enables our thinking, as of old, to sensuously connect with nature and thereby let nature help it recycle its contamination. This connection enables natural systems to dissolve the destructive addiction-bonds in our psyche and purify our thought processes.

As a practicing mental health counselor and educator I have, for the past five years, studied, observed and enjoyed a unique nature-connected psychology, an ecopsychology called the Natural Systems Thinking Process (NSTP) (Scull, 1999). I have, in addition, completed Doctoral studies and research in this field. My NSTP colleagues and I have applied NSTP modality in education, mental health, healing, outdoor education, social work and recreation settings, noting the personal and professional benefits similar to those that the founder of NSTP, Dr. Michael J. Cohen, describes below (Davies, 1997; Jones, 2002; McGinnes, 1999; Rowe, 2002; Schneider, 2001; Sweeney, 2002). Our research supports observations

describe in the article entitled "Who's the Boss of You" (Jones & Cohen, 2002). This article shows how psychologically addictive, nature disconnected, attachment bonds to our destructive ways prevent people from taking a giant step into wellness, sanity and integrity. The purpose of this paper is to further explain significant aspects of NSTP and provide additional references for them.

"We shall require a substantially new manner of thinking if mankind is to survive."
-Albert Einstein

Experts agree that contemporary civilization critically needs to engage in a way of thinking and relating that transforms our present personal, social and environmental destructiveness into constructive relationships (Abrams; Fox; Bateson; Bohm; Bowers; Berg; Berry; Capra; Clinefeld; Glendinning; Harmon; Hubbard; Lazlow; Lovins; McKibben; Meadows; Orr; Pearce; Quinn; Roszac; Schweitzer; Krutch; Scull; Seuss; Wald). What must deeply concern any clear thinking person is that when a new manner of thinking, like NSTP, produces desired effects and is readily available, why do so few leaders acknowledge, incorporate or teach it? One must conclude that, as might be expected, our leaders, like the rest of us, although they deny it, are addicted to a misguided way of thinking and relating that produces great troubles.

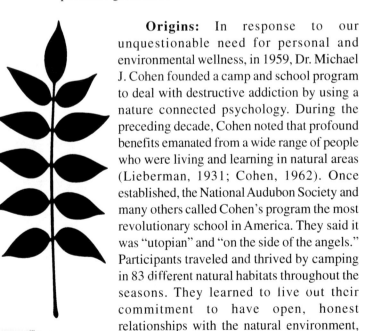

Origins: In response to our unquestionable need for personal and environmental wellness, in 1959, Dr. Michael J. Cohen founded a camp and school program to deal with destructive addiction by using a nature connected psychology. During the preceding decade, Cohen noted that profound benefits emanated from a wide range of people who were living and learning in natural areas (Lieberman, 1931; Cohen, 1962). Once established, the National Audubon Society and many others called Cohen's program the most revolutionary school in America. They said it was "utopian" and "on the side of the angels." Participants traveled and thrived by camping in 83 different natural habitats throughout the seasons. They learned to live out their commitment to have open, honest relationships with the natural environment, each other and with indigenous people(s), researchers, ecologists, the Amish, organic farmers, anthropologists, folk musicians, naturalists, shamans, administrators, historians and many others close to the land. The experience deeply reconnected their sensory inner nature to its origins in the whole of nature.

Results of the school community success were demonstrable:

Chemical dependencies, including alcohol and tobacco, disappeared as did destructive social relationships.

Personality and eating disorders subsided

Violence, crime and prejudice were unknown in the group.

Academics improved because they were applicable, hands-on and fun.

Loneliness, hostility and depression subsided. Group interactions allowed for stress release and management; each day was fulfilling and relatively peaceful.

Students using meditation found they no longer needed to use it. They learned how to sustain a nature-connected community that more effectively helped them improve their resiliency to stress and disease.

Participants knew each other better than they knew their families or best friends. Participants felt safe. They risked expressing and acting from their deeper thoughts and feelings. A profound sense of social and environmental responsibility guided their decisions.

When vacation periods arrived, neither staff nor student wanted to go home. Each person enjoyably worked to build this supportive, balanced living and learning utopia. They were home.Students sought and entered right livelihood professions.

All this occurred simply because every community member made sense of their lives by sustaining supportive, multisensory relationships that helped them restore contact with the recycling powers of the natural world within and around them.

From 30 years of travel and study in over 260 national parks, forests and subcultures, Cohen developed a repeatable learning process and psychology, (Cohen, 1987, pp. 57-59). This process unleashes one's ability to grow and survive responsibly with the natural systems within and around us. By documenting that it worked and could be taught, he earned his doctoral degree and his school evolved into a nationally recognized, accredited graduate and undergraduate degree program.

From 1985-92, Cohen translated his nature-connected psychology into the readily available Natural Systems Thinking Process (NSTP) for public use via the Internet or on site. Through NSTP, backyard or backcountry, people recover their natural integrity from readings and sharing sensory reconnection activities in local natural areas at home, work or school.

The value of NSTP is exemplified by research regarding its application to a group of at-risk students in an alternative school, (Davies, 1997). Three years of testing before and after the application of NSTP by a caring teacher or counselor showed increases in environmental literacy, academic and social skills, psychological improvement and the lasting cessation of chemical dependencies, (Cohen, 2002g).

PART TWO

Some of the factors that make it possible for NSTP to help us obtain the results I've described are listed below.

1. Addiction: Our disconnection from nature makes part of our mentality shut down by addictively rewarding us for detaching our thinking from its roots in the mutually supportive ways of Nature, (Wilson, 1984; Bateson, 1979). Unfortunately, like most addicts, we are in denial that we are addicted, (Cohen, 1993b; Glendinning, 1995; Marshall, 2001; Roszak, 1997). Our greatest problem is that because we are in denial we neither recognize nor treat as an addiction our psychological addiction to disconnectedness so we continue to suffer its hurtful effects, (Diego, 2000; Laing, 1967). Our addiction to destructive thinking creates critical troubles that many people say we must address for survival. Few, however, offer an enabling process to this end as exemplified by Abrams; Fox; Bateson; Bohm; Bowers; Berg; Berry; Capra; Clinefeld; Glendinning; Harmon; Hubbard; Lazlow; Lovins; McKibben; Meadows; Orr; Pearce; Quinn; Roszac; Schweitzer; Krutch; Scull; Seuss; Wilson; Wald.

2. Multiple Senses: Our addiction to disconnection from Nature pollutes our thinking by injuriously shutting down at least 53 vital sensitivities, natural intelligences we inherently register in our consciousness, (Cohen, 1997, pp. 37-50; Cohen, 1990; Barrett, 1998; Bekoff, 2000; Bower, 2002; Flom, 2001; Gardner, 1999; Giraud, 2001; Hewlett, 2000; Jaffe, 2001; Kinser, 2000; Kujala, 2001; Lipkin, 1995; Murchie, 1978; Pittenger, 2001, Rivlin, 1984; Rovee-Collie, 1992; Travis, 1997; Stern, 1998; Spelke, 1992; Samples, 1976). The biological imperative of these senses is to enable our thinking to help us survive in a mutually supportive balance with natural systems, as does everything else in nature.

3. Natural Attraction Energies: NSTP works because from sub-atomics to solar systems, all intact relationships, physical or otherwise, are held together by natural attraction energies, (Schombert, 2000; Unified, 2002; Einstein, 1997). What we call repulsion can just as easily be recognized as attraction to something more immediate and important. For example, when in a dangerous situation do we run away in fear or run for our life? Both are survival attractions. Was the "big bang" a profound explosion or a profound attraction to diversity? NSTP helps us create moments in nature that let genuine contact with attraction energies realign and recycle the misguided attachments in us that make us destructive addicts. A major solution to many problems is to genuinely enable our thinking to return to the "Garden of Eden" and use its wisdom to help us co-create a brighter future for it and ourselves, (Cohen, 2002b; Milius, 2002).

4. Recycling: Attractions feel good. Attraction energies are the heart of recycling and purification. For example, air recycles its purity as well as strengthens the diverse integrity of the plant, animal and mineral kingdoms, (Oxygen, 2001; Odum, 1971; Molles, 1999; Braswell et al, 1994). Nature's recycling of air is fueled, by attraction energies, nature's fundamental binding force (Capra 1997; Schewe & Stein 1999; Discovery 2001). Similarly, whenever we safely make contact with attractions in nature they trigger our brain to release dopamine, a neurotransmitter that triggers good feelings, (Powledge, 1999; Wise, R. A.; Bauco, P.; Carlezon, W. A.; Jr., & Trojniar, W.; 1992). Each attraction sensation, feeling or emotion is a rational, sensory, rewarding way of knowing and relating that we biologically inherit from and hold in common with Nature, (Encyclopedia, 2002; Irvine and Warber, 2002; Kinser, 2000). Neuroscientists identify attraction energies as Freud's "drives" that they call "seeking urges" (Guterl, 2002). Each encourages and shapes good citizenship in the global life community.

5 Pollution: We are mentally more than physically isolated from the natural world. The polluted way we think produces behavior that pollutes natural and social systems, (Pascale, 1999; Devall, 1986). We seldom recognize the need for our thinking to be connected with nature and thereby heal, purify and simultaneously contribute to life's welfare as part of nature's recycling process, (Sabini, 2000; Jung, 1964). This misjudgment produces a hurtful omission in our reasoning that pollutes and disables our ability to think attractively, like Nature works, (Ascione & Arkow; Cohen, 1993a; 1995, 2002u; Corum, 1997; Wheatley, 1992).

6. Natural Senses Make Sense: Over 85% of our mentality, the mammalian brain, biologically thinks and knows through natural senses, (Bekoff, 2000; Cohen, 1997; Washington, 2001). These sensitivities provide us with empirical knowledge and feelings about and from our relationship with plants, animals and minerals, (Krutch, 1956). That we experience these senses at birth or before demonstrates

that we inherit from nature, not society, the ability to enjoy and register them, (Stepp, 1996). Everything in Nature displays these sensitivities in some form, (Darwin, 1872). Some societies culture them to good effect (Kroeber, 1988; Farb, 1968). They can help us see that we are biologically part of nature, (Scull, 2000; Wilson, 1984; Washington, 2001). They also can motivate us to live cooperatively with natural systems in nature and each other, (Dwyer; Leeming; Cobern; Porter & Jackson, 1993; Encyclopedia, 2002).

7. Effects of Disconnection: Our disconnection deprives our thinking from recycling in nature, (Cohen, 2001b; Shaw, 2000; Vogel, 1999). Instead we become addicted to rewards from artifacts and beliefs foreign to nature. Their side effects are destructive to natural systems around and within us.

8. Denial: As addicts in denial, we neither approach nor treat our unsolvable problems as symptoms or results of our addiction to detachment. Instead, we consider our excessive detachment as normal, intelligence, and progress, (P.R. Newsletter, 2001). Contemporary people are addicted to live in buildings, towns and cities, void of sensory connection with Nature, (Glendinning, 1995). Over 99.99% of our thinking is disconnected from authentic nature's profound ability to create, purify, recycle, regenerate, cleanse and heal our mind, body and spirit. We spend, on average, 95% of our time indoors, (Wiley, 1994).

9. Wellness: The wellness and mental health improvements that result from reconnecting with nature are momentous, (Cohen, 1998, 2002h, f; Clay, 2001; Frumkin, 2001; Greenway, 1995; Irvine & Warber, 2002; Takano, T et al, 2002). Devoid of the responsible emotional rewards and information available from conscious contact with attractions in nature, our sensory unfulfillment generates our destructive wants hurt, greed, insensitivity and violence. It also prevents our disconnected thinking from recovering by recycling (Frumkin, 2001; Wilson, 1984; Durning, 1995).

10. Abstract Thinking: Our abstract thinking operates differently from Nature. Nature, being non-literate, rarely engages in our abstract verbal way of reasoning and relating, (Abram, 1997; Bohm, 1993; Kates, 2002; Environmental, 1994; Dewey, 1929). For example, at any given moment, everything in nature is always attracted to flowing and changing and therefore in a different place, shape and relationship from every other thing, (Morowitz, 1992). Thus, the abstract, the number "One" can not be correctly identified in nature except as constant flowing change, as John Dewey theorized. In addition, nowhere in nature do we find nothing; some attraction energy or material of nature exists everywhere.

Thus, the abstract Zero does not exist in nature. Since One and Zero don't represent nature, each time our thinking relies on them alone for information we further stray from living in balance with natural systems within and around us. Since our mathematics, logic, financial and computer systems are rooted in the mechanical, but unnatural, truth of One and Zero we produce our destructive side effects, (Cohen, 2002o). We may offset this irresponsible incompleteness by balancing One and Zero with additional sensory knowledge and rewards from attraction energies in nature, (Borhoo, 2001; Bradley, 2000).

NSTP researchers observe as well as directly experience and consider psychological, emotional and spiritual relationships between the natural systems in themselves, others and the environment, (Ingram, 1999). The social and environmental results of reconnecting these relationships in nature are the envy of responsible schools, therapies and social systems, (Cohen, 2002a). Any organization or person has the ability to enjoy the program's results by choosing to use Cohen's nature-reconnected thinking methods. NSTP empowers interested lay people or leaders with a science that works as well in backyards and local parks as it does back country, sometimes better. As practical as it is potent, the art of NSTP is available in five books written by Cohen, (Cohen, 2001). In addition, NSTP basics can be mastered in less than six weeks via the Institute's interactive Project NatureConnect classes on the Internet, (Cohen, 2002c).

11. Isolated Delusion: In our nature-disconnected, mentally isolated state we convince ourselves that we are wiser than nature but the deteriorated state of the environment and society tell a different story, (McKibben, 1999; Cohen, 1999; 2002z; Lavers, 2000; Wilson, 1993). Our addiction is a wanting, destructive juggernaut. Our great problems do not exist in nature or nature connected people(s), (Armen, 1971; Bower, 2002, Vol. 158; Farb, 1968; Kroeber, 1988; Cohen, 2002h).

12. Critical Questions: To correct our polluted thinking, Dr. Cohen and his workers have, with good success, sought, identified and introduced NSTP into contemporary thinking as a nature-reconnecting mental and social skill. When people include the use of this skill in their thinking, they think better and more successfully relate to the critical questions, below, that face us, (Cohen, 2000).

ENVIRONMENT: Since we are part of nature, what is, and how do we correct, the major difference that makes us destroy the environment while everything else in nature enhances it?

COMMUNITY: To be part of a community or system one must be in communication with it in some way. People are part of the global life system. How does it communicate with our thinking and vice versa?

SUSTAINABILITY: Can you cite a practical model, community or process that successfully produces sustainability for all of contemporary society?

ACCURATE INFORMATION: Since our polluted mathematics, language and perceptions are abstracts that distort empirical evidence, what is the greatest truth in your life that you can trust? (Hint: it is neither God, love, honesty nor nature)

PSYCHOLOGICAL DISORDERS: What produces the wanting void in our psyche, the discomfort, greed, and loneliness that fuels most human and, in turn, environmental disorders?

SPIRITUALITY: What is the psychological relationship between Nature, the Divine, and the Human Spirit?

EDUCATION: Since we learn to be who we are, what factor in modern education teaches us to produce our lasting problems?

RECOVERY: What important source of healing energy does our cultural bias omit thereby sustaining our dependency upon destructive substances and questionable healing programs?

ECONOMICS: What is the force that produces and makes us dependent upon environmentally and socially destructive economic relationships?

STRESS: What is the anxiety producing difference between a fact, a thought, a feeling and an act?

WAR: What omission makes us continue to assault nature and people when it doesn't make sense and we neither like doing it nor its hurtful effects?

LEADERSHIP AND CONFLICT RESOLUTION: If the thinking of a democratic society is polluted, how can the decisions of the majority, its leadership, or its foundations be in the society's best interest?

INTELLIGENCE AND CONSCIOUSNESS: How can we restore to our thinking our inherent but missing 53 or more natural sensory intelligences that contemporary society has hurtfully buried in our subconscious?

NATURAL SYSTEMS: Why does contemporary society often identify a person's love of nature as "escapist recreation" rather than "significant re-creation."

We don't respond adequately to these questions because most of our information and science is polluted by our bonded, abstract, separation from and conquest of nature, (Kahn 1999; Doman 984; Richmond 2000).

13. Regenerating Sanity: The regenerative abilities of natural systems peacefully produce nature's perfection, (Colwell, 2001; Stilgoe, 2001). In 1965, long-term exposure to natural attraction energies enabled Cohen to sense and reason that Earth acted like, and therefore no doubt was, a living organism, (Cohen, 1985, 1986a, 1987, pp., 49-78, 1994; Colwell, 2001; Irvine & Warber, 2002; Lovelock, 1987; Bower, 2002).

14. Mental Contamination: Mind pollution prevents the perfection of natural systems around and within us from operating normally, (Colman, 2002; Macphail, 1992).

15. Natural Antidotes: NSTP helps us meet the challenge of mind pollution through what some have called "a profound science of the obvious," (Cohen, 2000a; Cohen, 1993). It enables us to find and share natural antidotes to our contaminated thinking by thinking with NSTP while in conscious sensory contact with the attractions in natural systems found in ourselves, other people and natural areas, (Cohen, 1991, 1992; Batz, 2000; Dossey, 1997; Irvine, K & Warber, S, 2002; Lyman, 2002; Parsons, 1998; Ulrich, 1991). NSTP enables us to safely free the perfection of rewarding natural attraction energies within and around us to do what they do best, to recycle our polluted mentality so we may think more sensitively, like nature works, (Bateson, 1979).

16. Nature's Value: Most people don't recognize that personal or professional relationships that are genuinely connected with attractions in Nature are more enjoyable, successful and responsible than those isolated from Nature, (Holmes, 2000; Stepp, 1996; Greenway, 1995; Harrison, 1994). As seen below, for almost three thousand years our culture has been aware of nature's value but has prejudicially rewarded us for conquering it:

"The purpose of life is to live in agreement with nature."
- **Zen,** circa 520 B.C.

"What greater grief than the loss of one's native land."
- **Euripides** circa 450 B.C.

"And the true order of going, or being led by another, to the things of love, is to begin from the beauties of Earth. "
- **Plato** circa 400 B.C.

"If one way be better than another that you may be sure is nature's way."
- **Aristotle** 350 B.C.

"That which fills the universe I regard as my body and that which directs the universe I see as my own nature."
- **Chuang-Tzu** circa 370 B.C.

"Those things are better which are perfected by nature than those which are finished by art."
- **Cicero** circa 80 B.C.

17. Polluted Leadership: The intelligent leaders we appoint usually support our wayward path, (Terborgh, 1999). Cohen says, "If we don't genuinely reconnect our thinking to nature's rewards, trying to reverse our anti-nature bigotry and its effects is like a person of color trying to convince the KKK to embrace them."

18. Responsible Growth: People learning to use NSTP online have, within six weeks, reported that it makes a great difference for them, (Cohen, 1997c, 2002i; Colwel, 2001; Kaplan, 1995; Wheatley & Kellner-Rogers, 1999; Weil, 1996). They have learned to increasingly think with nature, (Davies, 1997; Jones, 2002; McGinnes, 1999; Rowe, 2002; Schneider, 2001; Sweeney, 2002). In the light of enjoying NSTP, they report that they, their family and world feel and relate better, (Brown, 1992; Bower, 2000; Carin, 2001; Frumkin, 2001; Greenway, 1995; Swanson, 1998; Taylors, 2000; Wiley, 1994). Destructive relationships with people, places and substances almost effortlessly diminish as they are replaced by responsible, non-polluting, purifying rewards from natural sensory attractions that previously lay hidden, (Cohen, 2002h; Nicodemus, 1999; Pearce, 1980; Wald, 1985; Wilson, 1984).

19. Alternatives: We have had, for decades, an abundance of affordable alternative technologies, social processes and models that would significantly increase our compatibility with natural systems and each other, (Lovins, 2000; Original Articles, 1984). These improvements continue to lie idle because we have not restored the consciousness necessary to motivate the public to insist upon their use, (Brown, 1992; Swanson, 2001; Todd, 1984).

20. Back to Basics: NSTP increases our mental capacity for gaining rewarding empirical knowledge directly from nature. Cohen designed the process while in the balance and beauty of bright stars and 87 different habitats in North America's national parks and forests, (Cohen, 2000a, 2001; National, 2001). NSTP helps us bring our thinking back to basics so we may recycle our mind pollution and travel a more sensible path in co-creation with natural systems, (Zev, 2000). The benefits of thousands of peoples' gratifying nature- connected transformative experiences, (Adams, 1996; Cohen, 1997a; Davies, 1997; Flannery, 1999; Slovic, 1999; Taylors, 2000) speak for themselves but only to minds willing to listen.

21. Resilience: Most writers seldom offer, and often disregard, a empirical thinking process, one that enables our polluted consciousness to identify, resist or change destructive bonding to disconnection, (Abram, 1997; Berg, 1995; Berry, 1990; Fox, 1996; Quinn, 1993; Roszac, 1995; Taylors, 2000). NSTP immunizes us to the callings of irresponsible attractions and seeks voluntary simplicity, (Pierce, 2000), It enables us to enjoy responsible rewards, (Additional Results, 2002).

22. Rebonding: To be effective, in addition to awareness messages, we must offer a potent psychological process that enables a person to achieve responsible goals by enjoying more responsible relationship satisfactions and bonds, (Cloran, 2000; Gifford, 2000; Laszlo, 2001; Hubbard, 1998). We seldom recognize that what we call cultural loves or bonds are actually natural sense attraction energies in us that have additively established cultural attachments, be they constructive or destructive, (Kaplan, 2000; Glendinning, 1995).

23. Core Problem: We deny that the most destructive parts of contemporary thinking and relationships result from our psychological addiction to rewards from nature-disconnected stories and technologies. This addiction separates our psyche from the renewing powers, purity and wellness enjoyed by the other members of natural systems, (Brown, 1992; Bower, 2000; Carin, 2001; Cohen, 2002c; Frumkin, 2001; Greenway, 1995; Taylors, 2000; Wiley, 1994).

PART THREE

Conclusion: Because I have mastered the NSTP experience, it is easy for me to recognize that excessive disconnection from natural system attraction energies in nature generate the hurt and omissions that underlie our greatest challenges. My familiarity with NSTP also enables me to conclude that reconnecting ourselves with natural system attraction energies makes perfect sense. It allows them to beneficially recycle and restore our integrity and thinking.

I can well remember, and still watch in others, the screen of disbelief that filtered and demeaned my attraction to NSTP when I first heard about it. That disbelief was countered, however, by recognizing that the way I felt and related when in natural areas was an important aspect of myself that I had learned to demean.

There was nothing to lose by trusting that part of me to show me where it thought I'd be happiest and most productive. With that in mind, I did the Orientation Course, (Cohen, 2002d). It opened new vistas that I found enjoyable and profound. I've remained on that path and conclude it is a valid way for people to reduce their stressful addictions and increase their integrity at every level. This gels with Nobel Peace Prize winners, Albert Schweitzer and Albert Einstein, who said in effect that, until mankind can extend the circle of his compassion to embrace all living creatures and the whole of nature and its beauty, he will never, himself, know peace, (Schweitzer, 1996; Einstein, 1997).

Author

Mardi Jones, Ph.D., is an environmental educator, writer and counselor who has pioneered the use of NSTP in her private practice in Washington State, USA.

Resource

Michael J. Cohen, Ed.D., an award winning author who directs several university programs in Applied Ecopsychology, conceived the 1985 International Symposium "Is the Earth a Living Organism" and is the recipient of the Distinguished World Citizen Award.

For further information, visit the NSTP website, http://www.ecopsych.com or contact the authors.

References:

Abram, D. (1997). The Spell of the Sensuous: Perception and Language in a More-Than-Human World. Vintage Books.

Adams, C. (1996). The Soul Unearthed. Sentient Publications: Boulder, Colorado.

Additional Results (2002). Survey of Participants http://www.ecopsych.com/survey.html

Armen , J.C. (1971). Gazelle Boy, Universe Books

Ascione, F.R. & Arkow, P. (ed) (1999). Child Abuse, Domestic Violence, and Animal Abuse: Linking the Circles of Compassion for Prevention and Intervention. Purdue University Press.

Barker, M. (2000). Religion and Order of Nature. (Review) The Ecologist, January 01, 2000.

Barrett, J.F. & Hoch, J. A. (1998). Antibacterial agents that inhibit two-component signal transduction systems. Proceedings of the National Academy of Sciences 95 (April 28): 5317.

Bateson, G. (1979). Every Schoolboy Knows, Mind and Nature: A Necessary Unit, Chapter 2, Bantam

Batz, J. (2000). It's hard to understand the nature of nature. National Catholic Reporter, December 15, 2000

Bekoff, M. (2000). Animal Emotions: Exploring Passionate Natures. Bioscience, Oct 2000, Vol. 50 Issue 10, p. 861.

Berg, (1995). Discovering Your Life-Place: A First Bioregional Workbook. Planet Drum Foundation.

Berry, T. (1990). The Dream of the Earth. Sierra Club Books.

Bohm, D. in Keepin, W. (1993). Lifework of David Bohm - River of Truth, ReVision, Summer http://www.shavano.org/html/bohm.html

Borhoo, (2001). The History of Zero, http://www.geocities.com/borhoo/History.htmBower, B (2002) The Eyes Have It: Newborns prefer faces with a direct gaze, Science News 07/01/2000Vol. 158 Issue 1, p8

Bowers, C. A. (1997). The Culture of Denial: Why the Environmental Movement Needs a Strategy for Reforming Universitites and Public Schools. Albany: State University of New York Press.

Bower, B. (2001). Into the Mystic. 02/17/2001, Vol. 159, Issue 7, p104 Science News.

Bower, B. (2000). Attachment disorder draws closer look. Science News 05/27/2000, Vol. 157, Issue 22, p. 343

Bower, B. (2000). Raising Trust, Science News 07/01/2000, Vol. 158, Issue 1, p8.

Bradley, E. (2000). The Computational Beauty of Nature: Computer Exploration of Fractals, Chaos, Complex Systems, and Adaptation. (book review) AI Magazine.

Braswell, (1993). Global Cycles of Biologically Active Elements. Schimel, David S, Holland, R. McKeown, D.S. Ojima, M.L Bender and P.P.Tans, 1993.

Brown, . (1992) The Journey 1992 / Berkley Publishing Group. http://www.spirittales.com/spirittales085.htm

Capra, F. (1997). The Tao of Physics: A New Understanding of Living Systems, pp. 132- 143 Doubleday. http://www.sciam.com/askexpert_directory.cfm

Carin, G. (2001). Nature's Path to Inner Peace Jul/Aug, Vol. 34, Issue 4, p62, Psychology Today.

Chawla, L. (1998). "Significant Life Experiences Revisited: A Review of Research on Sources of Environmental Sensitivity", The Journal of Environmental Education, 29, 3, pp. 11-21.

Clay, R. A. (2001), Green is good for you Monitor, Volume 32, No. 4 American Psychological Association April 2001 Clinebell, H, (1996) Ecotherapy: Heaing Ourselves, Healing the Earth, A Guide to Ecologically Grounded Personality Theory, New York, The Haworth Press.

Cloran, R. (2000). The Nature Photographer's Code of Practice. The Nature Division of the Photographic Society of America, PSA Journal, July 01 2000

Cohen, M. J. (2002). Natural Systems Thinking Process. POB 1605, Project NatureConnect, Friday Harbor, WA http://www.ecopsych.com/orient.html

a.   Introduction p.1

b.   Appendix p 8

c.   Prerequisites Survey http://www.ecopsych.com/survey.html

d.   Orientation Course Description p1 . http://www.ecopsych.com/orient.html

e.   Major questions, Course Description p2 http://www.ecopsych.com/orient.html

f.   Prerequisites Survey p2 http://www.ecopsych.com/survey2.html

g.   Prerequisites Survey p13 Davies http://www.ecopsych.com/survey5.html

h.   Prerequisites Survey p14 Cohen http://www.ecopsych.com/survey6.html

i.   Reference p1-1

j.   Appendix p.1-2

k.   Supportive reading Ch.1 p1-7 webstrings http://www.ecopsych.com/insight.html

l.   Process Ch.1 p.7

m.   Perceptions Ch. 2 p1 http://www.rockisland.com/~process/5grpercept.html

n.   Rewards Ch. 2 p4 http://www.rockisland.com/~process/

o.   Karen Ch. 2, p.6-7 http://www.rockisland.com/~process/5grnchkaren.html

p.   History Introduction, p.2

q.   Good feelings Ch.3 p.2-3

r.   Germine Ch.3 p.2-3 http://www.ecopsych.com/germine.html

s.   Permission respect Chr-p1 http://www.rockisland.com/~process/

t.   Ch. 4 Color Chart http://www.ecopsych.com/counseling.html

u.   Intelligence Ch. 5 ...http://www.ecopsych.com/ecoiq.html

v.   Respiration Ch. 6 p.1-9 http://www.ecopsych.com/trail.html

w.   Attractions Ch. 7 p.1-2 http://www.ecopsych.com/naturelov30greet.html

x.   NSTP Process Ch. 8 pp2-3

y.   Shock ppz. State of Earth Appendix p3-6 http://www.ecopsych.com/zombie2.html

Cohen, M. J. (2001). Books http://www.ecopsych.com/books.html

Cohen, M. J. (2001b). The Stairway to Sanity: Wellness means Wholeness. http://www.ecopsych.com/wholeness2.html

Cohen, M. J. (2000). Nature Connected Psychology Greenwich University Journal of Science and Technology Vol 1, No. 1, June 2000.

Cohen, M. J. (2000a). Einstein's World, Project NatureConnect, Box 1605, Friday Harbor, WA.

Cohen, M. J. (2000b). The personal page of an innovative scientist-counselor-ecopsychologist- http://www.ecopsych.com/mjcohen.html

Cohen, M. J. (1999). (Ed.) A Global Overview; The State of Planet Earth http://www.ecopsych.com/zombie2.html

Cohen, M. J. (1998). Who Needs To Be Educated? http://www.ecopsych.com/infonews.html

Cohen, M. J. (1997). Reconnecting With Nature: Finding Wellness through restoring your bond with the Earth, Ecopress, Corvallis, Oregon. (pp 89-98) http://www.ecopsych.com/newbook.html

Cohen, M. J. (1997a). How the Mind in Nature brings People to their Senses. Proceedings, International Conference of North American Association for Environmental Education, Washington, DC

Cohen, M. J. (1997c). Journalized Findings/ http://www.ecopsych.com/millecopstrand.html.

Cohen, M. J. (1995). Counseling Nature, A Greening of Psychotherapy, InterPsych Newsletter of Mental Health. Section C: Research http://www.ecopsych.com/counseling.html

Cohen, M. J. (1994). The Distinguished World Citizen Award: Responsible Fulfillment and Guidance from Nature Connections, Taproots, Fall 1994, Cortland, NY: Coalition for Education in the Out of doors. http://www.ecopsych.com/overview.html

Cohen, M. J. (1993). Well Mind, Well Earth, Roche Harbor, WA, World Peace University Press http://www.ecopsych.com/books.html

Cohen, M. J. (1993a). Integrated Ecology: The Process of Counseling With Nature. The Humanistic Psychologist, Vol. 21 No. 3 Washington, DC: American Psychological Association.

Cohen, M. J. (1993b). Counseling With Nature: Catalyzing Sensory Moments that Let Earth Nurture. Counseling Psychology Quarterly, Vol. 6, No. 1, Carfax Publishing, Abingdon Oxfordshire, England:

Cohen, M. J. (1992). New Roots for Personal Growth and Grounding Journal of the Oregon Counseling Association, Eugene, Oregon.

Cohen, M. J. (1991) Integrating Nature's Balance. The Journal of Environmental Education, v.22 #4, Washington, DC.9.

Cohen, M. (1990). Connecting With Nature: Creating Moments That Let Earth Teach. Portland, Oregon: World Peace University Press.

Cohen, M. J. (1987). How Nature Works, Stillpoint, Walpole, NH,

Cohen, M. J. (1986). Education as if Nature Mattered: Heeding the Wilderness Within, Proceedings, Association for Experiential Education Annual Conference, AEE, Boulder Colorado.

Cohen, M. J. (1986a). in Denness, B. (Ed.) The Maverick Genius Conference: Proceedings of the International Symposium on the Promotion of Unconventional Ideas in Science, Medicine and Sociology Bureau of Applied Sciences, Isle of Wight, UK.

Cohen, M. J. (1985). Reaffirming Kinship with Planet Earth, Proceedings of International Symposium "Is the Earth A Living Organism" Chapter 19 National Audubon Society.

Cohen, M. J. (1982). Prejudice Against Nature A Guide for the Liberation of Self and Planet, Cobblesmith, Freeport, ME

Cohen, M. J. (1974). Our Classroom is Wild America, Cobblesmith, Freeport, NY

Cohen, M. J. (1962). What's Wrong with Co-ed Camping? N.Y. Post Graduate Press.

Corum, H. G. (1997). Rehabilitating Vacant Lot Sparks Struggle at Alternative School. The Oregonian April 21, Portland, Oregonhttp://www.ecopsych.com/infonews.html

Colman J. (2002). Water Pollution in the Great Lakes,http://www.great-lakes.net/teach/pollution/water/water1.html

Colwell, R. (2001). "World Enough, and Time: A Global Investment for the Environment" in Dybas, C. L. From Biodiversity to Biocomplexity: A Multidisciplinary Step toward Understanding Our Environment.Bioscience Jun2001, Vol. 51 Issue 6, p. 426.

Darwin C. (1872). The Expression of the Emotions in Man and Animals.

Davies, L, (1997). Reconnecting With Nature: educational self-esteem activities for reducing drug use and irresponsible relationships in students at risk. ERIC 764 ED387752, U.S. Department of Education. http://www.ecopsych.com/restore.html

Dewey (1929). Experience and Nature Chapt 2 Dover, New York

Devall, B. (1986). Deep Ecology, Gibbs Smith

Diego, R. (2000).. Man In Denial New Century Publishing, http://www.insmkt.com/denial.htm

Discovery of the Unified Field (2001). http://www.worldpeaceendowment.org/invincibility/invincibility6.html

Doman R. J. (1984). Sensory Deprivation Journal of the National Academy for Child Development Vol. 4, No. 3

Dossey, L. (1997). The healing power of pets: a look at animal-assisted therapy. Alternative Therapy Health and Medicine, 3(4); 8-16.

Durning, A. T. (1995). Are We Happy Yet? inEcopsychology Restoring the Earth Healing the Mind. (pp. 68-76) San Francisco, Ca. Sierra Books.

Dr. Seuss, (1971). The Lorax, NY Random House

Dwyer, W. O., Leeming, F. C., Cobern, M. K., Porter, B. E., & Jackson, J. M. (1993). Critical review of behavioral interventions to preserve the environment: Research since 1980. Environment and Behavior, 25, 275-321.

Einstein, A. (1997). in Neligh, R.D. The Grand Unification: A Unified Field Theory of Social Order, New Constellation Press

Encyclopedia Britannica Sensory reception, (2002). Evolution of Sensory Systems http://www, britannica.com

Environmental Protection Agency, (1994). Pollution Brochure EPA-841-F-94-005, 1994 http://www.epa.gov/owow/nps/qa.html.

Fox, (1996). Original Blessing: A Primer in Creation Spirituality, Bear & Co.

Farb, (1968) Man's Rise to Civilization, Chapter 2, E.P. Dutton, New York, N.Y.

Flannery, M. C. (1999). The conservation aesthetic and the microscopic aesthetic.Oct99, Vol. 49 Issue 10, p801 Bioscience

Flom, R. A. & Bahrick, L. E. (2001). The global array: Not new to infant researchers. Behavioral and Brain Sciences 24(April): 221.

Frumkin, H. (2001). Beyond toxicity: Human health and the natural environment. American Journal of Preventive Medicine 20(3): 234-240 (March)

Gardner, H. (1999). Are There Additional Intelligences? The Case for Naturalist, Spiritual, and Existential Intelligences in Kane, J., Education, Information and Transformation, Prentice Hall, New Jersey

Giraud, A. L. (2001). The global array: Not new to infant researchers. Behavioral and Brain Sciences 24(April): 221.

Gifford, R. (2000). Why We're Destroying the Earth , Psychology TodayMar/Apr2000, Vol. 33 Issue 2, p68

Giraud, A. L., et al. (2001). Cross-modal plasticity underpins language recovery after cochlear implantation. Neuron 30(June): 657.

Glendinning, C. (1995). Technology, Trauma and the Wild in Roszak, Ecopsychology Restoring the Earth, Healing the Mind p. 44, San Francisco: Sierra Club Books

Germine, (1996). Reconnecting to Subconscious Origins http://www.ecopsych.com/germine.html

Greenway, R. (1995). The Wilderness Effect and Ecopsychology in Ecopsychology Restoring the Earth, Healing the Mind. p. 123, San Francisco: Sierra Club Books.

Guterl, F. (2002). What Freud Got Right, Newsweek, November 11, 2002, .New York.

Harman, W. (1998). Global Mind Change: The Promise of the 21st Century. Berrett-Koehler, Publishers, Inc., San Francisco.

Harrison, P. (1994). Natural Pantheism: a spiritual approach to nature and the cosmos. http://members.aol.com/Heraklit1/index.htm

Hewlett, B. S., Lamb, M. E. et al. (2000). Internal working models, trust, and sharing among foragers. Current Anthropology 41(April): 287.

Hubbard, B. M. (1998). Conscious Evolution: Awakening the Power of Our Social Potential, New World Library.

Holmes, (2000). Why are Natural Environments Special? Mental Health Resources, http://mentalhealth.about.com/library/weekly/aa011298.htm

Ingram, P. (1999). On the wings of a blue heron: religious reflections on the interdependence of nature) Cross Currents, June 22 1999

Irvine, K & Warber, S. (2002). "Greening Healthcare: Practicing as if the Natural Environment Really Mattered" reviewed in "Alternative Therapies in Health and Medicine" September/October 2002 (Volume 8, Number 5). .

Jaffe, J., et al. (2001). Rhythms of dialogue in infancy: Coordinated timing in development. Monographs of the Society for Research in Child Development 66:150.

Jones M. & Cohen, M. J. (2002). Who is the Boss of You? In press, http://www.ecopsych.com/wholeness66.html

Jung, C. G. (1964). Modern Man in Search of a Soul and Man and His Symbols by (Princeton University Press.

Kahn, P. H. (1999). The Human Relationship with Nature: Development and Culture. MIT Press, Cambridge, Massachusetts, USA.

Kaplan, S. (2000). Human Nature and Environmentally Responsible Behavior. Journal of Social Issues, September 22 2000 by Flom, R.A., and L.E. Bahrick. 2001. The global array: Not new to infant researchers. Behavioral and Brain Sciences 24(April): 221.

Kaplan, S. (1995). The Restorative Benefits of Nature: Toward an Integrative Framework. Journal of Environmental Psychology, 15, 169-182.

R.W. Kates, (2000). "Part and Apart: Issues in Humankind's Relationship to the Natural World," in F. Kenneth Hare, ed., The Experiment of Life: Science and Religion (Toronto, Can.: University of Toronto

Kinser, P (2000). Cerebral Cortex Wonders of the Brain, http://serendip.brynmawr.edu/bb/kinser/Glossary.html

Kujala, T. (2001). Brain science: A more direct way of understanding our senses. Behavioral and Brain Sciences 24(April): 224.

Kroeber, T. (1988). Ishi in Two Worlds, University of California Press

Krutch, J. W. (1956). The Moth and the Candle in Voice of the Desert, a Naturalist's Interpretation W. Sloane Associates, New York

Laing, R. D. (1967). The Politics of Experience Routledge & Kegan Paul http://www.mythosandlogos.com/Laing.html

Lavers, L. (2000). The Pangean Catastrophe. New Statesman, May 29 2000.

Lieberman, J. (1931). Creative Camping, Association Press, New York.

Lipkin, R. (1995). Bacterial Chatter. Science News, Vol. 147, No. 9 Washington DC: Science Service Inc.

Laszlo, E. (2001). Macroshift: Navigating the Transformation to a Sustainable World, Inc. San Francisco: Berrett-Koehler Publishers.

Lovelock, J. (1987). Gaia: A New Look at Life on Earth. Oxford.

Lovins, A. (2000). in Kumar Natural Capitalism Resurgence issue, 1980 January / February.

Lyman, F. (2002). The Geography of Health, Land and People, vol. 14 No. 2, Fall 2002.

Macphail, E. (1982)."Brain and Intelligence in Vertebrates". Oxford, England: Clarendon Press.

Marshall, G. (2001). The Psychology of Denial: our failure to act against climate change. The Ecologist, 22/10/2001.

Margulis, L. (1986). Microcosmos: Four Billion Years of Microbial Evolution. p. Intro, Summit Books.

Meyers, D. G. (1997). Does Economic Growth Improve Human Morale? The Consuming Passion, Rodney Clapp (Ed) InterVarsity Press http://www.newdream.org/newsletter/myers.html

Meadows, D. (2000). The Global Citizen, April 20, 2000 http://iisd1.iisd.ca/pcdf/meadows/earthday_plus_30.html

McKibben, W. (1999). The End of Nature Anchor Books/Doubleday.

McGinnes, M. (1999). Project NatureConnect, http://www.ecopsych.com/webst1ucsblttr.html

Milius, S. (2002). Corn Defenses: bitten plants deploy gut-rotting enzyme in Science News, Vol. 162 No. 11 p.166.

Molles, M.C. (1999). Ecology: Concepts and Applications. P .467. McGraw Hill.

Morowitz, H. (1992). Beginnings of Cellular Life. Yale Univ Press.

Murchie, G. (1978). Seven Mysteries of Life. Boston, Massachusetts: Houghton Mifflin.

National Park (2001). Visitation Statistics http://www.aqd.nps.gov/npstats/npstats.cfmmost

Nicodemus, T. (1999). Snoezelen: A Magical Place at Camp.Camping MagazineSep/Oct99, Vol. 72 Issue 5, p18

Odum, E. P. (1971). Fundamentals of Ecology. Third Edition. Saunders. p. 38

Original Articles (1984). New Alchemy Quarterly, No. 17 New Alchemy Institute, Inc.East Falmouth, MA 02536 http://gm.kqed.org/4/77/

Oxygen Cycle (2001). EncyclopÊdia Britannica http://www.britannica.com/eb/article? eu=59293

Parsons, R., Tassinary, L. G., Ulrich, R. S., M. R. Hebl, M. R. & Grossman-Alexander, M. (1998). The View from the Road: Implications for Stress Recovery andImmunization. Journal of Environmental Psychology , 18, 113-140.

Pascale, R. (Spring, 1999). Surfing the edge of chaos. Sloan Management Review, 40,3, p. 83-94.

Pearce, J. (1980). Magical Child. New York, NY: Bantam.

Pierce, L. B. (2000). Choosing Simplicity: Real People Finding Peace and Fulfillment in a Complex World Gallagher Press.

Pittenger, J. B. (2001). Three consequences of believing that information lies in global arrays and that perceptual systems use this information. Behavioral and Brain Sciences 24(April): 236.

Powledge, T. (1999). Addiction and the brain. Bioscience, Jul 99, Vol. 49 Issue 7, p513.

PR Newswire, (2001). Women Say Not Recognizing Addiction Is Major Barrier to Treatment. Nov. 19 / PRNewswire/ — From November 19 2001

Quinn, D. (1993). Ishmael. Bantam

Reconnecting With Nature (1999). May/Jun99, Vol. 29 Issue 3, p. 235, Ecologist.

Richmond, R. L. (2000). Honesty in Psychological Treatment A Guide to Psychology and its Practice http://members.aol.com/avpsyrich/honesty.htm

Rivlin R., Gravelle, K. (1984). Deciphering The Senses. New York, NY: Simon and Schuster.

Roland, A. L. (2001). Radical Therapy Origin Press, Mt. Shasta, CA

Rowe, (2002). Reconnecting With Nature Research, Costa Rica Outward Bound School. www.crrobs.org/

Roszak, T. (1995). Ecopsychology: Restoring the Earth, Healing the Mind, pp1-17 San Francisco, Sierra.

Roszak, T. (1997). Interview with Theodore Rozak (video) Voices of Change volume II by the Foundation for Global Community. Interview

Roszak, T. Interview with Theodore Roszak (video) Voices of Change volume II by the Foundation for Global Community. Interview

Rovee-Collier, C. (1992). Infant memory Shows The Power of Place, Developmental Psychology, March. Quoted in Science News, vol. 141 No. 16 p.244, Washington DC: Science Service.

Sabini, (2000). Soul and Nature - Resurgence, issue 198, January / February 2000 http://resurgence.gn.apc.org/issues/198.htm

Samples, B. (1976). The Metaphoric Mind. Reading, Massachusetts: Addison-Wesley Publishing Co.

Schewe, P. & Stein, B. (1999). Physics News UpdateThe American Institute of Physics Bulletin of Physics NewsNumber 454 (Story #1), October 26,

Schweitzer, A. (1961). The Decay and the Restoration of Civilisation and in Cousins, N. (1966) The Words of Albert Schweitzer Newmarket Press,

Schimel, D. S., Braswell, B. H., Holland, E. A., McKeown, R., Ojima, D. S., Painter, T. H., Parton, W. J., & Townshend, A. R. (1994). Climatic, edaphic and biotic controls over storage and turnover of carbon in soils. Global Biogeochem. Cycles, 8:279-293.

Schneider, R. (2001). The Mucherla Global School, Institute of Global Education http://mucherlaglobalschool.org

Schombert, J. (2000). The Unified Field Theory http://zebu.uoregon.edu/~js/glossary/unified_field_theory.html

Scull, J. (1999). Ecopsychology: Where does it fit in psychology? Malaspina University College Psychology Conference Proceedings, http://www.island.net/~jscull/ecointro.htm

Scull, J. (2000). Let a Thousand Flowers Bloom: A History of Ecopsychology, Gatherings, Winter 1999-2000 issue.http://www.ecopsychology.org/gatherings/history.htm

Shaw, Childhood and Nature (2000). Gatherings, International Community for Ecopsychology, Winter Issue: 1999 - 2000 http://www.ecopsychology.org/gatherings/childhoo.htm

Slovic, S. (1999). Giving expression to nature: voices of environmental literature. Environment, March 01 1999

Stern, K., & McClintock,, M. K. (1998). Regulation of ovulation by human pheromones. Nature 392 (March 12): 177.

Spelke, E. (1992). Infants Signal the Birth of Knowledge, Psychological Review, October, 1992 as quoted in Science News, November 14, 1992, Vol. 142 p. 325, Washington DC: Science Service.

Stepp, L.S. (1996). Where the Wild Thing Are: Using Nature to Build Living and Learning Skills. Washington Post, April 22.

Stilgoe, John R. (2001). Gone Barefoot Lately? Nature matters. American Journal of Preventive Medicine 20(3): 243-244.

Swanson, J. L. (1998). Prescribing Nature, Ecopsychology Online, No. 5 http://ecopsychology.athabascau.ca/0398/swanson.htm

Swanson, J. L. (2001). Communing with Nature: A guidebook for enhancing your relationship with the living earth. Corvallis, OR: Illahee Press, 2001.

Sweeney, T. (2002). Finding Truth in Nature, Doctoral Dissertation, Greenwich University

Ulrich, R. S. (1991). with R. F. Simons, B. D. Losito, E. Fiorito, M. A. Miles & M. Zelson. Stress Recovery during Exposure to Natural and urban Environments. Journal of Environmental Psychology, 11, 201-230.

Vogel, S. (1999). Unnatural Acts.The Sciences,

Takano, T et al, (2002). Urban residential environments and senior citizens' longevity in megacity areas: the importance of walkable green spaces Journal of Epidimiology and Community Health, December,

Taylors, (2000). Wilderness References http://www.c-zone.net/taylors/

Terborgh, (1999). Requiem for Nature, Island Press/Shearwater Books.Todd, John (1984). Ocean Arks: http://www.oceanarks.org/

Thoreau, (1992). Walden, NY: Barnes and Noble.

Travis, J. (1997). Biological clocks fly into view. Science News 152(Dec. 6): 365.

"Unified field theory" EncyclopÊdia Britannicahttp://www.britannica.com/eb/article? eu=76201

Wald, G. (1985). The Cosmology of Life in Cohen, (Ed,), Proceedings of the Conference "Is the Earth a Living Organism?" (pp. 72-14) National Audubon Society.

Washington, M. (2001). The Nature of Intelligence in the Second book of Genesis (http://mightymall.com/1st3seconds/intell.html

Weil, A. (1996). Spontaneous Healing, UNAPIX, November.

Wheatley, M. (1992). Leadership and the New Science: Learning about Organizations from an Orderly Universe. San Francisco: Berrett-Koehler.

Wheatley, M., & Kellner-Rogers, M. (1999). A simpler way. San Francisco, CA: Berret-Koehler.

Wilson , (1984). The Biophilia Hypothesis, Harvard Univ Press.

Wiley, J. A. et al (1994). at Holmes, California's children: Exposure to air pollution No. 94-6 Research Notes California Environmental Research Notes California Environmental Protection Agency Brief Reports to the Scientific and Technical Air Resources Board Community Study of Children's Activity Patterns. http://www.arb.ca.gov/research/resnotes/notes/94-6.htm

Wise, R. A., Bauco, P., Carlezon, W. A., Jr., & Trojniar, W. (1992). Self-stimulation and drug reward mechanisms. Annals of the New York Academy of Sciences, 654, 192-198.

Wynne-Edwards, (1991). Ecology Denies Darwinism. The Ecologist, May-June, Cornwall, England.

Zev, N. (2000). The Total Human Ecosystem: Integrating Ecology and Economics. Bioscience Apr2000, Vol. 50 Issue 4, p357

Appendix E: Organic Learning and Psychology
You may photocopy and distribute this page

The Web of Life Imperative

*Regenerative ecopsychology techniques that help people
think in balance with natural systems*

Michael J. Cohen, Ed.D. and 36 co-authors

An accredited book and course that teaches you the

Natural Systems Thinking Process

**FOUND: A unique, nature-connecting learning tool that
enables your psyche to authentically tap into the wisdom
and purifying powers of nature. This sensory science helps
you rejuvenate 48 subdued natural intelligences that
heighten your awareness and increase your responsibility.**

Backyard or backcountry, this book's practical process
empowers you to improve your health, inner-peace and self-
esteem.

Learn how to replace the
destructive blocks in your
thinking with dynamically
balanced ways of knowing.

Counteract your education's
omission of a much needed
organic psychology.

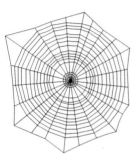

Master how to genuinely reconnect
your reasoning and senses to
their nurturing origins in
nature's restorative vigor,
sustainability and peace.

Help yourself, and those close to you, benefit from the renewal
that thrives in the magnificence of a beautiful day, the
wisdom of an ancient tree and the fortitude of a weed.

Let the higher power of nature's healing energies help your
thinking transform your harmful stress, disorders and
addictive bonds into the rewards from responsible personal,
social and environmental relationships.

Strengthen your inborn natural genius. Grow from hands-on,
biophilia-in-action, classes, essays, friendships, activities,
research, scholarships, ethics, counseling and healing.

Enjoy a satisfying, Earth-friendly job, career, internship or
teaching certification. Take advantage of online
scholarships, courses and degree programs.

To understand how and why the organic psychology in
this book will work for you as it has for so many others, consider the following key intelligence test question, one that ordinarily might help assess a person's mathematical aptitude:

*If you count a dog's tail as one of its legs,
how many legs does a dog have?*

"Five," of course, is the correct answer for a math test.
Intelligent people say "five" because it is valid in mathematical
systems and contemporary thinking and it is highly regarded
and rewarded by our society. However, we don't solely live
our lives or think in mathematical systems. Our natural sense
of reason can consider what we know from our actual contact

with a real, normal dog, too. That's when our multitude of 53
other natural senses come into play: senses of sight, touch,
motion, color, texture, language, sound, smell, consciousness,
community, trust, contrast, and love. They each provide further
information and help our sense of reason make more sense
and more informed decisions. They enable our thinking to
register that a tail is different than a leg, that a dog has four
legs, not five, no matter what is correct in mathematical
logic.

It is a grave mistake for anyone not to take seriously
the difference between 4-leg and 5-leg ways of knowing and
our learned prejudice for the latter. As this book shows, when
they are not in balance the schism between their different ways
of registering the world produces destructive relationships.

Four-leg knowing is a magnificent psychological and
physiological phenomenon with deep natural system roots into
the eons, the heart of Earth and our psyche. It brings our widely
diverse multiplicity of natural sensory experiences into our
awareness. *Five-leg knowing* produces important awareness
through abstract imagination, labels and stories. However,
when it does not find it reasonable to also seek and think with
4-leg knowledge it results not only in our desensitization but
in the separation of our thinking from the dynamically balanced
regenerative powers of Earth's natural systems within and
around us. This profound loss produces the many destructive
side effects of our artificial world that we can not readily solve.

Four-leg versus 5-leg discord creates an entrenched
conflict in our psyche between how we think and how nature
works. This is a point source of the stress and contamination
our society produces in the integrity of people and the
environment. It generates disorders and troubles that are seldom
found in nature.

It is important to recognize that by financially and
socially rewarding us for
getting "good grades" or for
"making the grade" by using
nature-isolated 5-leg thinking,
our socialization habitually
bonds, conditions, programs or
addicts us to 5-leg thinking. In
the process, 5-leg thinking often
learns to demean 4-leg
reasoning as childish,
unscientific, or environ-
mentalist (tree hugging, airy
fairy, earth muffin, fuzzy
thinking.) The result is that we
become dependent on 5-leg
knowing and relating as well as
go into denial. For example:

"Aristotle thought there were eight legs on a fly
and wrote it down. For centuries scholars were
content to quote his authority. Apparently, not one
of them was curious enough to impale a fly and
count its six legs."
-Stuart Chase

The Natural Systems Thinking Process (NSTP)
reverses this psychological schism and its harmful personal
and environmental effects by enabling us to reasonably gather
information from both 4-leg and 5-leg sources. This lets us

enjoy a whole, healing, 9-leg thinking process. The vital secret of NSTP is that by carefully following its instructions, we can enlist nature's restorative powers to overcome our bonded conditioning to half-truth 5-leg thinking. In time, 9-leg thinking becomes a habit, as healthful as brushing our teeth.

History of the Natural Systems Thinking Process.

In 1959, Dr. Michael J. Cohen founded a camp and school program based on reconnecting with nature. The National Audubon Society and many others called it the most revolutionary school in America. They said it was "on the side of the angels." Participants traveled and thrived by camping out in 83 different natural habitats throughout the seasons. They learned to honor their thoughts and feelings and to live out their commitment to have open, honest relationships with the  natural environment, each other and with indigenous people(s), researchers, ecologists, the Amish, organic farmers, anthropologists, folk musicians, naturalists, shamans, administrators, historians and many others close to the land. The experience deeply reconnected their 53 senses to their natural origins. They 9-leg reconnected their thinking and selves to the whole of nature.

The students loved to educate themselves this way and its effectiveness showed in its results:

- Chemical dependencies, including alcohol and tobacco, disappeared. Destructive social relationships were challenged and healed.

- Personality and eating disorders subsided. Violence, crime and prejudice were unknown in the group.

- Academics improved because they were applicable, hands-on and fun. Loneliness, hostility and depression subsided.

- Group interactions allowed for stress release and management; each day was fulfilling and relatively peaceful.

- Some students using meditation found they no longer needed to use it. They learned how to sustain a nature-connected community that more effectively helped them increase their resiliency to stress and disease. Others found the school experience increased the benefits of meditation by attaching it to the peace in global natural systems.

- Participants said they felt they knew each other better than they knew their families or best friends; they knew themselves better than they ever had before.

- Participants felt safe. They risked expressing and acting from their deeper thoughts and feelings. A profound, inborn sense of social and environmental responsibility guided their decisions.

- When vacation periods arrived, neither staff nor students wanted to go home. Each person enjoyed working to build this supportive, balanced living and learning utopia. *They were home.*

- Students entered right livelihood professions.

- All this occurred simply because community members made sense of their life by developing supportive, multiple-sensory relationships that restored contact with attractive callings from the natural systems within and around them.

The 9-leg secret to each participant's success was to discover how to thoughtfully learn through 4-leg natural sensations and feelings that arose from their newly regrown sensory roots in ecosystems of which they were part. These sensations acted as nature's guiding voice. The value and rewards of doing this freed the participants' 53 senses from their bonds to questionable 5-leg stories. It re-bonded them to their 4-leg sense of reason in congress with 52 other rejuvenated natural senses while these senses were connected to their nurturing origins and home in nature. This resulted in consensus-based 9-leg thinking, literacy and relating that included information from, and the regenerative, healing powers of, natural systems. To many 5-leg thinkers, this sounds crazy, but year after year the beneficial results still speak for themselves as they improve relationships and reduce stress, conflict and a wide range of associated disorders.

From 30 years of travel and study in over 260 national parks, forests and subcultures, Cohen developed a replicable learning process and psychology that anyone can use at home, work or school today. It unleashes our suppressed 4-leg ability to grow and survive responsibly with natural systems in ourselves, others and the environment. By documenting that it worked and could be taught, he earned his doctoral degree and the school became a nationally recognized graduate and undergraduate degree program.

From 1985-92, Cohen translated his nature-connected psychology program into the Natural Systems Thinking Process (NSTP) for public use, backyard or back country, via the Internet or in conjunction with local study groups in real time.

Through NSTP courses, people recover their natural senses and integrity by sharing their attractions to hands-on, sensory, nature-reconnections at home, work or school. This is done best with small study groups either over the Internet or in person.

Any reasonable person understands full well that we can't resolve our unsolvable problems using the same, nature-disconnected, 5-leg thinking that produces them. The critical contribution of NSTP is that it empowers  individuals to create moments that let Earth teach in its sensory voice. It helps us responsibly unify 5-leg and 4-leg thinking. This 9-leg amalgamation is a healthy, natural, super-intelligent way of knowing and relating. It's how nature works. It provides us with a missing essence of wellness, sustainable living and peace that we can enjoy personally, socially and globally.

* * *

For further information visit **www.webstrings.org.**
Contact the Institute to purchase copies of the *Web of Life Imperative* ($34.95) or for review or subsidized copies.

Institute of Global Education *Project NatureConnect*
Special NGO consultant to the United Nations Economic and Social Council.
P. O. Box 1605, Friday Harbor, WA. 98250
360-378-6313
www.ecopsych.com   nature@interisland.net

Appendix F

Online Orientation Course Sequence

The NatureConnect Base Camp

This page contains the course "Posting Schedule" for people doing the course online as the Orientation Course.

It's at this point that a consensus decision needs to be made by the group only if you find it is not convenient to keep to the default posting schedule of Wednesdays & Sundays from here to course completion in five weeks (see A below). The default schedule is usually best because it offers both adequate time and sustains momentum. It is also quite challenging to have to set up a new schedule by email. If you find this schedule is too fast, use Choice D, posting every five days (seven weeks total).

Once a schedule is selected, one of the course members should get the OK or take the initiative to make and submit to the group a schedule of the specific dates (month and day) for the course.

For most people, this course covers new ground and its momentum is important. Otherwise, the experiences get overwhelmed by the demands of daily life. Try and stay within the schedule framework upon which your group agrees. PLEASE inform your group if you will be late with one of your postings . . . don't be a missing ingredient. It causes a great deal of disarray that is often not apparent. Gaining and giving consent is the heart of the Interact group. It is also an essence of nature. It does, however, take time and patience.

Course Option Completion Times:

POSTING DAYS AND TOTAL COURSE DURATION

Choice A: Recommended (default) Wednesday and Sunday   5 weeks

Choice B: Monday, Wednesday, Friday   25 days

Choice C: Every day   12 days

Choice D: Every 5 days, a good alternative 7 weeks

Choice E: Once a week   11 weeks

Choice A, the default posting twice a week, is usually best for most groups and is automatically used if other options are not proposed.

This is the posting schedule for Choice A.

Day 1 posting and continuing (Sunday:) Post your prerequisite introductory paragraph and your survey attractions.
<u>Begin Chapter One</u>
Monday-Tuesday

Day 2 posting and continuing (Wednesday) Post <u>Chapter One</u> –Sensory experience
Carefully follow the Twelve Interact Catalysts referred to as "Thoughtful Verbalizations" on the last page of Chapter One (and repeated for convenience on the last page of this appendix) for guidance in writing your posts. Uniformity of posts helps you get used to what to look for in your own post and in the posts of others. Do this for all the postings on the course.
<u>Begin Chapter Two</u> "Psychological Bias" (do one or two sections every day for the next seven days and post some on Sunday and the rest on Wednesday a week from now)
Thursday-Friday-Saturday

Day 2 1/2 sub-post (Sunday)
Sub Post first half of Chapter Two (1-5)
Monday-Tuesday.

Day 3 posting and continuing (Wednesday)
Complete Posting Chapter Two – "Psychological Bias"
<u>Begin Chapter Three</u>
Thursday-Friday-Saturday

Day 4 posting and continuing
(Sunday): Post Chapter Three - "Feeling"
<u>Begin Chapter Four</u>
Monday-Tuesday

Day 5 posting and continuing (Wednesday)
Post Chapter Four - "Consent"
<u>Begin Chapter Five</u>
Thursday-Friday-Saturday

Day 6 posting and continuing (Sunday)
Post Chapter Five - "Intelligence"
<u>Begin Chapter 6</u>
Monday-Tuesday

Day 7 posting and continuing (Wednesday)
Post Chapter Six- "Inspire"
<u>Begin Chapter 7</u>
Thursday-Friday-Saturday

Day 8 posting and continuing (Sunday)
Post Chapter Seven – "Identity"
<u>Begin Chapter 8</u>
Monday- Tuesday

NOTE: ENROLL NOW IN THE ECO 501 COURSE THAT FOLLOWS THIS COURSE. Learn to integrate your thinking with NIAL using the book *Reconnecting With Nature.*

Day 9 posting and continuing (Wednesday)
Post Chapter Eight "Mentality"
<u>Begin Chapter 9</u>
Thursday- Friday-Saturday

Sometimes optionally available:
Day 10 posting and continuing (Sunday)
Post Chapter Nine – "Evaluation"
<u>Begin Part 10</u>
Monday-Tuesday-Wednesday

The core purpose of this course is for its participants to begin to learn and teach how to connect with natural systems in the environment, other course members and themselves.

We encourage you to continue with our four additional 4-12 week courses (with 7 credits optional) and/or as an Orientation Course facilitator for future participants on this course. It is an excellent learning experience. For details of the Courses that follow, see "Courses' on the www.ecopsych.com web site.

ECO 508 Natural Attractions: Einstein's World
ECO 501 Introduction to Educating and Counseling with Nature
ECO 502 Educating and Counseling with Nature 1 & 2

Thoughtful Verbalization:

Guidelines for completing chapters and posting:

Start your post to the group with the Subject (GROUP NAME OR NUMBER)_____: PART 1, YOUR NAME, so that other course member and readers can identify it, read it, and share their thoughts and feelings about your experiences with this page and vice versa.

Submit your attraction experiences, thoughts and feelings from the material on this page to your support group or

journal along with the following Twelve Interact Catalysts (repeated for convenience here from Chapter One):

1) a general description of how you did the activity and what happened, along with quotes you like from the readings and how they added meaning to the experience

2) the three most important things you learned from the chapter and webstring connections

3) how you would feel about having the webstring attractions you experienced in the activity taken away from you

4) whether or not the activity enhanced your sense of self-worth and your trustfulness of nature

5) the part of you, if any, the activity identified or re-educated inside or outside of you

6) your reactions to what you found attractive in the postings you read from the other group members. Be sure to save the Interact postings of yourself and others that are attractive to you so that you can refer to them and quote them in the final paper for this course

7) What value, if any, was there to doing the Summary Option (If you did it.)

8) Write one or two keywords that convey what important thing you learned from this assignment

9) Write one or more complete, single, short, power sentence "quotes" that convey a significant contribution that this assignment makes to improving our relationships

10) Integrating Dream Time: Get at least one night's sleep before doing the next activity. While your 5-leg mind sleeps, your 4-leg mind rides the inroads to consciousness made by the activity and reading. Note, upon awakening, whether any changes have occurred with respect to your outlook or the way you feel

11) Remember: You will increase your learning from this activity by 75% if you teach this activity to another person. This opportunity is available by interning as a co-facilitator for the course.

12) Conclude by identifying what things you have put into the trustable, uncontaminated, thought and feeling room/space you built into your psyche during Part/Chapter One. The use of these twelve Interact Catalysts will enhance your learning experience and that of the others in the course as well.

ISBN 141200185-4

9 781412 001854